new vegetarian cuisine

250 low-fat recipes for superior health

by linda rosensweig and

the food editors of

PREVENTION magazine

Rodale Press, Emmaus, Pennsylvania

Copyright © 1994 by Rodale Press, Inc.

Recipe photograph on front cover:

At left, Oven-Roasted Vegetables Pizza (page 317)

At right, Pepper and Mushroom Pizza (page 316)

Cover Photographer: Angelo Caggiano

Food Stylist: Mariann Sauvion

Library of Congress Cataloging-in-Publication Data

Rosensweig, Linda

New vegetarian cuisine: 250 low-fat recipes for superior health/by Linda Rosensweig and the food editors of Prevention magazine.

    p.   cm.

Includes index.

  ISBN 0–87596–168–1 hardcover

  1. Vegetarian cookery.   I. Prevention (Emmaus, Pa.)   II. Title.

TX837.R826 1993

641.5'636–dc20   93-17792

                                     CIP

Distributed in the book trade by St. Martin's Press

2 4 6 8 10 9 7 5 3 1 hardcover

—— OUR MISSION ——

We publish books that empower people's lives.

—— RODALE ❧ BOOKS ——

New Vegetarian Cuisine **Staff**

Editor: Jean Rogers
Executive Editor: Debora Tkac
Contributing Writers: Denise Foley, Eileen Nechas
Art Director: Jane Knutila
Book and Cover Designer: Elizabeth Otwell
Photographer: Angelo Caggiano
Food Stylist: Mariann Sauvion
Prop Stylist: Barbara Fritz
Illustrator: Julie Schieber
Home Economist, Rodale Food Center: JoAnn Brader
Research Chief: Ann Gossy Yermish
Research Associates: Susan Burdick, Christine Dreisbach, Karen Lombardi Ingle
Production Editor: Jane Sherman
Copy Editor: Susan G. Berg
Editor in Chief: William Gottlieb
Editor, *Prevention* **Magazine:** Mark Bricklin

To my husband, Dan, daughter, Rachel,
and faithful companion, Max

contents

acknowledgments

Food is my passion, particularly the creation of exciting, healthy new recipes for all food lovers.

Fortunately, I am surrounded by some special food lovers who made this project possible and fun.

First, my husband, Dan, who spent many Sunday mornings tasting these recipes. His desire for a neat kitchen was surpassed only by his desire to cheer me up when I had peeled too many carrots.

To my mother, Elaine Molzahn, who has supported my dream to become a chef and made this all possible.

And finally, I would like to thank my sisters, Carol and Barbara, and their husbands, Hal and Bob, and my nieces and nephew, Jessie, Meghan and Thomas, for all their support and encouragement.

Enjoy!

introduction

Let's get one thing straight right up front. You don't have to be a vegetarian to use and benefit from this book.

Of course, the odds are that you *are* a vegetarian at least some of the time—even if you think of yourself as a confirmed meat-and-potatoes person. Whenever you breakfast on pancakes, waffles or muffins instead of a ham omelet and whenever you opt for spaghetti with marinara sauce for dinner instead of a steak, you're taking a small step in the direction of the vegetarian lifestyle.

If you stop to think about it, you probably eat quite a few meatless meals during the course of any given week. You just don't consider them "vegetarian" because they're delicious, satisfying and a part of your regular repertoire. Foods like pizza with peppers and mushrooms, bean burritos, French toast and pasta salad are fun to eat, and they can stand on their own merits without an assist from meat, fish or poultry.

Doctors think that the types of foods plentiful in a vegetarian diet—grains, beans, vegetables, fruits—play a large part in the diet/health equation. *New Vegetarian Cuisine* can help you make sure that the equation is weighted in your favor.

Author Linda Rosensweig has drawn on her years as a food editor, recipe developer and, yes, *part-time* vegetarian to create 250 new and different meat-free dishes. She's thought of everything, including family dinners, home-alone suppers, breakfast and brunch fare, holiday feasts and easy fun foods. And she's marked which recipes you can prepare ahead to save time. Let her expertise give your menu plans a boost in the right direction. You might even find yourself serving more no-meat meals and reaping health benefits that will last a lifetime.

Jean Rogers
Food Editor, *Prevention* Magazine Health Books

the ultimate
food style

Vegetarianism is hot! It's so hot, in fact, that the
National Restaurant Association has urged its 150,000
member restaurants to feature meatless main dishes
and even to add whole vegetarian sections to their menus.
The advisory was prompted by a nationwide Gallup Poll show-
ing that one out of every five restaurant goers actively seeks
out eateries serving vegetarian food and that one out of every
three diners will order no-meat dishes if available.

The overwhelming success of vegetarian restaurants such as
Greens in San Francisco, Harmony Vegetarian Restaurant in
Philadelphia, the Chicago Diner in Chicago, Angelica Kitchen
in Manhattan and the pioneering Moosewood in Ithaca, New
York, proves that the American public is hungry for this type of
fare.

Indeed, the Hard Rock Cafe restaurant chain reports that
their veggie burger is a hot seller, and these days even truck
stops tend to sprout salad bars. The trend extends to the
crème de la crème, with such elegant restaurants as Jean-
Louis in Washington, D.C., featuring a five-course vegetarian
dinner for their discriminating clientele. Not to be outdone on
its own level, the military has developed shelf-stable vegetarian field rations.

The driving force behind this national trend is health—88 percent of those surveyed by Gallup cited it as a main reason for

choosing vegetarian meals. But just as interesting is the fact that 86 percent also mentioned taste preferences as a reason for choosing vegetarianism. That drives home an important point: Vegetarian food is *delicious.*

Certainly, vegetarian fare has come a long way from the bean sprouts, carrot juice and leaden lentil loaves that characterized the movement in the early 1970s. It has, in essence, evolved into a distinct cuisine in its own right—one defined by the pleasures and benefits of eating simply prepared seasonal foods.

The shift away from eating meat has been so pronounced in recent years that the beef industry has mounted a counter-attack, declaring beef "real food for real people." And the pork producers have promoted their product as "the other white meat" to interest people who avoid pork in favor of chicken, which is generally perceived as a healthier meat choice. In spite of such aggressive pro-meat campaigns, vegetarianism continues to gather momentum. Estimates vary, but somewhere between 3 and 20 percent of Americans are self-described vegetarians.

One recent survey, done in conjunction with *Vegetarian Times,* found that there are somewhere around 12.5 million people in this country who call themselves vegetarians. That's twice as many as there were in 1985.

The exact number is hard to pin down, admits Suzanne Havala, R.D., former chairperson of the Vegetarian Nutrition Dietetic Practice Group of the American Dietetic Association (ADA). "That's because there are so many people who are, to one degree or another, cutting back on their consumption of red meat, poultry or fish. Consequently, there is a marked increase in the number of people calling themselves vegetarians, whether they fit the strict definition or not," she says.

defining terms

There's more than one way to peg a vegetarian. That's because there are so many different types—and often a great deal of overlap among them. Here's a rundown of the most common types of vegetarians, along with the tongue-twister names used to designate them.

• A *lacto-ovo-vegetarian* is the most common vegetarian in the United States. This person does not eat meat, poultry, fish or seafood but does consume milk, milk products and eggs.

• A *lacto-vegetarian* is similar but excludes eggs.

• A *vegan* (pronounced *VEE-gun;* sometimes also called a strict, pure or total vegetarian) avoids all animal products, including dairy, eggs and possibly honey. This person may even refuse to wear fur, leather, silk or wool.

• A *semivegetarian* (or partial vegetarian) includes some animal foods, such as fish and poultry, in the diet. This person does, however, usually eschew red meat.

There are some more unusual variations on the vegetarian theme. There's the fruitarian diet, which includes only fruits, nuts, honey and oil. And then there's the matter of macrobiotics. Strictly speaking, the macrobiotic diet is not a subdivision of vegetarianism. It's just a diet that people tend to associate with vegetarianism because its practitioners do not eat meat. It is, in fact, a really limited diet, consisting mostly of cereal foods.

Unfortunately, says Havala, strict diets such as those two have contributed to misconceptions about the nutritional adequacy of more typical vegetarian diets. Certainly, the ultra-limited regimens have the potential for leading to many nutrient deficiencies. Broader-based vegetarian variations, however, have much to recommend them. Being based on healthy plant foods such as vegetables, fruits, grains, nuts and legumes, supplemented sometimes by dairy products or eggs, these diets have enough variety to meet the nutritional needs of most people.

In this book we'll deal mostly with lacto-ovo-vegetarian, lacto-vegetarian and vegan diets. And we'll concentrate on the health benefits of a vegetarian diet rather than the ethical aspects of avoiding animal products. The recipes that appear in the book were developed using dairy products and eggs (mostly egg substitute to keep cholesterol levels down) but no meat, fish or poultry. If you're avoiding all animal products, however, you'll find plenty of recipes that use neither dairy nor eggs. And there are a wide variety of soy-based cheeses, milk and such on the market that you could substitute for dairy products if you wanted.

By the way, you don't need to be a card-carrying vegetarian to benefit from this book. The recipes can help you cut back on the number of times per week you do eat meat. And you just may discover that meatless meals are so satisfying that you'll want to incorporate more of them into your diet.

when it's good, it's very good

Here's a common myth: A vegetarian diet is automatically healthier than a meat-based one. Not so. Like anything else worthwhile, adopting a vegetarian diet takes education and planning if you're going to do it right. After all, a diet of jelly doughnuts, potato chips and hot fudge sundaes *is* vegetarian, but no one would claim that it's health promoting. Even a more realistic vegetarian diet that relies heavily on whole-milk products, egg yolks and high-fat cheeses can do more harm than good.

Current scientific guidelines for promoting health and preventing disease focus on many important aspects of a well-rounded diet. The *Year 2000 Goals* issued by the United States Department of Health and Human Services, for instance, emphasize eating patterns that maintain appropriate body weight, reduce intakes of total fat, saturated fat, cholesterol and sodium and increase consumption of calcium, dietary fiber and iron.

These guidelines really stress the need to reduce the type and amount of fat eaten. They recommend that 30 percent or less of total daily calories come from fat. Of that total, 10 percent *or less* of calories should come from saturated fats (such as butter), and not more than 10 percent should come from polyunsaturates (such as corn oil). The rest of the fat calories should come from monounsaturates (such as olive oil).

"At present, individuals consuming a vegetarian, and especially vegan, diet usually come closer to achieving the recommended dietary patterns for fats than do people who eat both plant and animal

vegetarians versus meat eaters

This isn't a contest, just some curious bits of information that researchers at the University of Texas at Austin discovered when they asked 150 vegetarians and an equal number of nonvegetarians the same questions.

• More than twice as many nonvegetarians had been hospitalized during the previous five years.

• Twice as many nonvegetarians reported taking prescription medications.

• Almost three times as many vegetarians abstained from alcohol.

• Only half as many vegetarians smoked.

• Twice as many vegetarians took calcium supplements.

• Almost three times as many vegetarians practiced meditation on a regular basis.

• Vegetarians overwhelmingly believed that they are healthier.

• Vegetarians went out socially with friends and entertained friends at home more often than meat eaters did.

• More vegetarians had actively lobbied for legislation within the previous two years.

• Of those who had lobbied for legislation, more vegetarians were concerned with environmental and energy issues.

foods," says Johanna Dwyer, D.Sc., R.D., of the Tufts University School of Medicine and Frances Stern Nutrition Center at the New England Medical Center Hospital in Boston.

Indeed, to the degree that you can move in the direction of a diet that's high in fiber, high in complex carbohydrates and low in fat—and that you do it by eating a wide variety of plant foods—the more health benefits you can derive from it, adds heart disease researcher Dean Ornish, M.D., author of *Dr. Dean Ornish's Program for Reversing Heart Disease* and *Eat More, Weigh Less.* Dr. Ornish has been a vegetarian for the past 20 years.

vegetarians' first impressions

"Did you feel any different when you first became a vegetarian?" It's a question that meat eaters can't resist asking recent converts to the vegetarian way of life. And they ask it with a bit of skepticism thrown in. The answer to that question depends on whether the person you're quizzing became a vegetarian gradually or went "cold tofu," as some people describe the all-at-once approach. "You're more likely to feel a big difference if you make immediate and comprehensive changes in your diet," Dr. Ornish points out.

Adds Havala, who is also a nutrition advisor for the Baltimore-based Vegetarian Resource Group and who has been a vegetarian since her teen years: "Although there is no scientific proof for it, I have talked to enough people who either became full-fledged vegetarians or cut back markedly on their consumption of meat to know that there is a common theme to their first impressions. Universally, people talk about feeling 'lighter.' That's the best word they can think of to describe how they feel—and I hear it used over and over again.

"People feel better about themselves, too. Maybe it's because they believe they are doing something nice for themselves. Or perhaps it's because they're doing something that's good for the environment, too. While some of the feelings of well-being might be psychological," she admits, "there are also many people who experience a noticeable improvement in their physical health as well. My sister is a good example. She became a vegetarian a few years ago. Before that, she had been following a diet that was very high in fat, and she had been plagued with chronic heartburn. Once she changed her diet, her heartburn seemed to disappear literally overnight."

Dr. Ornish says that when he became a vegetarian, he felt more energetic, was able to think more clearly and was less depressed. And although he admits that he has never lost his taste for meat, he believes giving it up was a choice worth making. "The improvement in how I feel just isn't worth losing for the momentary pleasure of eating meat," he insists.

Even the switch to partial vegetarianism may reward you with physical benefits. Robert Lang, M.D., medical director of the Osteoporosis Diagnostic and Treatment Center in New Haven, Connecticut, experienced dramatic improvement in several health conditions—even though he still eats an occasional piece of chicken and some seafood. "I eat no red meat at all and practically no dairy products," he says. "Once I adopted that diet, my allergies cleared up by about 90 percent, and my asthma by 95 percent. My colitis problems are practically nonexistent."

debunking the myths

It wasn't too long ago that vegetarians were considered weird, eccentric folks who were probably damaging their health by not eating animal products. Today, according to the ADA, the medical community recognizes that there is indeed a positive relationship between a vegetarian lifestyle and risk reduction for chronic degenerative diseases such as obesity, heart disease, high blood pressure, diabetes, colon cancer and more.

The myths surrounding vegetarianism—which are still alive and well in some circles—generally center around the nutritional adequacy of what the ill-informed consider restricted diets. And that's in spite of the fact that the ADA has stated emphatically that "vegetarian diets are healthful and nutritionally adequate when appropriately planned."

Since nutrition is at the root of these persistent myths, let's look at them one by one and see how they hold up to scientific fact.

Myth: If you don't eat meat, you won't get enough protein. *Truth:* In this country, it's more likely that you're getting too much protein rather than too little if you eat meat. In fact, experts estimate that meat eaters consume about twice the recommended daily requirement. So although dropping meat from your diet will decrease your protein consumption, says the ADA, vegetarian diets still usually meet or even exceed the recommended amount of this nutrient.

And believe it or not, an overdose of protein does have disadvantages, including an increased risk of the brittle-bone disease osteoporosis. What's more, says the ADA, many foods high in protein are correspondingly high in fat. So a lower protein intake generally translates into a lower-fat diet, with all its inherent advantages.

If you don't consume eggs or dairy products, you still can easily meet your daily protein requirement (about 50 grams for adult women, 63 grams for adult men) by eating a variety of nuts, seeds, legumes (including lentils and all kinds of beans), tofu and commercial soy milk. All are high in protein. Other vegetables plus breads and cereals supply somewhat less but are still good sources.

Myth: Vegetarian diets don't supply "complete" protein. *Truth:* This myth is based on research done decades ago, says Havala, and persists even today among less well informed folks. It was believed that only animal products could supply the eight essential amino acids—the so-called complete protein—in the correct proportions for humans.

Today it is acknowledged that almost all plant foods contain all the essential amino acids, although some have greater amounts than others, says Havala. If you simply eat a wide variety of these foods over the course of a day—not even at the same meal—and get enough food to meet your energy needs, you can be confident that you will get the complete protein your body requires, Havala adds.

Even the ADA put its stamp of approval on this concept in its 1988 position paper on vegetarian diets. (And it reaffirmed that position several years later.) Although it was once thought that you were risking malnutrition if you didn't consciously combine proteins at every meal and within a strict time interval, the ADA now states that a plant-based diet provides adequate amounts of amino acids when a varied diet is consumed on a daily basis. Besides, the body maintains a "protein pool"—a natural reservoir of amino acids ready and waiting to combine with whatever protein you get from the foods you eat.

"The fact is," says Havala, "you would have to carefully plan and calculate *not* to get enough complete protein in your diet."

Myth: Vegetarians can't get enough calcium. *Truth:* For those on a lacto-vegetarian or lacto-ovo-vegetarian diet, getting enough calcium is not a problem. In fact, intakes of calcium tend to be quite high, says Dr. Dwyer. Vegans present the reverse case.

Theoretically, vegans, who consume no milk or milk products, should be courting danger with respect to adequate calcium intake. "Vegans often have low intakes of both vitamin D and calcium. In addition, they have very high intakes of dietary fiber and its components, including oxalates (in spinach and chocolate) and phytates (in wheat bran)," says Dr. Dwyer. "Fiber may inhibit calcium absorption and is thought to place vegans at particular risk of deficiency. However, protective factors also exist in vegan lifestyles."

Take the case of vitamin D. This nutrient, which helps regulate the metabolism of calcium, is not naturally found in many foods. Most people get theirs from dairy products, but even that is present only through fortification. Fortunately for vegans, it's not necessary to consume dairy foods to get adequate D—exposure to sunlight can achieve the same effect.

As for calcium itself, a deficiency is rare in vegetarians—even among vegans, according to the ADA. "There are reasons why vegans seem protected from calcium deficiency," says Havala. "If you hold a vegan's intake of calcium up against American Recommended Dietary Allowance (RDA) standards, by all accounts she should be in trouble. But the problem lies with the RDA—American standards may not always be appropriate for vegetarians. The RDA for calcium was devised for those eating a typical American diet, which includes an excessive amount of protein. Too much protein causes an increased loss of calcium through the urine. Vegetarians, who typically eat more moderate amounts of protein, absorb and retain more calcium than nonvegetarians."

A vegan, whose diet is much lower in protein, with no animal protein at all, may require only half the RDA—which would come to 400 to 500 milligrams—to maintain healthy bones. It is not difficult at all for a vegan to meet those needs from plant sources, explains Havala.

Another concern of many vegetarians is that the whole wheat products prevalent in their diets rob whatever milk they do drink of valuable calcium. But that's not so, according to a study conducted by Connie M. Weaver, Ph.D., professor of foods and nutrition at Purdue University in West Lafayette, Indiana. "Our results contradict the widely accepted conclusions of studies done in England during the 1950s. Those studies concluded that when whole wheat is eaten with foods that provide calcium—as in the case of milk poured over whole wheat cereal—the grain's phytic acid binds with the calcium and carries most of the nutrient out of the body, unused."

In the study conducted by Dr. Weaver and her colleagues, volunteers drank milk

that contained a specific calcium isotope—a "marked" form of calcium—so that the amount absorbed could be monitored. "We found that when the milk was consumed with whole wheat, its calcium was absorbed as well as when milk was fed alone, despite the presence of the wheat's phytic acid," she says.

Dr. Weaver notes, in fact, that absorption of calcium from wheat flour compares favorably with absorption from milk. The big exception concerns wheat products with a greater-than-normal phytate concentration, such as wheat bran: Apparently, straight bran *does* interfere with the absorption of calcium eaten at the same time. So take that into consideration when eating bran-packed foods.

Myth: You can't get enough usable calcium out of dark green leafy vegetables. *Truth:* Dr. Weaver and her colleagues have put this myth to rest, too. "Many dark green leafy vegetables are known to have relatively high calcium densities and, except for spinach, have been presumed to be good sources of calcium," she says. The question is whether the calcium can be absorbed by the body.

Dr. Weaver decided to test kale for its calcium absorbability because it's high in calcium and low in calcium-binding oxalates and also because it's in the same family as other commonly eaten vegetable greens—turnip, collard and mustard greens. "Our studies showed that the body actually uses about 30 to 38 percent

of the calcium contained in a serving of milk. A regular serving of kale—which contains just as much calcium as milk—has about a 40 percent rate of absorption," Dr. Weaver says.

Myth: Vegetarians risk anemia because they can't get enough usable iron. *Truth:* "It seems difficult for American women to meet the RDA for iron, regardless of whether they're vegetarian or not," admits Havala. That's probably because women lose blood each month through menstruation, and iron is a major component of red blood cells. What's more, although iron is plentiful in many foods, it is generally poorly absorbed, adds Elaine Monsen, Ph.D., R.D., professor of medicine and nutrition at the University of Washington in Seattle. Yet in spite of these factors, vegetarians are not necessarily at risk for anemia.

Food iron falls into two distinct classifications—heme and nonheme, says Dr. Monsen, who is also editor of the *Journal of the American Dietetic Association.* Heme iron is well absorbed by humans, but it is found only in meat, fish and poultry—clearly unacceptable sources for full-fledged vegetarians. Nonheme iron, which is not absorbed as well, is found in many more sources. All the iron in vegetables, fruits, grains, nuts, eggs and dairy products is nonheme iron.

"The so-called animal protein factor increases absorption of nonheme iron when meat, fish or poultry is eaten at the same meal," says Dr. Dwyer. But all is not lost if you avoid meat sources of iron. And in fact, you can greatly increase the amount of nonheme iron you absorb by eating it at the same time as certain other foods. For instance, some amino acids (such as cysteine in milk and eggs) and citric acid (in citrus fruits) enhance nonheme iron absorption. But it's vitamin C that really shines in this department. Studies have shown that as little as 25 to 75 milligrams of vitamin C consumed at the same time enhances the intestinal absorption of nonheme iron two to four times.

Dr. Dwyer points out that one milligram of vitamin C is approximately equivalent to one gram of meat, fish or poultry in its ability to enhance absorption of nonheme iron. (However, she adds, animal foods also contribute other nutrients, such as calcium, so this is not the only consideration.)

To put this equivalency factor into useful terms: 1 ounce of meat weighs 28 grams; therefore, 2½ ounces of meat—a modest but realistic serving—weighs 70 grams. A single orange, with its 70 milligrams of vitamin C, would theoretically have the absorption-enhancing ability of 2½ ounces of meat.

Be aware that there are other substances in foods that can *inhibit* the absorption of iron, and these should be taken into consideration when you plan your meals. The tannic acid found in tea and coffee, for example, forms a tight chemical bond with nonheme iron, preventing its absorption through the cell walls of the digestive tract, says Dr. Monsen. So anyone at risk for iron deficiency would be prudent to minimize the use of coffee and tea with meals.

Likewise, the phytates commonly found in whole grains, bran and soy products can inhibit absorption. So can some forms of dietary fiber. Nevertheless, says Dr. Monsen, "most people, including vegetarians, can get enough iron if they construct their diets carefully. The main exception would be women with extremely heavy menstrual blood losses, who are likely to need supplements in order to get the amount of iron they need." If you do opt for iron supplements, advises Dr. Monsen, choose one containing easily absorbed ferrous sulfate. And take them on an empty stomach with a glass of orange juice.

Myth: Complex carbohydrates (including fiber) inhibit mineral absorption. *Truth:* Despite some evidence that certain chemicals in whole grains can inhibit the absorption of some minerals, the issue is not clear-cut.

Dietitian Suzanne Havala wanted to find out if diets that are high in fiber have an adverse effect on iron absorption. In fact, she did her master's thesis on the subject, using data from a long-term Chinese study. "The people in China take in as much as 77 grams of fiber a day," she says, "which is far more than what Americans consume. Yet contrary to what you might expect, the study showed that as total dietary fiber intake increased, hemoglobin levels increased as well." Hemoglobin is the iron-containing substance in the blood. Your hemoglobin level is one of the lab values used to determine whether or not you're anemic.

"The Chinese, on average, get 34 milligrams of iron in their diets per day—more than *double* the American RDA," says Havala. "Nearly all of it comes from plant sources. But the Chinese also take in very large amounts of vitamin C, which probably helps them absorb the iron."

In another study, researchers from King's College in London examined the effect of increased intake of complex carbohydrates (cereals, vegetables and fruits) on the metabolism of iron and zinc. The doctors studied 15 women who ate either a normal-fiber diet (about 20 grams per day) or a high-fiber diet (about 30 grams per day). The study, which lasted 14 weeks, demonstrated that "while there was much individual variation in iron and zinc absorption, overall balances and absorption did not change significantly." A moderate increase in complex carbohydrate intake using common foods had no adverse effects on the availability of iron and zinc, say the researchers. In fact, there appeared to be a tendency toward improvement in both iron and zinc balance after 12 weeks on the high-fiber diet.

Other studies, like Havala's, have also shown that populations habitually consuming diets high in complex carbohydrates do not have mineral deficiencies. The London researchers speculate that "even if a diet high in complex carbohydrates reduces mineral absorption in the short term, the body may respond in the longer term by gradually increasing the efficiency of absorption."

While we're on the subject of minerals, we should note that some studies *do* point to the possibility of inadequate zinc levels among vegetarians. Excessive intake of fiber, phytates, oxalates and soy products can have an unfavorable impact on zinc bioavailability, according to researchers. "Serum zinc levels do often tend to be lower among vegetarians than they are among omnivores, but they're still adequate," says Dr. Dwyer. A study of Trappist monks, who are lacto-vegetarians, showed that dietary counseling allowed

them to maintain adequate zinc levels in spite of high intakes of phytates and other zinc inhibitors.

Havala devised a sample vegetarian meal plan for the ADA and believed it to be adequate for all vitamins and minerals. "When it was analyzed, it came out below the RDA for zinc," she admits. "So I added two tablespoons of wheat germ to breakfast, and the zinc content skyrocketed."

Myth: Vegetarians wind up with vitamin B_{12} deficiencies. *Truth:* Actually, this qualifies as a partial myth, depending upon which type of vegetarian you are. Adequate vitamin B_{12} intake *is* a legitimate concern for vegans, says the ADA, but not for lacto-vegetarians or lacto-ovo-vegetarians. Vitamin B_{12} is available only from animal sources. Consequently, if you consume dairy products or eggs, you will get all the nutrient that your body requires, especially since it requires so little to begin with. For vegans, however, you can see the potential problem: No animal foods translates to no B_{12}.

Experts warn that you don't want to get shortchanged on vitamin B_{12}. When your body becomes depleted, you're at risk for severe anemia as well as for generalized weakness, fatigue, anorexia, indigestion, diarrhea and weakness in the extremities. What's more, some of the symptoms of B_{12} deficiency can become irreversible if left untreated.

The liver stores almost all the vitamin B_{12} you have in your body, which is enough for approximately 1,000 days, say researchers from Central Emek Hospital in Afula, Israel, who studied levels of the vitamin in vegans. Consequently, people who have been on a vegan diet for 3 or more years could deplete their internal stores. Indeed, when the researchers studied people who had been vegans for between 5 and 35 years and who had consumed no source of the vitamin for all that time, they found that the vegans did have low levels of B_{12} in their blood. Although these vegans had normal blood cells—as would be expected at first—they did complain of weakness, fatigue and poor mental concentration.

What's curious, though, is that these long-term vegans had *any* vitamin B_{12} in their blood at all. There are some highly speculative theories to explain this occurrence. But until any definitive explanations arise, the experts agree that vegans should not take chances with B_{12}. Havala counsels vegans to eat a reliable source of the vitamin a few times a week—that might be a B_{12}-fortified breakfast cereal or fortified soy milk. An alternative, she says, is to take a B_{12} (cyancobalamin) supplement. But check labels before you buy. Some brands, she says, contain very high amounts—many times the RDA. If that's all you can get, you can break the tablets into pieces or take just one whole tablet every week or so. You might want to discuss supplementation with your doctor.

a weapon against disease

Ask a typical group of vegetarians why they decided to adopt that food style and the vast majority will say they did it for their health. Indeed, 88 percent of those surveyed in a nationwide Gallup Poll cited health as *the* reason for choosing vegetarian meals. And why not? Studies abound that show vegetarians live longer, weigh less and have fewer chronic diseases than their meat-eating counterparts. In fact, the closer you get to a vegetarian diet—eating a wide variety of plant foods with a minimum of animal foods—the better off you're likely to be, according to medical research.

One comprehensive, ground-breaking study conducted by researchers at Cornell University in Ithaca, New York, over a seven-year period underscores what vegetarians have suspected for years. This study of over 6,000 Chinese people (who eat few animal products) examined the relationship between diet and the risk of developing certain diseases. Here's what the researchers found.

• The average Chinese adult, whose fiber intake is three times greater than ours, is two to three times less likely to develop colon cancer than an American.

• Although rural Chinese consume more calories than we do, they're much thinner—in part, no doubt, because less than 15 percent of their calories come from fat. Americans, by contrast, routinely consume 40 percent of their calories as fat.

• The Chinese have cholesterol levels almost half those of typical Americans. Not surprisingly, heart disease is much rarer in China than here.

• Osteoporosis, the bone-thinning disease, is also far less common in China, in spite of the fact that the Chinese eat few dairy products and consume only half as much calcium as Americans.

• Americans eat one-third more protein than the Chinese do. About 70 percent of our protein intake comes from animals. The Chinese, on the other hand, get only 7 percent of theirs from animal sources. As expected, those Chinese who eat the most protein, especially animal protein, also have the highest rates of heart disease, cancer and diabetes.

Of particular importance, according to Cornell University's T. Colin Campbell, Ph.D., a coauthor of the China study, is that a diet with lots of protein, especially animal protein, may have the greatest potential for enhancing the risk of cancer, heart disease and diabetes—the so-called diseases of affluence.

What *do* the Chinese eat most? An impressive 75 percent of their calories come from complex carbohydrates—the rice, grains and vegetables that are the mainstay of a vegetarian diet.

A more recent study done in Germany also has exciting news for vegetarians.

Researchers there conducted a five-year study of 1,900 vegetarians in what was formerly West Germany. These people classified themselves as either strict or moderate vegetarians. Many never ate fish, poultry, meat or eggs. Others did consume eggs and dairy products, with occasional amounts of fish or meat. In general, the group had healthy lifestyle habits, such as not smoking or being overweight. At the end of five years, the group experienced only *one-third* the deaths from heart disease that would normally have been expected. And they suffered half the expected deaths and diseases related to respiratory and digestive disorders.

Closer to home, the Seventh-Day Adventists have also shown us what a vegetarian lifestyle can do for your health. This conservative religious group is prohibited from using alcohol, tobacco and pork and is encouraged to follow a lacto-ovo-vegetarian diet. Through numerous studies of this special group, researchers have found that Seventh-Day Adventists have lower death rates from cancer, heart disease, stroke, diabetes and other chronic diseases than other Americans who do not follow the Adventists' dietary practices.

The fact is that a vegetarian diet can heal certain ailments, lessen their severity or sometimes even prevent them altogether. So the closer you come to eliminating meat from

your diet, the better it is for your overall health.

To stress this point, we've put together a list of 15 ailments or conditions—from arthritis to stroke—that can benefit from a vegetarian diet. All the information presented is based on medical research from doctors and universities studying the connection between diet and health.

One final note: Some of the scientific studies cited here did not specifically deal with a vegetarian diet. But they did the next best thing. They tested the foods most commonly found as the major components of a vegetarian diet—whole grains, vegetables, fruits and other complex carbohydrates. Where would your health be without them?

arthritis

People who suffer from the pain, swelling and stiffness of rheumatoid arthritis have often said that what they eat has an effect on their level of discomfort. And for the most part, their observations have been dismissed or, at best, viewed with skepticism. But now a study from a group of researchers in Oslo, Norway, may finally help turn the skeptics around. Over a period of 13 months, the researchers found that arthritis sufferers assigned to a week-long fast followed by a vegetarian diet had a significant improvement in their symptoms compared with a similar group who ate their usual diets.

In their experiment, the researchers studied 53 patients (45 women and 8 men) with rheumatoid arthritis. To be included in the study, the patients had to have active disease—three or more swollen joints, six or more tender joints, morning stiffness that lasted longer than 45 minutes and altered blood-test values typical of rheumatoid arthritis. The participants were then split into two groups. Twenty-six were told to simply eat the diets they had always eaten. The remaining 27 immediately began dietary modifications, and that's where the study got really interesting.

Fast, then feast. For the first seven to ten days, the diet group fasted, consuming only herbal teas, garlic, vegetable broth and juice extracts from carrots, beets and celery. No fruit juices were allowed. "After the fast, the patients reintroduced a 'new' food item every second day," the researchers explained. "If they noticed an increase in pain, stiffness or joint swelling within 2 to 48 hours, this item was omitted from the diet for at least seven days." If symptoms worsened on a second tryout of the food, it was excluded from the person's diet for the rest of the study period.

What's more, during the first 3½

months, the diet group patients were asked to refrain from eating foods that contain gluten, meat, fish, eggs, dairy products, refined sugar or citrus fruits. And they were told to avoid salt, strong spices, preservatives, alcoholic beverages, tea and coffee. At the end of that time period, however, some of the forbidden foods—specifically milk, other dairy products and gluten-containing items—were carefully reintroduced into the people's diet. In other words, the patients became lacto-vegetarians.

The outcome of this study was nothing short of astonishing. After four weeks, the patients in the vegetarian group showed a significant improvement in the number of tender and swollen joints as well as in the duration of morning stiffness. Also, their grip-strength and blood-test results improved. Best of all, those benefits were still present after one year on the modified diet. Indeed, say the researchers, there were significant advantages for the diet group in all measured areas.

What about the group that *didn't* change their diets? Although they did experience a decrease in pain after the first month, this improvement did not last until the end of the study. What's more, none of the other measurements used to gauge arthritis showed any significant improvement throughout the year. Consequently, the researchers concluded that fasting followed by an individually adjusted vegetarian diet can be a "useful supplement to con-

ventional medical treatment of rheumatoid arthritis."

cancer

As mentioned before, Seventh-Day Adventists tend to follow a strict, largely vegetarian diet. Because they do for religious reasons what many health experts advise the rest of us to do for our health—eat a low-fat diet containing lots of whole grains, fruits and vegetables as well as refrain from smoking and drinking—they've become a fertile ground of study for scientists interested in the relationship between diet and disease.

The researchers haven't been disappointed. Studies dating back to 1960 have found that the Adventists are healthier than the average American. They have significantly lower death rates from heart disease, diabetes and many forms of cancer, including lung and breast cancers.

Paul K. Mills, Ph.D., studied cancer among the Adventists for eight years at Loma Linda University, an Adventist institution in Loma Linda, California. When he first began his work, he says, he and his colleagues expected to find that the lack of animal fat in the Adventists' diet was responsible for the low incidence of the killer cancers. Many cancer researchers have long believed that dietary fat may play a key role in causing cancer, largely because populations eating high-fat diets tend to have high cancer rates.

But among the Adventists, the evidence

to date suggests there's something more to the equation than just avoiding animal fat.

"Although we have found a fat link for some cancer sites, it isn't true for all of them," says Dr. Mills, who is now a researcher for the Cincinnati office of the Centers for Disease Control and Prevention. "Probably the most striking result of our work is that no matter what cancer site we examine, there seems to be a very strong *protective* association with the consumption of fruits and vegetables."

The evidence collected from the Adventist studies and from other research prompted the National Cancer Institute (NCI) to establish the Diet, Nutrition and Cancer Program in 1975. Its aim was to pursue the dietary links to cancer and, among other things, to make recommendations for further research. A few years later, NCI commissioned the National Academy of Sciences to review all the scientific information on diet and cancer and

to issue interim dietary guidelines for reducing the risk of cancer. At this point, those guidelines are well known: Reduce your intake of fat to no more than 30 percent of calories, eat foods high in fiber (20 to 35 grams daily), include fresh fruits and vegetables and whole-grain cereals in your daily diet, decrease consumption of cured foods, and drink alcoholic beverages only in moderation.

Though the dietary link to cancer is still the subject of intense study, says Carolyn Clifford, Ph.D., chief of NCI's Diet and Cancer Branch, experts believe that if every American followed these dietary guidelines to the letter, there would be a 50 percent reduction in colorectal cancer, a 25 percent reduction in breast cancer and a 15 percent reduction in cancers of the prostate, endometrium and gallbladder.

In addition, notes Dr. Clifford, studies are under way to investigate which plant compounds may act as inhibitors of the carcinogenic process in the body. "We're looking at some of the more well known ones—vitamins A, C and E, beta-carotene and dietary fiber," she explains. "But there are other types of compounds in foods that are not classed as essential nutrients— such as plant estrogens; indoles, which are found in vegetables such as cabbage and broccoli; and flavonoids and phenols—which seem to exert a protective effect against cancer."

In fact, in March 1992, a team of researchers at Johns Hopkins University

School of Medicine in Baltimore made the front page of the *New York Times* with its discovery: A potent compound—sulforaphane—in broccoli and other cruciferous vegetables causes cells to speed up their production of enzymes known to protect against cancer-causing chemicals. "Although the story is not yet complete," says researcher Paul Talalay, M.D., a molecular pharmacologist who heads a program at Johns Hopkins to develop strategies for protection against cancer, "our *prediction* is that sulforaphane will block tumor formation in animals and presumably man."

All that from broccoli? Yes—and there's more. Studies have shown that many of the staples of the vegetarian diet contain compounds that have cancer-fighting properties. Legumes, for instance, contain a substance that suppresses the activity of genes known to cause cancer and interferes with abnormal cell growth, the hallmark of malignancy. There's evidence, too, that components of cruciferous vegetables may

detoxify estrogens, which are thought to cause breast cancer. In many cases, one "good" food component may protect against another known to cause cancer. Ellagic acid, for instance, found in fruits such as strawberries, may protect the body against a carcinogenic assault from aflatoxins, a natural food contaminant associated with liver cancer.

The vegetarian diet may work in other ways as well. A German study of male vegetarians found that their white blood cells—the immune system's frontline troops against disease and infection—were twice as deadly to tumor cells as those of meat eaters. The researchers speculated that for some reason, the vegetarians may have either more "natural killer cells" among their white cells or more ferocious natural killer cells—or both.

Not all cancers seem to have a food link. "The association is most marked for epithelial cancers—those of the gastrointestinal and respiratory tracts," says Dr. Clifford. "But those are most of the major ones."

Here's a brief rundown of some of the major research on cancers that have a strong dietary link.

Lung cancer. Among the Adventists, increased fruit consumption is strongly associated with a large decrease in lung cancer risk, says Dr. Mills. In fact, he says, even among former smokers there was "a very dramatic decrease with the consumption of fruits."

This is a very important finding because

lung cancer is the leading cause of cancer death in this country, linked almost entirely to smoking. Lung cancer rates are declining among men but are increasing among women, probably because of different smoking patterns. Prevention appears to be the only weapon against this killer, which has a low 13 percent survival rate after five years. Detection is difficult, and most lung cancers are discovered only when the disease is in an advanced stage.

Other studies, notably those among a multiethnic group of Hawaiians, have found a link between increased consumption of vegetables and decreased lung cancer risk. Early studies led researchers to look at beta-carotene as the constituent possibly responsible for this protective effect. But a number of other studies, including the Hawaiian research, have suggested there may be another fruit or vegetable compound responsible. No matter what's actually doing the trick, this is one more strong reason to eat lots of vegetables.

Breast cancer. Adventist women have breast cancer rates 15 to 20 percent lower than other women. A study done among German vegetarians found death from breast cancer to be rare. But so far, the studies examining the dietary link to breast cancer have been equivocal. Many experts believe that a high-fat diet may cause breast cancer, largely through estrogen production. Many breast cancers are, in effect, "fueled" by estrogen, and estrogen production increases on high-fat diets.

A number of studies, including the ten-year, $25 million Women's Health Initiative, will explore the role of fat in breast cancer.

Prostate cancer. Prostate cancer is the second most common malignancy among American men, ranking behind only lung cancer. But unlike lung cancer rates, which are dropping among men, prostate cancer has shown a steady increase over the past several decades. And this cancer is responsible for 11 percent of all cancer deaths among men.

Researchers have noted a strong correlation between dietary fat intake and prostate cancer risk. In fact, in the United States, the highest death rates from prostate cancer are in those counties with the highest fat consumption. There also seems to be a link to age, socioeconomic status, race, marital status and incidence of venereal disease.

In a study financed by the NCI, Dr. Mills and his colleagues analyzed the dietary and lifestyle characteristics of 14,000 Adventist men, who were monitored for six years. The researchers looked particularly at the 180 confirmed cases of prostate cancer among the men in the group. They found that men who had more education were at a significantly decreased risk of developing prostate cancer. But no other factor, including consumption of dietary fat, was as profound as the effect of a vegetarian diet. "It was the frequent consumption of fruits and vegetables that was associated with the decreased risk of prostate cancer," says Dr. Mills.

The researchers found strong protective relationships with the increasing consumption of dried beans, lentils or peas; fresh citrus fruits; raisins, dates and other dried fruits; nuts; and tomatoes. A daily green salad and use of vegetarian protein products—soy or gluten-based meat substitutes—also had some protective effect.

Colon cancer. Colon cancer is the second leading cause of cancer death among Americans. Fortunately, the evidence linking diet with prevention of colon cancer is quite convincing. A study published in the *Journal of the National Cancer Institute* reviewed all the major studies done in this area up until 1990. The conclusion? An appreciable protective effect was associated with high intake of fiber or vegetables.

Too late to be included in that analysis were two studies done by Walter C. Willett, M.D., and his colleagues at Harvard Medical School in Boston. One study involved 88,751 women in what is called the Nurses Study; the other was among 7,284 men in the Health Professionals Follow-Up Study. Both studies found that animal fat is strongly associated with colon cancer and that fiber from all sources—vegetables, fruits and grains—exerts a protective effect against colon cancer.

For semivegetarians who eat only fish or chicken, the news is still good. Dr. Willett found that the women in the Nurses Study who ate chicken or fish but no red meat cut their colon cancer risk by as much as 50 percent.

Dr. Mills, who recently finished his own colon cancer study, says he has achieved similar results. "These studies are so dramatic that Walt Willett—who is not given to making wild statements—is often quoted as saying the optimum amount of red meat in the American diet should be zero."

Pancreatic cancer. Cancer of the pancreas is the fifth leading cause of cancer death in the United States. Very little is known about this cancer, except that risk increases after age 50 and is higher among smokers. It is usually detected when it is in an advanced stage, which may be why only 3 percent of all pancreatic cancer patients live more than five years after diagnosis.

But in his studies among the Adventists, Dr. Mills found that traditional Adventist fare—legumes, dried and fresh fruits, vegetables and soy products—had "a very protective effect" against this cancer that is almost impossible to cure.

Bladder cancer. Bladder cancer is more common among men than women. In a significant number of cases, it's linked to smoking. But Dr. Mills and his colleagues, looking at bladder cancer among the Adventists, found another startling association: meat. "One thing we thought we would see is a strong protective association with fresh fruits and vegetables, but actually, meat consumption turned out to be very risk enhancing. A twofold increase in bladder cancer risk was associated with frequent meat consumption," he says.

constipation

As the old laxative ad used to say, constipation can be a problem. And it certainly is, according to a survey of 14,407 Americans by the National Institute of Diabetes and Digestive and Kidney Diseases, which found 23 percent of the women and 9 percent of the men suffered. Older people were five times more likely to be constipated than younger people.

Constipation, which is defined as infrequent and difficult bowel movements, can be caused by many things, ranging from a blockage in the digestive system to lack of exercise to a diet deficient in fiber. For less serious causes, constipation lends itself to self-help cures. According to the National Institutes of Health, Americans spend an estimated $750 million annually on laxatives. But laxatives aren't meant to

be a long-term solution to constipation problems. In fact, they can make the problem worse because they are habit-forming. Once the body begins relying on laxatives to prompt bowel movements, the body's natural mechanisms effectively shut down, and the user becomes dependent on drugs to have a bowel movement.

But constipation is rarely, if ever, a problem among vegetarians. In fact, a Finnish study aimed at assessing the health effects of a vegetarian diet found that the few constipated subjects who switched to a lacto-ovo-vegetarian diet weren't constipated anymore.

A high-fiber diet, full of fruits (especially dried ones), vegetables and grains—along with exercise and drinking plenty of liquids—is accepted as the best natural remedy for constipation, according to the National Institutes of Health. The fiber tends to make stools softer and bulkier, so they pass more easily and frequently.

diabetes

Perhaps more than any other ailment, diabetes responds to treatment with diet.

And that's true whether you're talking about type I (juvenile-onset; insulin-dependent) or type II (adult-onset; non-insulin-dependent) diabetes. Nevertheless, for the 14 million people in the United States who have diabetes (and for the 750,000 who will develop it each year), therapy is more likely to revolve around insulin and drugs. Too bad.

"Diet therapy is cost effective, well tolerated and safe," says noted cholesterol researcher James W. Anderson, M.D. Along with his colleagues at the Veterans Affairs Medical Center in Lexington, Kentucky, Dr. Anderson has proposed an ideal diet to help manage and control blood sugar fluctuations as well as the complications often associated with diabetes (high cholesterol and heart disease). The diet, which is also advocated by the American Diabetes Association, has all the hallmarks of a vegetarian regimen. It leans heavily on complex carbohydrates

and fiber, and it's low in fat.

In fact, studies have shown that vegetarians have a distinct advantage over nonvegetarians when it comes to diabetes: They're less likely to die of the dis-

ease than are their meat-eating brethren. In one long-term study, researchers from the School of Public Health at the University of Minnesota in Minneapolis observed more than 22,000 Seventh-Day Adventists for 21 years. After all that time, the rate of diabetes as an underlying cause of death among the Adventists was only 45 percent of the rate for all white Americans. In addition, the study also suggested that the rate of development of new diabetic cases is lower in vegetarians than in meat eaters.

Why vegetarian diets work. What is it about a vegetarian diet that helps control diabetes and its complications? It's more than the fact that vegetarians are thinner than nonvegetarians, says Johanna Dwyer, D.Sc., R.D., of the Tufts University School of Medicine and Frances Stern Nutrition Center at the New England Medical Center Hospital in Boston.

"Vegetarian diets tend to be higher in complex carbohydrates and dietary fiber from beans, legumes, whole-grain bread, fruits and other plant foods" than typical American diets, says Dr. Dwyer. This type of diet probably influences carbohydrate metabolism for the better because it lowers blood sugar. Also, eating legumes slows digestion and absorption of carbohydrates and helps slow down the rise in blood sugar that often follows a meal, she notes.

What's more, the diets of most vegetarians are usually low in both total fat and saturated fat, which keeps cholesterol levels low and reduces the risk of heart disease, a frequent and often deadly complication of diabetes.

Sounds a lot like Dr. Anderson's dietary therapy for diabetes. While it's not strictly vegetarian, it's quite close. Besides being low in fat and cholesterol, "the diet we use contains commonly available foods and provides 70 percent of calories as carbohydrates and 35 grams of dietary fiber per 1,000 calories eaten," says Dr. Anderson. That's a lot of fiber, but it's gotten results. "In our studies, it improved blood sugar control and also reduced insulin requirements by 30 to 40 percent for patients with type I diabetes and by 75 to 100 percent for those with type II diabetes. In most instances, insulin was discontinued after 10 to 21 days of diet treatment in type II patients," he states.

The studies also showed that as an added benefit, the diet lowered blood cholesterol levels an average of 30 percent in people with type I diabetes and 24 percent in those with type II. And it also helped peel off pounds, the only thing many type II diabetics have to do to eradicate or control their disease.

diverticular disease

Diverticular disease is a painful intestinal disorder rare in the Third World but common in developed countries such as the United States.

Though the connection hasn't been proven, most researchers believe that

diverticular disease is caused by a low-fiber diet. It may be for that reason that the disease is uncommon among vegetarians, whose consumption of fiber, especially cereal fiber, is so great. Interestingly, studies have found that as the Japanese have abandoned their semivegetarian diets for more high-fat, low-fiber Western fare, the prevalence of diverticular disease has increased.

Though it didn't look at vegetarians per se, a study done in Greece comparing 100 patients with diverticular disease and 110 other people found that the problem-free people were eating diets higher in fiber-rich foods. And they consumed significantly less meat, milk and milk products than their counterparts.

Other research has found that high-fiber diets reduce the frequency, recurrence and complications of diverticular disease, though most scientists remain cautious about calling fiber a cure until further studies are done.

fatigue

Although there are no scientific studies that prove you can increase your level of pep with a vegetarian diet, increased energy still ranks high on the list of positive changes experienced by those who adopt this food style.

"Nearly one out of every three vegetarians reports an enhanced level of energy, stamina and endurance, making this the most commonly mentioned health-related benefit," write Paul R. Amato, Ph.D., and Sonia A. Partridge in their book *The New Vegetarians: Promoting Health and Protecting Life.* "Many people who notice an improvement in energy are involved in sports or athletics. Not surprisingly, they find that giving up meat is associated with better performance."

And at least in the particular case of athletic prowess, there *is* scientific research. According to David Nieman, D.H.Sc., professor of health promotion at Appalachian State University in Boone, North Carolina, endurance athletes who are also vegetarians have a distinct advantage over their meat-eating competitors.

"Athletes in heavy training are urged to consume 70 percent of their calories as complex carbohydrates," says Dr. Nieman. Studies show that a diet high in complex carbohydrates maximizes the body's glycogen stores and, consequently, enhances the ability to perform. "For those who engage in running, cycling or swimming, for example, a vegetarian diet simply makes it easier to get the fuel their muscles need," he says.

What about the rest of us? Forget the

kind of carbo loading that endurance athletes in training require. That won't give ordinary Joes and Josephines more pep, says Dr. Nieman. Instead, look at your diet more closely, "because certain foods can worsen fatigue, while others can actually combat it," says Susan Lark, M.D., director of the PMS Self-Help Center in Los Altos, California, and author of *The Menopause Self-Help Book.*

The diet to beat fatigue. New vegetarians often make the mistake of eating large quantities of dairy products and whole wheat to make up for the calories and protein they used to get from meat, says Dr. Lark. "Unfortunately, dairy and wheat are the primary foods that can cause low energy." So can sugary foods, alcohol, coffee and other caffeine-containing beverages.

"Alcohol depletes stores of B complex vitamins and magnesium, both of which help convert food into usable energy," she says. "Sugar and caffeine also deplete B vitamins." What's more, as you probably know, eating sugar may provide an initial rush of energy, but it's typically followed by a drop in blood sugar, with a resulting energy dip. Coffee has a similar effect.

Dr. Lark says that an ideal fatigue-free vegetarian diet should avoid wheat, dairy foods and eggs and be high in foods containing magnesium and potassium, B vitamins and vitamin C. "I would stock my pantry with staples such as dried beans and peas, raw nuts and seeds, ample fruits and vegetables, plus complex starches such as white potatoes and sweet potatoes."

Low blood levels of iron can also cause fatigue. So women in particular, who tend to lose iron when they menstruate, should fuel up on iron-rich foods such as beans baked in molasses, lima beans, prunes and greens.

It's also quite common to feel an energy dip late in the afternoon, adds Ralph LaForge, director of health promotion at the San Diego Cardiac Center Medical Group. "That's often a result of what and how much is eaten at lunch. Vegetarians usually eat less of the calorie-dense foods that tend to slow you down.

"Eating too many rich, fatty calories at lunch—as nonvegetarians often do—leads to what I call the Jacuzzi effect. In order for you to digest this heavy, fatty meal, blood is diverted to the stomach and intestines and away from the brain," he explains. "In addition, research has shown that changes in blood sugar levels alter specific brain neurotransmitters (such as serotonin). The result is like being in a Jacuzzi, all cozy and relaxed. A great feeling, but not what you want at work."

gallstones

Fair, fat, forty, female and fertile. Doctors call them the five Fs. These traits represent some of the greatest risk factors for developing gallstones—lumps of solid material, usually cholesterol, that form in the gallbladder. Not that those with the five Fs are the only ones who get gallstones. Men do, too, and those of Native American ancestry are particularly susceptible. But vegetarians, it seems, appear to have some protection against stone development.

In one study, Fiona Pixley, M.B., and her colleagues from Oxford University in Oxford, England, compared 632 women who ate meat with 130 women who were vegetarians. The researchers found that the meat eaters' risk of developing gallstones was twice that of the vegetarians. The difference could not be explained by the patients' social or economic status or by what region of the country they came from.

Dr. Pixley notes that Africans, who have a traditional diet that is high in fiber, rarely develop gallstones. Other studies have implicated the quantity of food eaten as well as the intake of cholesterol, simple sugars and fats as contributing to the formation of the stones. "Vegetarians," she points out, "tend to eat less saturated fat in addition to not eating meat and have a higher intake of fiber than nonvegetarians." This suggests that some dietary factor associated with vegetarianism affords a strong, independent protective effect against this common condition, she concludes.

Vegetarians also tend to be thinner, adds Harris Pastides, Ph.D., associate professor of epidemiology at the University of Massachusetts School of Public Health in Amherst. "It's well known that gallbladder disease is a fat-dependent disease. It could be that there is a problem with fat metabolism that leads to the accumulation of gallstones," he explains. "Therefore, the more dietary fat that is being ingested, the more likely you are to overload the system. Studies have shown that people who consume a greater proportion of their food from vegetables, beans and other legumes such as lentils have a lower risk of gallbladder disease than those who eat more meats and animal fats."

Protection by vegetable protein.

Malcolm Maclure, Sc.D., associate professor at the Harvard School of Public Health in Boston, speculates that vegetable protein might also be involved in the protective nature of a vegetarian diet. Dr. Maclure, who studied the relationship of diet to gallstones in over 88,000 nurses, admits that "something connected with vegetarianism seems to be protective. Whether it's the protein or the kind of fat or the fiber is not totally clear. It will take a few more years of study, and a few thousand more gallstones, to have enough statistical power to begin to clarify these questions."

Nevertheless, Dr. Maclure speculates that vegetable protein might be a key ingredient because—at least in hamsters—it reduces both the amount of cholesterol in the bile (the fluid inside the gallbladder) and also the incidence of gallstones. What's more, vegetable protein lowers the amount of cholesterol in the blood of those with high levels.

"There are vast numbers of compounds in vegetables. When you eat a vegetable, you're eating a very complex mixture. Although most attention has been paid to the substances in largest quantity—the proteins and fats, for example—it is very possible that others present in lesser amounts might be contributing to these study outcomes," says Dr. Maclure.

Whatever the reason, if you're in a high-risk group for developing gallstones, it seems prudent to decrease the proportion of fat in the diet and to increase the proportion of vegetables, says Dr. Pastides.

heart disease

This could be the single most important reason to become a vegetarian.

Scientifically, the proof is irrefutable—a low-fat vegetarian diet is a heart saver, indeed, a lifesaver. Experts have known for years that something in the diet affects the rate of heart disease. Countries with the highest consumption of animal fats also have the highest incidence of heart disease deaths. But a country like Japan, whose diet is traditionally low in fat, has had only one-tenth the rate of coronary heart disease as the United States. However, as fat consumption in Japan has increased, so has the rate of heart disease.

Consider these alarming statistics from the American Heart Association.

• Every 34 seconds, someone dies of heart disease (cardiovascular disease).

• Cardiovascular disease is the number one killer of Americans.

• More than six million people alive today have a history of heart attack, chest pain or both.

• This year, as many as 1.5 million Americans will have heart attacks. About one-third of them will die.

• More than 100 million American adults have blood cholesterol values of 200 milligrams or higher (considered borderline high). About 49 million have levels of 240 or above (considered high).

There's no doubt that a low-fat vegetarian diet is protective against cardiovascular disease, says heart disease researcher Dean Ornish, M.D. "I think the optimal amount of dietary animal products is prob-

ably zero or close to it. So the more you can move in that direction, the better off you are likely to be," he contends.

Dr. Ornish also conducted a ground-breaking study that proved the validity of his message. He wanted to see whether comprehensive lifestyle changes could affect hardening of the arteries (atherosclerosis) within a time frame of one year. To do that, he placed 28 patients with atherosclerosis in an experimental group that incorporated diet and lifestyle changes into their lives. Another 20 people with the same condition were assigned to a group that received the usual medical care.

The diet that heals. The patients in the experimental group were asked to eat a low-fat vegetarian diet, which was composed of fruits, vegetables, grains, legumes and soybean products. "No animal products were allowed, except egg whites and one cup per day of nonfat milk or yogurt," says Dr. Ornish. The diet contained only about 10 percent of calories from fat. That's dramatically less than the typical American diet, which hovers around 40 percent. And it was far less than that eaten by the usual-care group, which followed the conventional recommendation of 30 percent.

The diet also contained less than five milligrams of cholesterol a day. "Cholesterol is found only in animal products, which also tend to be high in saturated fat. Saturated fat, in turn, is converted by your body into blood cholesterol. In addition," Dr. Ornish notes, "people found it easier to go totally vegetarian than to cut back to two or three ounces of meat a day. When you eat a little meat, you tend to want more."

Lifestyle changes in the experimental group also included stress management and moderate exercise, such as walking.

Unclogging arteries. At the conclusion of the year's experiment, even Dr. Ornish was surprised by some of the results. At the beginning of the study, both groups had about the same severity of heart disease. Not so at the end.

Eighty-two percent of the patients who followed the low-fat vegetarian diet experienced a *regression* of their clogged arteries. In other words, their arteries were *less clogged* than before the study began. The usual-care group, on the other hand, ended up with arteries that were *more clogged*. The biggest surprise came, however, when the researchers discovered that those whose arteries were most closed to begin with (and who therefore had the most severe heart disease) showed the greatest improvement.

Of particular interest were the amazing statistics that follow. It's noteworthy that most of the improvements occurred in the first week or two. The patients in the vegetarian group reported:

- A 91 percent reduction in the frequency of chest pains (angina).
- A 42 percent reduction in the duration of angina.
- A 28 percent reduction in the severity of their angina.

In contrast, the patients in the usual-care group reported:

- A 165 percent rise in the frequency of angina.
- A 95 percent rise in its duration.
- A 39 percent rise in the angina severity.

Dr. Ornish believes his results suggest that "conventional recommendations for patients with heart disease (such as a 30 percent fat diet) are not sufficient to bring about disease reversal in many patients. In fact, seven other studies found that the majority of people with heart disease who follow a 30 percent diet become measurably worse. However, more comprehensive lifestyle changes may begin to reverse coronary atherosclerosis in as little as a year." And he says that improvements may continue as long as people maintain their healthy ways.

Feeling is believing. So how do you get former meat eaters to willingly accept not only a vegetarian diet but also one that is extremely low in fat? "We try to emphasize the short-term gains that come from changing your lifestyle," says Dr. Ornish.

"There's no point giving up something you enjoy unless you get back something else that's even better. If someone has heart disease, those choices become clearer because the chest pains begin to diminish very quickly. Within a few days to a few weeks, even those people with severe heart disease notice that they feel much better and have much less chest pain. In some cases, it goes away completely. People will say to me 'Yes, I like meat, but not *that* much. I feel so much better than before that it's a choice worth making.' "

Critics of Dr. Ornish's plan say that it's only because of his hands-on involvement with his patients that they're able to change and improve. But Dr. Ornish doesn't believe that. He says he gets letters from people all over the country who have maintained these changes on their own for as long as ten years. "One man who literally couldn't walk across the room without getting severe angina wrote to tell me he just got back from a two-week cross-country skiing trip carrying a 100-pound backpack in the Swiss Alps," he says.

Cholesterol drops, too. Need more proof? Consider what a vegetarian diet can do for high cholesterol levels. Cholesterol is the soft, fatlike substance present in all animal products that can build up on the insides of your arteries. It's unquestionably associated with heart disease. The higher your blood cholesterol level, the more likely you are to suffer from heart disease.

Furthermore, studies show that for every 1 percent reduction in blood cholesterol levels you can bring about, there is an estimated 2 percent reduction in your chances of heart disease. And a vegetarian diet can help you achieve those lower levels.

In one study, researchers from Australia examined the effect of three different diets on patients' cholesterol levels. One diet was high in fat and contained meat. Another was lacto-ovo-vegetarian. The third was a modification of the second in which 60 percent of the plant protein was replaced with *lean* meat.

At the end of the experiment, the researchers found that both of the prudent diets—the vegetarian and the lean meat—significantly lowered total cholesterol as well as undesirable low-density lipoprotein (LDL). The vegetarian diet, however, had the added benefit of producing a "greater cholesterol-lowering effect than did the lean meat diet (10 percent versus 5 percent)."

Prudent diets, if widely adopted, have

the potential for reducing the burden of heart disease in many Western countries, the researchers conclude.

Cholesterol levels can be lowered even more, however, if you're willing to go one step further—to a vegan diet. In a study of vegan Seventh-Day Adventists, researchers from the American Health Foundation in New York City compared Adventists' cholesterol levels with those of people who ate a typical American diet. Not surprisingly, they found that the Adventists' average total cholesterol was 25 percent lower and their average LDL levels were 38 percent less.

hemorrhoids

It's been estimated that 50 to 90 percent of the civilized world suffers from hemorrhoids, a condition that's been bothering folks since the beginning of time. There's even a reference in the Bible to those sometimes painful, sometimes itchy anal swellings.

Although hemorrhoids can be caused by heavy physical labor, pregnancy or prolonged periods of sitting or standing, the most common cause is simple constipation. Straining at something that Mother Nature never intended to be an eye-bulging experience can cause veins inside or outside the anus to bulge with blood, producing hemorrhoids. They're just like varicose veins, only hemorrhoids can remain your own personal secret.

As common as they are, however, relief

from existing hemorrhoids or prevention of future ones may be as simple as adding more fiber to your diet. Something in the neighborhood of 20 to 25 total grams of fiber a day is what most experts recommend for a happier, healthier bottom. Naturally, that means eating more whole-grain breads, whole-grain cereals, beans, fruits and vegetables—the same foods that vegetarians eat in abundance.

Why does increasing your fiber intake improve your chances of a hemorrhoid-free bottom? As food is digested, the waste products pass through the large intestine on their way to the rectum, where they stay until you move your bowels. As the waste materials move along, the intestine absorbs water from them. If the bulk moves too slowly, too much water can be removed, making the mass hard and irritating to pass. If it travels too quickly, not enough water is removed, and diarrhea may result.

When fiber is added to the diet, it helps

form the right consistency—not too hard, not too loose—and waste moves through the colon at just the right speed. The result is a bowel movement that is effortless and comfortable.

One study conducted in Sweden proved the point. Nineteen patients with a history of hemorrhoids participated in an experiment to measure the time for digested food to move through the intestine (what's known as transit time). Times were measured both before and after six weeks on a diet supplemented with ten grams of fiber daily. According to the researchers, patients with hemorrhoids often complain of transit time that is either too slow or too fast—meaning a problem of either constipation *or* diarrhea. As it turns out, an increase in fiber helped both situations. No strain equals no pain from hemorrhoids.

high blood pressure

Right now more than 62 million Americans have high blood pressure, but 46 percent of those people don't even know it. Of those with hypertension (another name for high blood pressure), two-thirds are not on any special diet or drugs, and another 22 percent are being treated inadequately.

What this means is that millions of Americans are asking their hearts to work harder than normal, putting both their hearts and arteries under great strain. Eventually, this strain will translate to

heart attacks, strokes and hardening of the arteries—and ultimately to life cut short. In 90 to 95 percent of the cases of high blood pressure, doctors have no idea what's causing it. Some, however, have an idea about how to lower it—and it doesn't involve drugs. You guessed it—the "therapy" is a vegetarian diet.

In one study, researchers from Harvard Medical School and Brigham and Women's Hospital in Boston compared two different groups of vegetarians with others who ate meat. One group of vegetarians followed a strict diet consisting mainly of cereal grains and vegetables. The other group included dairy products in their diet. Those who followed the strict vegetarian regime had blood pressures slightly lower than the lacto-vegetarians, but both groups had blood pressures about 10 to 15 points lower than the nonvegetarians.

Why does it work? The researchers were curious to know what it was in the meat eaters' diet that caused blood pressure to rise (or, conversely, what it was in the vegetarian diets that lowered blood pressure). So they looked at a few possibilities and found that the beneficial effects did not seem to be directly related to the avoidance of meat or to the intake of plant protein, salt, fiber or polyunsaturated fat.

"It seems likely," say the researchers, "that a nutrient or nutrients eaten in greater amounts in vegetarian than nonvegetarian diets lower blood pressure. Our

hypothesis is that there are minerals and perhaps vitamins in cereal products, fruits and vegetables that may lower blood pressure." Perhaps combinations of nutrients may be needed to produce enough of a blood pressure lowering to be detected in dietary studies, they suggest. "However, the low blood pressures of vegetarians are so striking that efforts must be expended to determine why they occur."

Whatever the reason turns out to be, researchers also know that a vegetarian diet can be beneficial for those with normal blood pressures as well as for those with mild high blood pressure. Doctors at the University of Western Australia Medical School in Perth studied the diets of Seventh-Day Adventists and concluded there is strong evidence that a lacto-ovo-vegetarian diet lowers blood pressure. The effect, they say, is independent of both salt intake and amount of food eaten each day. They also recognize that a vegetarian diet may be important in terms of both preventing and treating hypertension.

There's another benefit, adds Dr. Ornish. "People with high blood pressure who adopt a vegetarian diet are often able to reduce or even discontinue their blood pressure medications—under a doctor's supervision, of course. Because those medications sometimes have unpleasant side effects, people who can reduce or eliminate them are in for a double benefit," he claims. "They'll feel better because of the nature of the vegetarian diet and also because they no longer have to endure any potential drug side effects."

Another study underscores Dr. Ornish's contention that a vegetarian diet can help reduce or eliminate the need for blood pressure medications. Researchers from the Weimar Institute in Weimar, California, found that 36 out of 46 men and 40 out of 56 women in their study were able to discontinue their medications after adopting a vegan diet.

kidney stones

While the evidence is still scanty, a vegetarian diet seems to protect against kidney stones, pebblelike substances that form in the kidneys and cause excruciating pain when they pass through the urinary tract. Studies have shown that lacto-vegetarians have fewer episodes of calcium oxalate stones (the most common kind of kidney stone) than meat eaters.

Some studies indicate that people prone to stone formation eat more animal protein than others, but the relationship between animal protein and kidney stones is little understood. A possible link: The intake of animal products increases the amount of uric acid in the body and also leads to calcium being pulled out of the bones. Both uric acid and calcium are associated with stones.

osteoporosis

Here's a disease that's virtually preventable if you start young enough. And even if you don't do much until later in life, you can still produce a positive change—especially if you're a strict vegetarian.

Osteoporosis is the thinning of bone that often accompanies old age. While men can get it, too, osteoporosis is far more prevalent in women, whose bone density takes a dramatic nosedive during the decade or so following menopause. About one in three women can expect to suffer a hip fracture by age 75, thanks to osteoporosis. The same number of women will also shrink by inches due to vertebral fractures in their spines that they probably aren't even aware of. Indeed, that's one of the most devastating features of osteoporosis: Most people don't even know they have it until they break a bone.

Even if you're at greatest risk for getting osteoporosis—small-boned Caucasian and Oriental women are particularly vulnerable—you don't have to wait helplessly for it to strike. On the contrary, adopting a vegetarian diet can give you a leg up on preventing this disease. "It's quite well known that vegetarians get far less osteoporosis than people who eat animal protein on a regular basis," says Robert Lang, M.D., medical director of the Osteoporosis Diagnostic and Treatment Center in New Haven, Connecticut.

In one study, 1,600 postmenopausal women who had followed a lacto-ovo-vegetarian diet for at least 20 years had only 18 percent less bone mineral by age 80 than they had previously. A group of similar women who were meat eaters had *35 percent* less bone mineral.

In a more recent study, the same group of researchers sought to find out *why* vegetarians seem far less prone to osteoporosis. Researchers from Andrews University in Berrien Springs, Michigan, compared a group of ten healthy postmenopausal lacto-ovo-vegetarian women with a group of similar women who were meat eaters. The two groups ate about the same number of calories each day and took in the same amount of protein. And their calcium, iron and fiber intakes were about the same. As expected, the vegetarians consumed far less cholesterol, and the fat they ate was more likely to be polyunsaturated than saturated.

Clues to the puzzle. But there were two things that set the groups apart. And they're perhaps the major reasons that vegetarians are more protected against osteoporosis. The vegetarians' calcium-to-phosphorus ratio was more favorable, and they had an alkaline diet rather than an acidic one.

Here's what that means. "The calcium-phosphorus ratio is important for several reasons," says Dr. Lang. "Phosphorus in excess amounts interferes with your ability to absorb bone-building calcium from the intestines. Phosphorus (which is found in animal protein, dairy products and cola soft drinks) also activates the release of a hormone that in turn causes the body to pull calcium out of the bones. So when intakes of calcium are borderline or low and phosphorus intakes are high, bone loss is more likely to occur."

Meat eaters also have a more "acid" diet, continues Dr. Lang. The more acidic the diet, the more calcium is lost through the urine, a loss which upsets the body's acid-base balance. Acidic by-products of meat digestion have to be "buffered" when they are absorbed into the body. And it's bicarbonate from your bones that does the buffering. The problem is, when bicarbonate comes out, calcium comes along with it and is promptly excreted by the kidneys. Vegetable protein, on the other hand, does not require buffering and therefore does not deplete your bones of calcium, Dr. Lang explains.

Further evidence of a vegetarian diet's protective effect against osteoporosis comes from a Yale University School of Medicine study. The researchers there were looking for an association between eating meat and the incidence of hip fractures in women over age 50. They found it. After analyzing the data from 16 countries, they concluded that countries where little animal protein is eaten had a low incidence of hip fractures. Conversely, countries where most of the protein eaten is from animal sources had the highest rate of hip fractures. These researchers, like others, point to the acid-forming nature of meat digestion as the probable culprit.

Women who are strict vegans probably have the greatest potential for bone health, says Dr. Lang. That's because they simply have fewer phosphorus-containing foods in their diets. "I have patients who are vegetarian or nearly so who have actually *increased* their bone mass," he notes. He points out that other diet and lifestyle modifications are also beneficial to bone health. "I counsel my patients to keep their egg intake to a minimum, to get plenty of calcium and other minerals (especially magnesium, manganese, boron and zinc) and to exercise on a regular basis," he says.

Of course, the longer you've been a vegetarian, the better. Still, says Dr. Lang, becoming a vegetarian can produce bone benefits, even if you don't adopt that food style until you're past age 50. "The optimal age to start? Before your mother is pregnant with you," he quips.

overweight

Along with all the other health benefits of a vegetarian diet is one that should interest weight watchers everywhere: Vegetarians are almost invariably lean.

A survey done a few years ago by Dr. Amato found that 53 percent of the women and 54 percent of the men who adopted a vegetarian diet had lost weight. Their weight losses ranged from 2 to 90 pounds.

But how vegetarians get thin and stay that way remains a mystery. Although people who switch to a vegetarian diet often lose weight, studies in which overweight participants are placed on a vegetarian diet to lose weight aren't overwhelmingly successful.

There haven't been any studies that conclusively prove the leading theories—that vegetarians eat less, that their high-fiber diet promotes satiety, that they eat less fat or that they exercise more. In fact, some studies have just added to the mystery of vegetarians' leanness. One done at Purdue University in West Lafayette, Indiana, found that vegetarians who ate roughly the same number of calories as nonvegetarians and exercised about as often were still thinner. The average vegetarian, who ate 2,340 calories daily, 30 percent from fat, weighed in at 143 pounds. The average meat eater, who had three or four servings of meat a week and ate fewer calories (2,225), weighed 15 pounds more!

Considering all the health advantages of a vegetarian lifestyle, you've got nothing to lose (but pounds) by giving up meat.

premenstrual syndrome

It's not a disease, nor does it seem to affect any two women in the same way. But nearly every woman has had some symptom—whether it's bloating, breast pain, depression or something else—she associates with her period. Little is known about what causes premenstrual syndrome—in shorthand, PMS—but a study at the Massachusetts Institute of Technology suggests a high-carbohydrate, low-protein diet may reduce or eliminate some of the more troubling symptoms.

Though researcher Judith Wurtman, Ph.D., wasn't specifically studying a vegetarian diet, she wanted to learn if a carbohydrate meal with *no* protein would improve the moods of the 19 subjects who lived at her lab for three to five days before their periods. So she gave them a bowl of cornflakes moistened with nondairy creamer. "It worked like Valium," she reported.

Women who were morose and sluggish suddenly became alert and happier, says Dr. Wurtman, who has done extensive research on the effects of carbohydrates on mood and appetite. Moreover, the cornflakes had that effect only when the women were premenstrual. After their periods, a bowl of cornflakes wasn't a mood-elevating drug. It was just a bowl of cornflakes.

Carbohydrates raise the level of a brain chemical called serotonin, a mood and sleep regulator. The reason Dr. Wurtman gave her subjects cornflakes without protein (which would have been supplied by milk) is that protein curtails serotonin production.

There's no evidence that a vegetarian diet is the answer to every woman's PMS troubles, but some physicians who treat PMS do so with a diet that is low in fat and protein and high in complex carbohydrates such as fruits, vegetables and whole grains, the staples of vegetarian fare.

stroke

A stroke is a form of cardiovascular disease, but instead of the coronary arteries being blocked, it's the arteries to the brain that are affected. According to the American Heart Association, a stroke occurs when a blood vessel bringing oxygen and nutrients to the brain bursts or is clogged by a blood clot. When this happens, part of the brain doesn't get the flow of blood and oxygen it needs, and nerve cells in the affected area die. When the nerve cells can't function, the part of the body controlled by those cells can't function either. The loss is often permanent.

Current estimates show that about 500,000 people each year suffer a new or recurrent stroke. And it's not only really old people who get them. Twenty-eight percent of victims are under age 65.

Two of the biggest risk factors for stroke are heart disease and high blood pressure. Obviously, your best chances for stroke prevention lie with avoiding those two conditions. For details, see the sections that cover them on pages 26 and 31.

"The risk of stroke is much lower in vegetarians," says Dr. Ornish. "The Framingham Heart Study and studies conducted with Seventh-Day Adventists have shown that. The same processes that cause blockages to build up in the arteries that feed the heart also affect the arteries that supply blood to the brain. We have found that the benefits of a low-fat vegetarian diet extend beyond reversing or preventing heart disease and high blood pressure. We have simply focused our research on heart disease as a model that helps demonstrate how powerful simple changes can be."

making the switch with ease

Whether it's your conscience or your cholesterol prompting you to become a vegetarian, the transition from omnivore to herbivore doesn't have to be difficult. Of course, there's more to going meatless than not eating anything from the animal kingdom.

For one thing, you can't eat like a vegetarian while you're still thinking like a meat eater. Consider for a moment the typical American meal. We don't eat "steak, potato and a salad." We have a "steak dinner." It's a "roast turkey dinner," not "turkey, sweet potatoes, stuffing and a green bean casserole." Meat is the star of a meal, with vegetables merely supporting players. But what happens when the star is gone? What's the understudy?

"When you become a vegetarian, you are not just taking meat off the plate and eating what's left," says Reed Mangels, Ph.D., R.D., a nutrition advisor for the Baltimore-based Vegetarian Resource Group, the largest nonprofit, nonsectarian vegetarian group in the country. She often winds up counseling new—and confused—vegetarians who call for help.

"I've had people tell me 'Without that pork chop, I have a vegetable and a potato, and I'm still hungry.' They think they need to eat the same kind of meals as they ate before: 'something' plus a vegetable, a starch and a dessert," says Dr. Mangels, who generally follows a vegan diet. "Menu planning is different when you're a vegetarian. We tend to eat a lot more mixed dishes and casseroles with vegetables and grains or beans."

where's the beef substitute?

For an average American used to seeing vegetables as the colorful stuff that accompanies the steak on the plate, learning to regard the "garnish" as the meal may take some time. At first, a plate of pasta and vegetables may look as though it's missing something.

Of course, there *are* ways you can eat pretty much the way you did before. "A lot of people are concerned about this change in food habits. They wonder if they'll have to eat all sorts of weird foods," says Charles Stahler, who is codirector of the Vegetarian Resource Group and has been a vegan since 1977.

Some new vegetarians simply put a meat substitute in the spot where the pork chop used to be. Meat substitutes, which are made from vegetable protein, can be quite tasty. They come in every meat guise, from hot dog to turkey. For some people who find meatless too dramatic a change, a slice of soy turkey nestling up to some cranberry sauce and mashed potatoes can be comforting.

"I came from a meat-and-potatoes family," says Stahler, whose parents are now vegetarians. "Today we are a meat-substitute-and-potatoes family. The way

my mother cooks is the way she used to cook. There just isn't any actual meat in her meals."

Although most experts will tell you to do what makes you feel most comfortable, the secret behind a successful transition to a healthy vegetarian diet is variety. For most vegetarians, a constant diet of meat substitute and potatoes gets boring.

"Some people do like to use those foods when they're making the switch. They're transition foods," says Suzanne Havala, R.D., former chairperson of the Vegetarian Nutrition Dietetic Practice Group of the American Dietetic Association and a nutrition advisor to the Vegetarian Resource Group. "In some ways, I find those foods a hindrance because they delay the change in the mindset that says there has to be a high-protein focal point to the meal."

That's not to say soy dogs and fib ribs should be forbidden foods. "Even I keep frozen veggie burgers on hand because they make a quick meal," says Havala.

Besides being the spice of life, variety is what guarantees you'll get all the nutrients you need. When a vegetarian eats a salad, it's rarely a clump of iceberg lettuce with a few anemic tomato slices and some grated carrots. There may be deep green spinach or kale and some marinated pinto beans to help supply iron. And you'll probably find a sprinkling of nuts or wheat germ for zinc, not to mention zip.

In the long run, what's going to keep your meatless diet healthy and interesting are the many and varied foods that may be new to your palate now—tofu, kasha, bulgur, tempeh, basmati rice, mustard greens—but which, in a matter of weeks, you'll wonder how you lived without.

start slowly or jump in?

Should you give up meat today or taper down to the vegetarian lifestyle? The experts don't always agree—and the advantages to both approaches are equally good.

When heart disease researcher Dean Ornish, M.D., decided to become a vegetarian at the age of 19, he did so to feel better, not out of a fear of dying. As director of the Preventive Medicine Research Institute in Sausalito, California, Dr. Ornish puts patients with severe coronary artery disease on a vegetarian diet. They not only feel better but also experience an improvement—sometimes even a reversal—of their heart disease.

Dr. Ornish finds that people are better off making big changes rather than small ones. "If people make moderate changes, they often have the sense they're being deprived, not being able to eat everything they want. But they're not making changes *big enough* to enable them to feel that much better," he says. "When you make comprehensive changes, you often feel *so* much better, so quickly, that the choices you make are easier because the benefits are clearer."

Of course, for those who are making the switch for ethical reasons, doing so gradually is generally unthinkable. But if you're changing for health reasons, you might find it easier to make the switch gradually—especially if you're not savvy about nutrition or vegetarianism. After all, you're going to be changing the eating habits of a lifetime.

the biggest mistake

Perhaps the biggest mistake new vegetarians make is to substitute full-fat cheese and whole eggs for meat as their primary

protein. That is the absolute wrong thing to do if your goal is to eat healthier. "People who feel they have to replace meat with a lot of cheese and eggs end up with a diet as high—or higher—in fat and cholesterol as they had before. They're not doing themselves any favors," says Dr. Mangels.

If you're not becoming a vegan, you can turn to nonfat or low-fat cheeses and skim milk. And you can take advantage of egg substitutes. But don't limit yourself to those changes. Beans and bean products such as tofu and tempeh are good sources of protein.

But what if you don't like beans and think of tofu as something for Zen monks but not for you? Don't worry, say the experts. You're unlikely to suffer a protein deficiency if you eat a wide variety of other foods, including other soy products. "Tofu is not going to make or break you," says Havala.

What if you like beans but they don't agree with you? They are, after all, known as "the musical vegetable" and can produce gas in the digestive tract. Adding beans to the extra fiber you're eating as you increase your intake of fruits and vegetables can leave you bloated and full, not to mention discouraged. After all, you expected your new vegetarian diet to make you feel better, not worse.

"Not everyone experiences excess gas when making the switch," says Havala. "But for some people, there is an increased amount of flatulence, which generally sub-

sides as the body adapts to the higher intake of fiber. It varies according to the individual. You need to remember that while some people see excess flatulence as a social problem, biologically there's nothing wrong with it."

If you don't find that comforting, there are some things you can do to avoid excess gas. One way is to *slowly* increase your intake of fiber, particularly beans. "Don't start out eating two cups of beans a day," suggests Dr. Mangels. Soy products are more easily digested—even though they're derived from a bean—so you can eat them while you build your fiber intake. Also, there is a product called Beano, which contains an enzyme that helps you digest beans. Add a few drops to your first bite of cooked beans for gas control.

In addition, there are some cooking methods that help cut beans' gas potential. Soaking dried beans overnight in water helps. Drain the beans, then cook them in fresh water. Midway through cooking,

drain them again and add new water. All that helps reduce some of their ballistic power by getting rid of the water-soluble compounds that cause gas.

doing too much

Another mistake new vegetarians make is to try to do too much too fast, says Dr. Mangels. "People have the idea that they need to make every change on the spot. Not only are they now vegetarians, but they're going to eat only whole, unprocessed, organic foods, cooked from scratch. The whole thing becomes so much of a task that they get discouraged and give up."

Becoming a vegetarian may mean you're going to spend a little more time contemplating what you're going to eat. Eating is a habit, and the recipes you grew up eating and cooking may have to be discarded or changed to reflect your new style. "A lot of people can whip up a batch of beef spaghetti sauce while they're talking on the phone and not give it a second thought," says Havala. "If they're making a lentil loaf or bean chili, however, they have to pay more attention to what they're doing the first few times. It takes a little longer than something you've made 10 or 20 times."

To save time, become a weekend cook, says Havala. Many working people do this already, cooking a big batch of food on Sundays and freezing it in portions that can be microwaved after work.

For those who aren't willing to go cold tofu, a shift away from red meat and toward chicken and fish is a good start. Even if you intend to go meatless eventually, phasing out meat dishes gradually is a nontraumatic approach. And it's certainly not difficult to substitute nonmeat pasta dishes for steaks or burgers several times a week. In fact, many health-conscious Americans are doing just that, with no intention of ever becoming full-time vegetarians.

While you're painlessly weaning yourself from animal products, start gathering good resources on the healthy vegetarian diet. The Vegetarian Resource Group publishes a number of pamphlets and booklets—some free, some at a charge—as well as the *Vegetarian Journal,* a bimonthly magazine that carries articles on nutrition, recipes and helpful hints for vegetarians. You can contact them at P.O. Box 1463, Baltimore, MD 21203.

You'll want to learn more about the wide variety of beans and grains that can be turned into tantalizing meals. Unless you're an adventuresome gourmet, you might want to start by simply adding vegetables to your favorite pasta dish. Or you can make your favorite stir-fry without meat. (The bold can toss in a little tofu.) Exploring cookbooks and ethnic restaurants as well as experimenting with new foods will ease the transition into this brave new world of eating.

Meal planning and shopping may also be a little more time-consuming, since you're altering those habits as well. But to eat a healthy vegetarian diet, there is no need to cook everything from scratch and buy all your food from specialty stores. "Specialty stores do carry some of the more uncommon items and some of the vegetarian convenience foods, but they tend to be more expensive," says Havala. "Anything you're going to need to eat a healthy vegetarian diet can be gotten at the neighborhood grocery store."

Many stores now even carry products that were once available only in health food stores, such as basmati rice and tofu. Supermarkets have recognized that American eating habits are changing. Further, an influx of Asian and Latino immigrants in many areas has forced stores to stock more exotic items. Since many of these ethnic groups eat little meat, you can benefit from the cultural—and culinary—diversity of your neighborhood.

Even if you never buy any exotic products, produce can be expensive. To cut down on your food bill, suggests Havala,

buy fruits and vegetables only in season, when they're plentiful and cheap—and at the height of their flavor, so you don't need to perk them up with lots of salt, sugar or fat. Strawberries and asparagus, for example, are costlier in the winter because they must be shipped from warmer climes.

In the spring and summer, you can pick up local produce at roadside stands, farmers' markets and many supermarkets, often for half the winter price. That's also a good time to consider doing some canning or freezing, so you can enjoy summer's bounty—at reduced cost—all year long.

Don't be afraid to rely on low-fat convenience foods. Dinner doesn't have to be a three-course meal cooked from scratch. Sometimes you might just want to microwave a potato and serve it with a hearty salad. Not every meal has to be a big production, says Dr. Mangels.

the nutritional rules

Many people approach vegetarianism with trepidation because they believe they'll have to turn meal planning into some complex chemistry experiment, mixing this food with that to get just the right nutrients. That's not true. Most experts agree that a diet that contains a variety of foods will supply most of the nutrients you need. There are only a few nutritional rules you may need to adhere to. They include:

• Keep your intake of empty calories—such as sweets and high-fat foods—to a minimum. Those filler-uppers don't leave you much room for all the good things you should be eating, such as fruits and vegetables, which supply more nutrients.

• Choose whole-grain rather than refined products. Again, you get more nutrients in food that is less processed.

• Eat a variety of fruits and vegetables. Include plenty of dark green leafy vegetables, which contain iron and calcium. Try to eat something containing vitamin C with the greens because C helps to increase iron absorption, suggests Havala. Also eat deep yellow or orange fruits and vegetables, such as carrots, sweet potatoes, peaches and cantaloupe, because they're good sources of cancer-preventing beta-carotene.

• If you're eating eggs and cheese, limit yourself to three egg yolks a week and use nonfat or low-fat cheeses. Egg substitutes are made from egg whites, so they contain no cholesterol and can be used freely for protein.

• Eat a variety of nuts and seeds, especially if you're a vegan. These items contain the zinc, calcium and iron that you'd usually get from animal foods. But remember that nuts and seeds are high in fat, so don't go overboard.

• Don't forget about beans, which provide zinc, calcium and iron. When choosing tofu (which is made from soybeans), opt for a type processed with calcium sulfate—a good source of calcium.

stock up

Once you've decided to become a vegetarian, it's a good idea to restock your cupboards and freezer. That way you'll have the supplies you need to whip up meals in a hurry. Among the staples you'll find handy:

• Ready-to-eat whole-grain cereals fortified with vitamin B_{12}

• Quick-cooking whole-grain cereals, such as oatmeal

• Whole-grain breads and crackers

• Canned beans, such as kidney, pinto, black and white

• Canned vegetarian soups or soup mixes

• Pasta, rice and tortillas

• Plain frozen vegetables

• Tomato sauce

• Frozen fruit juice

• Frozen meat substitutes (available extensively in health food stores and in some supermarkets)

• Nuts and seeds, such as sunflower seeds

• Spices and herbs

★ pasta galore

Welcome to the infinitely diverse realm of pasta. There are so many ways to serve America's favorite noodles that you'll never be at a loss for quick lunches as well as sophisticated dinners.

Pasta fits beautifully into a vegetarian diet. It's got protein, lots of filling complex carbohydrates and very little fat. Whole wheat pasta has more fiber than white, but even white is an admirable source. I've included recipes for both types. Egg noodles that contain no yolks are free of cholesterol and lower in fat than regular egg varieties.

I've cut fat considerably in my recipes by substituting low-fat cheese, yogurt and other dairy products for heavy cream, butter and full-fat cheese. I've also been generous with my pasta serving sizes, allotting three ounces per person instead of the usual two. When you're eating low-fat, meatless meals, you want them to be hearty and to leave you feeling satisfied when you get up from the table.

sun-dried tomato and parsley pesto

Be sure to buy dehydrated sun-dried tomatoes rather than those steeped in oil, which are much higher in fat. If you can't find tricolor tortellini, substitute plain white or green. I like to use a mini food processor when dealing with small amounts, as in this sauce, but a regular-size one will work just as well.

Preparation time: 15 minutes
Cooking time: 10 minutes
Makes 4 servings.
Per serving: 378 calories, 8.1 g. fat (18% of calories), 2.6 g. dietary fiber, 41 mg. cholesterol, 327 mg. sodium.

12	sun-dried tomatoes	1	tablespoon grated Parmesan cheese
1	cup boiling water	1	tablespoon pine nuts
2	plum tomatoes, cut into quarters	2	teaspoons red wine vinegar
¼	cup chopped fresh flat-leaf parsley	12	ounces fresh tricolor cheese tortellini

1. In a small bowl, combine the sun-dried tomatoes and water. Let stand for 2 minutes. Drain, reserving the soaking liquid.

2. Transfer the soaked sun-dried tomatoes to the work bowl of a food processor. Add the plum tomatoes; process until coarsely chopped. Add the parsley, Parmesan, pine nuts, vinegar and 2 tablespoons of the reserved tomato soaking liquid. Process until smooth. Set aside.

3. In a large pot of boiling water, cook the tortellini for 5 to 8 minutes, or until tender. Drain.

4. Place the tortellini in a large serving bowl. Add the tomato mixture; toss to mix well.

creamy lemon primavera

Stirring a little corn-starch into yogurt prevents it from curdling when mixed with hot ingredients.

Preparation time: 10 minutes
Cooking time: 10 minutes

Makes 4 servings.
Per serving: 443 calories, 5.5 g. fat (11% of calories), 6.6 g. dietary fiber, 1 mg. cholesterol, 60 mg. sodium.

1 cup nonfat yogurt	2 cups thinly sliced yellow squash
¼ cup low-sodium vegetable stock	1 cup chopped sweet red peppers
2 tablespoons lemon juice	½ cup chopped scallions
2 teaspoons cornstarch	1 teaspoon no-salt lemon-herb blend
12 ounces short fusilli	
1 tablespoon canola oil	
2 cups snow peas	

1. In a small bowl, stir together the yogurt, stock, lemon juice and cornstarch; set aside.

2. In a large pot of boiling water, cook the fusilli for 8 to 10 minutes, or until tender. Drain.

3. Meanwhile, in a large no-stick frying pan over medium heat, warm the oil. Add the snow peas, squash, peppers and scallions; cook, stirring frequently, for 7 minutes.

4. Remove the frying pan from the heat. Stir in the fusilli, yogurt mixture and herb blend; toss to mix well.

spaghetti with spinach cream sauce

This sauce goes nicely with most any type of pasta. I like to use vegetable-flavored varieties, such as tomato, whenever I have them on hand.

½ cup nonfat or part-skim ricotta cheese	½ cup diced onions
2 teaspoons grated lemon peel	1 box (10 ounces) frozen chopped spinach, thawed and squeezed dry
⅛ teaspoon grated nutmeg	1½ tablespoons grated Parmesan cheese
1 cup skim milk, divided	12 ounces spaghetti
2 teaspoons margarine	

Preparation time: 15 minutes
Cooking time: 10 minutes
Makes 4 servings.
Per serving: 429 calories, 6.7 g. fat (14% of calories), 3.7 g. dietary fiber, 12 mg. cholesterol, 187 mg. sodium.

1. In a food processor, blend the ricotta, lemon peel, nutmeg and 1 tablespoon of the milk.

2. In a 2-quart saucepan over medium heat, melt the margarine. Stir in the onions; cook, stirring frequently, for 4 to 5 minutes, or until tender. Stir in the ricotta mixture, spinach, Parmesan and the remaining milk. Cook, stirring constantly, for 4 to 6 minutes, or until the liquid is reduced by half.

3. Meanwhile, in a large pot of boiling water, cook the spaghetti for 8 to 10 minutes, or until tender. Drain. Place in a serving bowl. Add the spinach sauce; toss to mix.

hot antipasto linguine

This is a cross between antipasto and pasta primavera. One reason I like it is because you can save time by cooking the vegetables right in with the noodles. If you have any leftovers, add them to a brown-bag lunch.

2 tablespoons red wine vinegar	2 cups cauliflower florets
2 tablespoons olive oil	2 cups thinly sliced carrots
1 tablespoon coarse Dijon mustard	2 cups cut (2" pieces) green beans
1 teaspoon dried marjoram	1 cup canned chick-peas, rinsed and drained
½ teaspoon dried basil	2 tablespoons shredded provolone cheese
¼ teaspoon freshly ground black pepper	¼ teaspoon red-pepper flakes
12 ounces linguine	

Preparation time: 15 minutes
Cooking time: 10 minutes
Makes 4 servings.
Per serving: 508 calories, 11.3 g. fat (20% of calories), 9.1 g. dietary fiber, 5 mg. cholesterol, 347 mg. sodium.

1. In a small bowl, combine the vinegar, oil, mustard, marjoram, basil and black pepper; set aside.

2. In a large pot of boiling water, cook the linguine, cauliflower and carrots for 4 minutes. Add the beans; cook for 4 to 6 minutes longer, or until the linguine and vegetables are just tender. Drain.

3. Place in a large serving bowl. Add the chick-peas, provolone, pepper flakes and vinegar mixture; toss to mix well.

caponata-stuffed shells

Caponata is an eggplant and tomato mixture popular in Italy. Here I use a similar combination to stuff pasta shells. This is a great make-ahead dish. You can even freeze the baked shells to reheat when unexpected guests arrive for dinner.

MAKE AHEAD

Preparation time: 15 minutes
Cooking time: 40 minutes
Baking time: 35 minutes
Makes 8 servings.
Per serving: 237 calories, 3.8 g. fat (14% of calories), 2.7 g. dietary fiber, 4 mg. cholesterol, 170 mg. sodium.

1 tablespoon olive oil	1 tablespoon capers, rinsed and drained
1 medium eggplant, peeled and cubed	1 tablespoon honey
1 can (28 ounces) low-sodium tomatoes with juice	½ teaspoon dried basil
1 cup diced celery	½ teaspoon dried oregano
1 cup diced carrots	12 ounces jumbo shells
½ cup chopped onions	½ cup chunky tomato sauce
2 tablespoons red wine vinegar	¼ cup shredded Fontina cheese

1. In a large no-stick frying pan over medium heat, warm the oil. Add the eggplant; cook, stirring frequently, for 6 to 8 minutes, or until the eggplant is very tender. Add the tomatoes (with their liquid), celery, carrots, onions, vinegar, capers, honey, basil and oregano.

2. Bring to a boil. Reduce the heat to low. Simmer, partially covered, for 25 to 30 minutes, or until the mixture thickens and excess liquid has evaporated.

3. Meanwhile, in a large pot of boiling water, cook the shells for 10 to 12 minutes, or until just tender. Drain and rinse with cold water. Set aside.

4. Preheat the oven to 350°. Spread the tomato sauce in the bottom of a 9" × 13" baking dish. Using a spoon, evenly divide the caponata mixture among the shells. Place the shells upright in the baking dish. Sprinkle with the Fontina. Bake for 30 to 35 minutes, or until the cheese is bubbly.

pasta with broccoli and arugula

This makes a great first-course dish. I like my pasta spicy, but you may vary the pepper according to your own taste. This recipe calls for cutting arugula in *chiffonade,* which means very thin strips. The easiest way to do that is to stack a bunch of leaves, then use a chef's knife to thinly shred the whole stack.

Preparation time: 20 minutes
Cooking time: 15 minutes
Makes 4 servings.
Per serving: 307 calories, 6.1 g. fat (17% of calories), 2.7 g. dietary fiber, 0 mg. cholesterol, 93 mg. sodium.

3 teaspoons olive oil, divided	10 kalamata olives, pitted and coarsely chopped
2 garlic cloves, minced	
½–1 teaspoon red-pepper flakes	8 ounces lasagna noodles, coarsely broken
2 cups canned low-sodium stewed tomatoes	2 cups broccoli florets
¼ cup tomato sauce	1 bunch arugula, cut in chiffonade
1 tablespoon chopped sun-dried tomatoes	¼ cup chopped fresh basil

1. In a large no-stick frying pan over medium heat, warm 2 teaspoons of the oil. Add the garlic and pepper flakes; cook, stirring constantly, for 1 minute.

2. Stir in the stewed tomatoes, tomato sauce, sun-dried tomatoes and olives. Cook over medium-low heat, stirring frequently, for 10 to 12 minutes, or until the sauce thickens slightly and excess liquid has evaporated.

3. Meanwhile, in a large pot of boiling water, cook the noodles for 5 minutes. Add the broccoli; continue cooking for 5 to 7 minutes longer, or until the noodles and broccoli are tender. Drain.

4. Place the arugula and basil in a large serving bowl. Add the noodles, broccoli and the remaining 1 teaspoon oil; toss to mix well. Spoon the tomato mixture on top; toss to mix well.

vegetable kasha and bow ties

Sometimes when I make this dish, I replace the bow tie noodles (also known as farfalle) with sesame rice spirals. The spirals, which can be found in specialty food stores, add a wonderful nutty flavor. *Kasha* is another name for toasted buckwheat groats and is widely available in supermarkets.

Preparation time: 10 minutes
Cooking time: 40 minutes
Makes 4 servings.
Per serving: 369 calories, 5 g. fat (12% of calories), 4.5 g. dietary fiber, 0 mg. cholesterol, 213 mg. sodium.

2 teaspoons olive oil	2½ cups low-sodium vegetable stock
½ cup chopped scallions	1 tablespoon chopped fresh thyme
½ cup chopped celery	
½ cup thinly sliced mushrooms	2 teaspoons low-sodium soy sauce
½ cup chopped green peppers	Pinch of freshly ground black pepper
6 ounces bow tie noodles	
1 cup kasha	
½ cup egg substitute	

1. In a large no-stick frying pan over medium heat, warm the oil. Add the scallions, celery, mushrooms and green peppers; cook, stirring frequently, for 5 to 7 minutes, or until the vegetables are tender.

2. Meanwhile, in a large pot of boiling water, cook the noodles for 8 to 10 minutes, or until tender. Drain and set aside.

3. In small bowl, combine the kasha and egg; mix well.

4. Push the vegetables in the frying pan over to one side. Add the kasha on the other side. Cook, stirring constantly, for 4 to 5 minutes, or until the egg is cooked and the kasha grains have separated. Mix the kasha with the vegetables.

5. Stir in the stock, thyme, soy sauce and black pepper; mix well. Reduce the heat to low. Cover the pan and cook, stirring occasionally, for 20 to 25 minutes, or until the kasha is tender and the liquid has been absorbed.

6. Stir in the noodles. Cook for 1 minute, or until heated through.

herbed grilled vegetables with spaghetti

To save time when preparing dinner, you may grill the vegetables at your leisure and refrigerate them until needed. Let them come to room temperature while you prepare the rest of the ingredients. You may cook the vegetables indoors using a stove-top grill unit or a ridged cast-iron pan, or you may do them outside with a standard grill.

Preparation time: 25 minutes
Cooking time: 20 minutes
Makes 4 servings.
Per serving: 325 calories, 7 g. fat (20% of calories), 4.4 g. dietary fiber, 4 mg. cholesterol, 81 mg. sodium.

2 small Japanese eggplants, cut into ½" thick lengthwise slices	1½ tablespoons olive oil
2 heads Belgian endive, cut in half lengthwise	2 garlic cloves, finely chopped
2 sweet red peppers, cut in half lengthwise	1 small head radicchio, coarsely chopped
1 large red onion, sliced crosswise into ½" rounds	¼ cup low-sodium vegetable stock
1 cup chopped fresh basil	1 tablespoon balsamic vinegar
2 tablespoons chopped fresh chives	1 tablespoon Dijon mustard
8 ounces thin artichoke spaghetti	2 tablespoons crumbled goat cheese or shredded provolone cheese

1. Coat a charcoal grill rack with no-stick spray. Place over hot coals.

2. Working in batches if necessary, grill the eggplant, endive, peppers and onions until tender, turning the vegetables once. Set aside until cool enough to handle.

3. Coarsely chop all the vegetables except the onions; separate the onions into rings. In a large bowl, combine the vegetables, basil and chives. Toss well and set aside.

4. In a large pot of boiling water, cook the spaghetti for 6 to 8 minutes, or until tender. Drain.

5. Meanwhile, in a large no-stick frying pan over medium heat, warm the oil. Add the garlic; cook for 1 minute. Add the radicchio; cook, stirring constantly, for 2 minutes, or until wilted. Stir in the stock, vinegar and mustard; cook for 1 minute.

6. In a large serving bowl, toss together the spaghetti, grilled vegetables and radicchio mixture. Sprinkle with the goat cheese or provolone; toss to mix well.

cellophane noodles with sprouts

Here's a different side dish to add to a summer buffet. Cellophane noodles are also known as bean thread noodles.

Preparation time: 15 minutes
Cooking time: 5 minutes
Makes 4 servings.
Per serving: 215 calories, 3.5 g. fat (15% of calories), 1.3 g. dietary fiber, 0 mg. cholesterol, 157 mg. sodium.

2 tablespoons minced scallions	$\frac{1}{8}$–$\frac{1}{4}$ teaspoon red-pepper flakes
1 tablespoon sesame oil	2 packages (3$\frac{1}{2}$ ounces each) cellophane noodles
1 tablespoon oyster sauce	$\frac{1}{2}$ cup mung bean sprouts
1 tablespoon minced fresh ginger	$\frac{1}{2}$ cup shredded zucchini
2 teaspoons rice wine vinegar	

1. In a large bowl, combine the scallions, oil, oyster sauce, ginger, vinegar and pepper flakes; set aside.

2. In a medium pot of boiling water, cook the noodles for 5 minutes, or until translucent and tender. Drain and place in a serving bowl. Add the scallion mixture, sprouts and zucchini; toss to mix well. Serve warm or chilled.

penne with fresh vegetable sauce

This light and refreshing pasta is especially good when it's made with summer-ripe plum tomatoes and fresh herbs.

1 pound plum tomatoes, diced	1 tablespoon olive oil
1 green pepper, diced	2 teaspoons white wine vinegar
1 medium yellow squash, diced	2 garlic cloves, minced
1 medium cucumber, peeled, seeded and diced	$\frac{1}{4}$ teaspoon freshly ground black pepper
$\frac{1}{2}$ cup chopped fresh basil	12 ounces penne
10 kalamata olives, pitted and coarsely chopped	$\frac{1}{4}$ cup shredded smoked mozzarella cheese
2 tablespoons chopped fresh oregano	

Preparation time: 20 minutes
+ marinating time
Cooking time: 10 minutes

Makes 4 servings.
Per serving: 435 calories, 8.4
g. fat (17% of calories), 4.9 g.
dietary fiber, 4 mg. cholesterol, 95 mg. sodium.

1. In a large serving bowl, combine the tomatoes, green peppers, squash, cucumbers, basil, olives, oregano, oil, vinegar, garlic and black pepper. Set aside at room temperature for at least 30 minutes.

2. In a large pot of boiling water, cook the penne for 8 to 10 minutes, or until tender. Drain and transfer to the serving bowl. Toss with the vegetable mixture. Sprinkle with the mozzarella.

orange cilantro fettuccine

Not all pasta has to have an Italian flavor. This is a great side dish for a Mexican meal. Cilantro is a pungent green herb also known as fresh coriander and Chinese parsley. If it's not available, you may substitute parsley, but the flavor won't be the same.

Preparation time: 10 minutes
Cooking time: 10 minutes

Makes 4 servings.
Per serving: 387 calories, 3.9
g. fat (9% of calories), 2.4 g.
dietary fiber, 0 mg. cholesterol, 201 mg. sodium.

1 cup orange juice	2 teaspoons Dijon mustard
½ cup low-sodium vegetable stock	½ teaspoon powdered ginger
¼ cup chopped fresh cilantro	12 ounces fresh spinach fettuccine
1 tablespoon grated orange peel	2 tablespoons toasted sesame seeds
1 tablespoon cornstarch	
1 tablespoon low-sodium soy sauce	

1. In a 2-quart saucepan, whisk together the juice, stock, cilantro, orange peel, cornstarch, soy sauce, mustard and ginger. Bring to a boil over medium heat. Reduce the heat to low and cook, stirring often, for 2 to 3 minutes, or until the sauce thickens. Keep warm over low heat.

2. Meanwhile, in a large pot of boiling water, cook the fettuccine for 3 to 5 minutes, or until tender. Drain and place in a large serving bowl. Toss with the orange sauce and sesame seeds.

shredded vegetable lo mein

Here's a really low-fat version of a Chinese favorite. Soba noodles are made from buckwheat flour, which gives them a brownish gray color and an interesting flavor. They're available in Oriental markets, health food stores and many large supermarkets. If you can't find them, substitute spaghetti. The miso and sesame oil are available in the same types of stores. If you can't find them, just omit them for a slightly different flavor.

Preparation time: 15 minutes
Cooking time: 15 minutes

Makes 4 servings.
Per serving: 303 calories, 6.9 g. fat (19% of calories), 3.6 g. dietary fiber, 0 mg. cholesterol, 755 mg. sodium.

8 ounces soba noodles	1 tablespoon minced fresh ginger
½ cup low-sodium vegetable stock	1 cup shredded carrots
1 tablespoon low-sodium soy sauce	1 cup shredded zucchini
2 teaspoons soybean miso	2 cups shredded napa cabbage
½ teaspoon sesame oil	½ cup sliced water chestnuts
1 tablespoon peanut oil	½ cup chow mein noodles
2 garlic cloves, minced	

1. In a large pot of boiling water, cook the soba for 5 to 8 minutes, or until tender. Drain and set aside.

2. Meanwhile, in a small bowl, combine the stock, soy sauce, miso and sesame oil; set aside.

3. In a wok or large frying pan over high heat, warm the peanut oil. Add the garlic and ginger; cook, stirring constantly, for 1 minute. Stir in the carrots and zucchini; stir-fry for 2 minutes.

4. Add the cabbage and 2 tablespoons of the stock mixture; stir-fry for 1 minute, or until the cabbage is wilted. With a slotted spoon, remove the vegetables from the pan.

5. Stir the remaining stock mixture into the pan; bring to a boil. Boil for 1 minute, stirring constantly. Add the soba, vegetables and water chestnuts; cook for 1 minute longer, stirring to blend the flavors. Sprinkle with the chow mein noodles.

creamy peanut butter noodles with vegetables

Serve this entrée hot or cold. Leftovers make a great lunch to take along to work.

MAKE AHEAD

Preparation time: 15 minutes
Cooking time: 15 minutes

Makes 4 servings.
Per serving: 468 calories, 12.8 g. fat (25% of calories), 5.3 g. dietary fiber, 0 mg. cholesterol, 379 mg. sodium.

½ cup low-sodium vegetable stock	3 teaspoons sesame oil, divided
3 tablespoons smooth peanut butter	1 cup chopped scallions
2 tablespoons rice wine vinegar	1 tablespoon grated fresh ginger
2 tablespoons low-sodium soy sauce	2 cups thinly sliced carrots
¼ teaspoon red-pepper flakes	1 cup snow peas
12 ounces no-yolk medium egg noodles	1 cup thinly sliced mushrooms
	¼ cup water
	1 tablespoon toasted sesame seeds

1. In a small bowl, combine the stock, peanut butter, vinegar, soy sauce and pepper flakes; set aside.

2. In a large pot of boiling water, cook the noodles for 8 to 10 minutes, or until tender. Drain and keep warm.

3. Meanwhile, in a large no-stick frying pan over medium heat, warm 2 teaspoons of the oil. Add the scallions and ginger; cook, stirring frequently, for 2 minutes. Add the carrots and snow peas; cook, stirring constantly, for 4 minutes. Stir in the mushrooms and water; cook for 2 minutes, or until the vegetables are tender.

4. Place the noodles in a large serving bowl. Toss with the remaining 1 teaspoon oil. Add the vegetables, peanut butter sauce and sesame seeds; toss to mix well.

saffron and raisin whole wheat noodles

This is my version of a traditional dish popular in Sicily. Whole wheat noodles have more fiber and a firmer texture than regular pasta. If you don't have any whole wheat noodles on hand, you may use regular broad noodles.

Preparation time: 15 minutes
Cooking time: 10 minutes
Makes 4 servings.
Per serving: 370 calories, 9.9 g. fat (24% of calories), 10.6 g. dietary fiber, 0 mg. cholesterol, 170 mg. sodium.

¼ cup dried currants
1 cup warm water
1 tablespoon olive oil
1½ cups chopped fennel
1 cup chopped celery
½ cup chopped onions
¼ cup walnut halves, coarsely chopped
1 cup low-sodium vegetable stock
¼ teaspoon saffron threads, crushed
Pinch of freshly ground black pepper
8 ounces no-yolk whole wheat broad egg noodles
1 cup fresh bread crumbs

1. In a small bowl, soak the currants in the water for at least 5 minutes.

2. In a large no-stick frying pan over medium heat, warm the oil. Add the fennel, celery, onions and walnuts; cook, stirring frequently, for 4 to 5 minutes, or until the vegetables are tender. Stir in the stock, saffron and pepper.

3. Drain the currants and reserve the soaking liquid; add the currants to the frying pan. Bring to a boil. Reduce the heat to low; simmer for 2 to 3 minutes, or until the liquid is reduced by half.

4. Meanwhile, in a large pot of boiling water, cook the noodles for 10 to 12 minutes, or until tender. Drain. Add the noodles to the frying pan; toss to combine. Stir in about ⅓ cup of the reserved currant soaking liquid. Sprinkle with the bread crumbs.

bitter greens with dressing (p. 206), stuffed shells (p. 48)

cellophane noodles with sprouts (p. 52)

pasta e fagioli (p. 82)

farfalle with mushrooms (p. 73), bruschetta (p. 146)

vermicelli with chunky vegetable sauce (p. 80) 65

creamy goat cheese risotto (p. 90)

millet-stuffed grape leaves (p. 105)   **67**

curried brown rice and peas (p. 92)

asian fried rice with bok choy (p. 91)

brown rice egg rolls (p. 106)

farfalle with porcini mushrooms

This hearty dish has a strong earthy taste, thanks to the porcini mushrooms. If they're not available at your market, substitute other dried mushrooms (or use about a pound of thinly sliced fresh mushrooms and sauté them in a teaspoon of oil). *Farfalle* is the Italian name for bow tie noodles. Serve this entrée with a light tossed salad.

Preparation time: 10 minutes
Cooking time: 10 minutes
Makes 4 servings.
Per serving: 418 calories, 6.2 g. fat (13% of calories), 1.3 g. dietary fiber, 3 mg. cholesterol, 71 mg. sodium.

1 cup boiling water	1 teaspoon dried oregano
2 ounces dried porcini mushrooms	2 tablespoons skim milk
1 tablespoon olive oil	12 ounces bow tie noodles
4 garlic cloves, thinly sliced	2 tablespoons grated Parmesan cheese
¼ teaspoon freshly ground black pepper	2 tablespoons chopped fresh flat-leaf parsley
Pinch of grated nutmeg	

1. In a small bowl, combine the water and mushrooms. Set aside for 10 minutes to soften. Drain the mushrooms, reserving the soaking liquid. Coarsely chop the mushrooms.

2. In a large no-stick frying pan over medium heat, warm the oil. Add the garlic, pepper and nutmeg; cook, stirring constantly, for 1 minute. Stir in the mushrooms, ½ cup of the reserved mushroom soaking liquid and the oregano; simmer for 2 minutes. Stir in the milk; cook for 1 minute.

3. Meanwhile, in a large pot of boiling water, cook the noodles for 8 to 10 minutes, or until tender. Drain and place in a large serving bowl. Spoon the mushroom sauce on top; toss to mix well. Sprinkle with the Parmesan and parsley. Toss with more of the reserved mushroom soaking liquid if desired.

artichoke lasagna

A good dish for a large crowd. Just add a simple tossed salad and some crusty garlic bread for a quick party meal. Don't use a metal pan for this dish because the artichokes will become discolored from it. You may assemble the lasagna ahead of time and bake it later. Cover it well and refrigerate for up to one day or freeze for up to a month.

MAKE AHEAD

9 lasagna noodles	1 cup chopped roasted sweet red peppers
2 teaspoons olive oil	1 teaspoon margarine
1 medium onion, chopped	1½ tablespoons unbleached flour
3 garlic cloves, minced	
1 cup low-sodium vegetable stock	1 can (12 ounces) evaporated skim milk
¼ cup chopped fresh basil	1½ tablespoons grated Parmesan cheese
2 boxes (9 ounces each) frozen artichoke hearts, partially thawed	⅛ teaspoon grated nutmeg
1 box (10 ounces) frozen chopped spinach, partially thawed	3 tablespoons seasoned dry bread crumbs

1. In a large pot of boiling water, cook the noodles for 10 to 12 minutes, or until just tender. Drain and rinse with cold water. Set aside.

2. Meanwhile, in a large no-stick frying pan over medium heat, warm the oil. Add the onions and garlic; cook, stirring frequently, for 2 to 3 minutes, or until tender. Stir in the stock and basil; bring to a boil. Add the artichokes, spinach and peppers; cover and cook for 5 minutes. Remove the lid and cook until all the liquid has evaporated. Set aside.

3. In a 1-quart saucepan over medium heat, melt the margarine. Whisk in the flour; cook for 1 minute. Slowly whisk in the milk, Parmesan and nutmeg; cook, stirring constantly, for 5 to 7 minutes, or until the sauce boils and thickens.

4. Preheat the oven to 350°. Coat a 9" × 13" glass or ceramic baking dish with no-stick spray.

5. To assemble the lasagna, spread ⅓ cup of the sauce in the bottom of the prepared baking dish.

6. Top with 3 of the noodles; spread with half of the artichoke mixture. Spoon ⅓ cup of the sauce over the artichoke

Preparation time: 20 minutes
Cooking time: 20 minutes
Baking time: 45 minutes

Makes 8 servings.
Per serving: 235 calories, 3.3 g. fat (10% of calories), 1.8 g. dietary fiber, 3 mg. cholesterol, 164 mg. sodium.

mixture and sprinkle with 1 tablespoon of the bread crumbs. Repeat the procedure.

7. Top with the remaining 3 noodles. Spread with the remaining sauce and sprinkle with the remaining 1 tablespoon bread crumbs.

8. Cover with foil and bake for 30 minutes. Uncover and bake for 10 to 15 minutes, or until bubbly. Let stand for 10 minutes before serving.

ravioli with sautéed peppers

Here's a nice change from typical ravioli topped with tomato sauce.

Preparation time: 15 minutes
Cooking time: 15 minutes

Makes 4 servings.
Per serving: 319 calories, 10.9 g. fat (30% of calories), 2.4 g. dietary fiber, 100 mg. cholesterol, 355 mg. sodium.

1 pound fresh cheese ravioli	3 garlic cloves, minced
1 tablespoon olive oil	1 cup low-sodium vegetable stock
1 sweet red pepper, julienned	1 tablespoon lemon juice
1 yellow pepper, julienned	1 teaspoon dried tarragon
2 medium carrots, julienned	¼ cup chopped fresh flat-leaf parsley
1 medium red onion, thinly sliced crosswise and separated into rings	

1. In a large pot of boiling water, cook the ravioli for 5 to 8 minutes, or until tender. Drain and keep warm.

2. Meanwhile, in a large no-stick frying pan over medium heat, warm the oil. Add the red peppers, yellow peppers, carrots, onions and garlic; cook, stirring frequently, for 4 to 5 minutes, or until tender. Stir in the stock, lemon juice and tarragon; simmer for 3 to 5 minutes, or until the liquid is reduced to approximately ¼ cup.

3. Place the ravioli in a flat serving dish. Spoon on the pepper mixture. Sprinkle with the parsley.

a pair of perfect sauces

Tomato sauce straight from a jar is the most convenient pasta topper around. But it's certainly not your only option when you want dinner in a hurry. Besides, you can get awfully bored with canned varieties. The following two sauces are a delightful change of pace. The first gets a rich creaminess from evaporated skim milk. And the second has an unusual ingredient: red lentils, which add interesting texture. You can make either sauce ahead and store it in the refrigerator for up to a week. Or you can freeze either type in 1-cup portions for quick defrosting on busy days.

creamy roasted red pepper tomato sauce

1 tablespoon olive oil	1 can (28 ounces) low-sodium tomatoes with juice
1 small onion, thinly sliced crosswise and separated into rings	1 cup coarsely chopped roasted sweet red peppers
3 garlic cloves, minced	½ cup evaporated skim milk
¼ cup chopped fresh flat-leaf parsley	
¼ cup chopped fresh basil	

1. In a large no-stick frying pan over medium heat, warm the oil. Add the onions and garlic; cook, stirring frequently, for 2 to 3 minutes, or until tender. Stir in the parsley and basil; cook for 1 minute.

2. Stir in the tomatoes (with their liquid) and peppers; bring to a boil. Reduce the heat to low. Simmer, crushing the tomatoes with the back of a wooden spoon and stirring them frequently, for 25 to 30 minutes, or until the sauce thickens slightly. Stir in the milk; cook for 2 minutes.

MAKE AHEAD

Preparation time: 10 minutes. Cooking time: 40 minutes.
Makes 4 cups.

Per 1 cup: 118 calories, 4.2 g. fat (29% of calories), 2.7 g. dietary fiber, 1 mg. cholesterol, 363 mg. sodium.

With 3 ounces pasta: 433 calories, 5.5 g. fat (11% of calories), 3.9 g. dietary fiber, 1 mg. cholesterol, 369 mg. sodium.

hearty red lentil sauce

2 cups low-sodium vegetable stock
½ cup water
1 cup red lentils, rinsed and drained
2 teaspoons olive oil
½ cup chopped shallots
½ cup finely chopped fennel
¼ cup finely chopped celery

¼ cup finely chopped carrots
1 can (28 ounces) low-sodium tomatoes, drained
½ cup spicy vegetable-cocktail juice
2 teaspoons lemon juice
1 teaspoon dried basil

1. In a 2-quart saucepan over medium heat, bring the stock and water to a boil. Stir in the lentils. Cover and simmer for 30 to 35 minutes, or until the lentils are tender and the liquid has been absorbed; set aside.

2. Meanwhile, in a 3-quart saucepan over medium heat, warm the oil. Add the shallots, fennel, celery and carrots; cook, stirring frequently, for 4 to 5 minutes, or until the vegetables are tender. Stir in the tomatoes, vegetable juice, lemon juice and basil; simmer for 5 minutes, crushing the tomatoes with the back of a wooden spoon.

3. Gently stir in the lentils; cook for 1 to 2 minutes, or until heated through.

MAKE AHEAD

Preparation time: 15 minutes. Cooking time: 35 minutes.

Makes 6 cups.

Per 1 cup: 182 calories, 2.7 g. fat (12% of calories), 5.7 g. dietary fiber, 0 mg. cholesterol, 268 mg. sodium.

With 3 ounces pasta: 496 calories, 3.9 g. fat (7% of calories), 6.9 g. dietary fiber, 0 mg. cholesterol, 274 mg. sodium.

orzo with broccoli-mint pesto

You may serve this as either a main course or a side dish. The mint and broccoli sauce is a nice change from traditional basil pesto—and it's much lower in fat. Orzo is a type of small pasta that resembles grains of rice.

Preparation time: 15 minutes
Cooking time: 15 minutes
Makes 4 servings.
Per serving: 395 calories, 6.8 g. fat (15% of calories), 3 g. dietary fiber, 1 mg. cholesterol, 61 mg. sodium.

2 cups broccoli florets, lightly steamed	1 tablespoon grated Parmesan cheese
¼ cup chopped fresh flat-leaf parsley	2 teaspoons dried mint
4 garlic cloves	Pinch of ground red pepper
½ cup low-sodium vegetable stock	12 ounces orzo
¼ cup coarsely chopped walnuts	1 teaspoon onion powder
	¼ teaspoon garlic powder

1. In the work bowl of a food processor, combine the broccoli, parsley and garlic; process until coarsely chopped. With the motor running, add the stock, walnuts, Parmesan, mint and pepper; process until smooth. Set this pesto mixture aside.

2. In a medium pot of boiling water, cook the orzo for 10 to 12 minutes, or until tender. Drain and place in a serving bowl. Sprinkle with the onion powder and garlic powder; toss to mix well. Add the pesto mixture and toss well.

elbows with peas and smoked mozzarella

This is a great use for leftover cooked macaroni.

1 tablespoon olive oil	1 cup thawed frozen peas
¼ cup chopped shallots	1 tablespoon grated Parmesan cheese
2 garlic cloves, minced	3 cups cooked macaroni
1 medium carrot, chopped	2 ounces smoked mozzarella cheese, shredded
1 cup chopped zucchini	
2 medium tomatoes, chopped	

Preparation time: 20 minutes
Cooking time: 15 minutes
Makes 4 servings.
Per serving: 246 calories, 7.1 g. fat (25% of calories), 5.1 g. dietary fiber, 9 mg. cholesterol, 150 mg. sodium.

1. In a large no-stick frying pan over medium heat, warm the oil. Add the shallots and garlic; cook, stirring constantly, for 1 minute. Stir in the carrots and zucchini; cook, stirring frequently, for 4 to 5 minutes, or until tender.

2. Add the tomatoes, peas and Parmesan; cook for 2 minutes, or until the tomatoes release their liquid. Stir in the macaroni; cook for 2 to 3 minutes, or until heated through. Sprinkle with the mozzarella; toss well.

wagon wheels with mexican salsa

This no-cook sauce is perfect for hot summer nights. Serve it chilled or at room temperature.

MAKE
AHEAD

Preparation time: 15 minutes + marinating time
Cooking time: 10 minutes
Makes 4 servings.
Per serving: 492 calories, 9.7 g. fat (17% of calories), 9.6 g. dietary fiber, 0 mg. cholesterol, 356 mg. sodium.

1 medium tomato, coarsely chopped	1 tablespoon chopped canned chili peppers (wear plastic gloves when handling)
1 medium avocado, diced	
1 can (19 ounces) black beans, rinsed and drained	
	Juice of 1 lime
½ cup drained canned corn	1 teaspoon ground cumin
2 tablespoons chopped fresh cilantro	4–5 drops hot-pepper sauce
	12 ounces wagon wheel pasta

1. In a large bowl, combine the tomatoes, avocados, beans, corn, cilantro and peppers. Stir in the lime juice, cumin and hot-pepper sauce; set aside at room temperature for at least 1 hour.

2. In a large pot of boiling water, cook the pasta for 8 to 10 minutes, or until tender. Drain.

3. Place the pasta in a large serving bowl. Add the salsa mixture; toss to mix well.

vermicelli with chunky vegetable sauce

This might seem like a lot of ingredients, but the finished dish is well worth it. I first made this sauce on a night when it seemed there was nothing in the house to eat. You could call it a creation made straight from the pantry.

Preparation time: 20 minutes
Cooking time: 30 minutes
Makes 4 servings.
Per serving: 441 calories, 5.5 g. fat (9% of calories), 4.7 g. dietary fiber, 0 mg. cholesterol, 128 mg. sodium.

1 tablespoon olive oil	½ cup chopped roasted sweet red peppers
2 cups broccoli florets	
1 cup chopped green peppers	6 sun-dried tomatoes, minced
2 garlic cloves, minced	1 tablespoon capers, rinsed and drained
1 can (14½ ounces) low-sodium stewed tomatoes	1 teaspoon dried basil
	1 teaspoon dried oregano
1 box (9 ounces) frozen artichoke hearts, thawed	⅛ teaspoon red-pepper flakes
	12 ounces vermicelli

1. In a large no-stick frying pan over medium heat, warm the oil. Add the broccoli, green peppers and garlic; cook, stirring frequently, for 3 to 4 minutes, or until the vegetables are crisp-tender.

2. Stir in the stewed tomatoes, artichokes, red peppers, sun-dried tomatoes, capers, basil, oregano and pepper flakes; bring to a boil. Reduce the heat to low; partially cover and simmer for 20 to 25 minutes, or until the sauce thickens slightly.

3. Meanwhile, in a large pot of boiling water, cook the vermicelli for 6 to 8 minutes, or until tender. Drain.

4. Place the vermicelli in a large serving bowl. Add the vegetable sauce; toss to mix well.

asparagus and feta with cavatelli

If asparagus is out of season, substitute broccoli florets.

Preparation time: 15 minutes
Cooking time: 15 minutes

Makes 4 servings.
Per serving: 460 calories, 11 g. fat (21% of calories), 2.5 g. dietary fiber, 25 mg. cholesterol, 426 mg. sodium.

10 sun-dried tomatoes	2 tablespoons capers, rinsed and drained
1 cup boiling water	2 teaspoons dried oregano
¼ cup chopped fresh flat-leaf parsley	⅛ teaspoon freshly ground black pepper
4 ounces feta cheese	12 ounces cavatelli pasta
2 tablespoons balsamic vinegar	10 thin asparagus spears, cut into 2" pieces
1 tablespoon olive oil	

1. In a small bowl, combine the tomatoes and water. Let stand for 2 minutes. Drain, reserving 2 tablespoons of the soaking liquid.

2. Transfer the tomatoes to a food processor. Add the parsley and process until coarsely chopped.

3. Crumble the feta into a large serving bowl; drizzle with the vinegar and oil. Sprinkle with the capers, oregano and pepper. Stir in the tomato mixture.

4. In a large pot of boiling water, cook the cavatelli for 5 minutes. Add the asparagus; cook for 5 to 7 minutes longer, or until the pasta and asparagus are tender. Drain.

5. Transfer the cavatelli and asparagus to the serving bowl. Toss with the tomato mixture and the reserved tomato soaking liquid; mix well.

pasta e fagioli

Fagioli is the Italian word for beans. Pasta e fagioli is a traditional dish combining, obviously, pasta and beans. This version reminds me of one served at my favorite restaurant in New York City's Little Italy. I like to use bucatini for the pasta. It's hollow, like macaroni, but much thinner. If your store doesn't carry it, substitute linguine.

Preparation time: 10 minutes
Cooking time: 15 minutes
Makes 4 servings.
Per serving: 459 calories, 8.7 g. fat (17% of calories), 6.5 g. dietary fiber, 0 mg. cholesterol, 273 mg. sodium.

2 tablespoons olive oil	½ cup low-sodium vegetable stock
1 teaspoon dried rosemary, crumbled	1 can (19 ounces) white kidney beans, rinsed and drained
½ teaspoon dried thyme	
1 cup quartered mushrooms	
½ cup chopped scallions	12 ounces bucatini, coarsely broken
2 garlic cloves, minced	

1. In a large no-stick frying pan over medium heat, warm the oil. Add the rosemary and thyme; cook for 1 minute. Stir in the mushrooms, scallions and garlic; cook, stirring frequently, for 2 to 3 minutes.

2. Add the stock; bring to a boil. Stir in the beans; simmer, stirring frequently, for 4 to 5 minutes, or until the sauce thickens slightly.

3. Meanwhile, in a large pot of boiling water, cook the bucatini for 8 to 10 minutes, or until tender. Drain.

4. Add the bucatini to the frying pan; cook for 1 minute, stirring to coat evenly. If the sauce gets too thick, thin it with 1 or 2 tablespoons water.

whole wheat linguine with creamy roquefort sauce

This flavorful sauce is ideal for Roquefort lovers. Roquefort is a blue cheese traditionally made from sheep's milk. If your supermarket doesn't carry authentic Roquefort, substitute another type of blue cheese.

Preparation time: 15 minutes
Cooking time: 10 minutes
Makes 4 servings.
Per serving: 438 calories, 8 g. fat (16% of calories), 11 g. dietary fiber, 25 mg. cholesterol, 598 mg. sodium.

1	cup nonfat cottage cheese	12	ounces whole wheat linguine
3	ounces Roquefort cheese		
2	tablespoons lemon juice	15	cherry tomatoes, halved
½	teaspoon onion powder		
	Pinch of freshly ground black pepper		

1. In the work bowl of a food processor, combine the cottage cheese, Roquefort, lemon juice, onion powder and pepper; process until smooth. Set aside.

2. In a large pot of boiling water, cook the linguine for 10 to 12 minutes, or until tender. Drain, reserving 2 tablespoons of the cooking liquid.

3. Place the linguine in a large serving bowl. Add the cheese sauce, tomatoes and the reserved linguine cooking liquid; toss to mix well.

radiatore with three-onion sauce

This pasta dish gets interesting flavor depth from the combination of three types of onions. And it's well worth all the onion chopping required!

Preparation time: 15 minutes
Cooking time: 20 minutes
Makes 4 servings.
Per serving: 434 calories, 6.1 g. fat (13% of calories), 4.7 g. dietary fiber, 2 mg. cholesterol, 120 mg. sodium.

1 tablespoon olive oil	⅛ teaspoon freshly ground black pepper
1 large red onion, chopped	12 ounces tricolor radiatore pasta
1 large yellow onion, chopped	
½ cup chopped scallions	½ cup low-sodium vegetable stock
2 tablespoons balsamic vinegar	1 cup frozen peas
1 teaspoon brown sugar or honey	2 tablespoons grated Parmesan cheese
½ teaspoon dried thyme	

1. In a 2-quart saucepan over medium heat, warm the oil. Add the red onions, yellow onions and scallions; reduce the heat to medium-low. Cook, stirring frequently, for 5 to 7 minutes, or until the onions just begin to brown.

2. Reduce the heat to low and stir in the vinegar, sugar or honey, thyme and pepper; cook, stirring frequently, for 8 minutes, or until the onions begin to caramelize.

3. Meanwhile, in a large pot of boiling water, cook the radiatore for 8 to 10 minutes, or until tender. Drain.

4. Stir the stock and peas into the onions; cover and simmer for 5 minutes.

5. Place the pasta in a large serving bowl. Add the onion mixture. Sprinkle with the Parmesan; toss to mix well.

creamy ziti vegetable bake

This is "comfort food" made healthy. Tofu adds creaminess usually supplied by heavy cream and fatty cheeses. This one-dish meal needs only a large green salad to accompany it.

Preparation time: 25 minutes
Cooking time: 15 minutes
Baking time: 40 minutes
Makes 6 servings.
Per serving: 460 calories, 9.3 g. fat (18% of calories), 4.8 g. dietary fiber, 13 mg. cholesterol, 250 mg. sodium.

8 ounces firm tofu, well drained and squeezed dry between paper towels	1 small head broccoli, separated into florets
½ cup nonfat cottage cheese	1 sweet red pepper, chopped
¼ cup hot water	1 green pepper, chopped
2 tablespoons coarse Dijon mustard	1 medium zucchini, chopped
2 tablespoons grated Parmesan cheese	½ cup chopped scallions
1 pound ziti	1 cup shredded low-fat Cheddar cheese
	1 tablespoon seasoned dry bread crumbs

1. In the work bowl of a food processor, combine the tofu, cottage cheese, water, mustard and Parmesan; process until smooth. Set aside.

2. In a large pot of boiling water, cook the ziti for 5 minutes. Add the broccoli; cook for 5 to 7 minutes longer, or until the ziti and broccoli are just tender. Drain and return to the pot. Off heat, add the red peppers, green peppers, zucchini, scallions, Cheddar and tofu mixture; stir to mix well.

3. Preheat the oven to 350°. Coat a 3- or 4-quart casserole with no-stick spray. Add the ziti mixture; sprinkle with the bread crumbs. Bake for 35 to 40 minutes, or until bubbly and heated through.

tomato-basil linguine with rapini

Rapini is a green leafy vegetable with scattered clusters of broccoli-like buds. It's also known as broccoli raab, broccoli rabe and rape. If your market doesn't carry it, you could substitute small broccoli florets. If you can't find tomato-basil linguine, substitute spinach or plain linguine.

Preparation time: 10 minutes
Cooking time: 10 minutes
Makes 4 servings.
Per serving: 344 calories, 6.1 g. fat (16% of calories), 5.6 g. dietary fiber, 0 mg. cholesterol, 337 mg. sodium.

1 tablespoon olive oil	2 tablespoons water
¼ cup chopped fresh flat-leaf parsley	1 can (19 ounces) chick-peas, rinsed and drained
¼ cup chopped fresh basil	½ cup low-sodium vegetable stock
2 sprigs fresh rosemary, finely chopped	8 ounces tomato-basil linguine
2 tablespoons chopped fresh thyme	2 tablespoons balsamic vinegar
2 garlic cloves, minced	
1 small bunch rapini, tough stems removed	

1. In large no-stick frying pan over medium heat, warm the oil. Add the parsley, basil, rosemary, thyme and garlic; cook, stirring frequently, for 2 minutes. Stir in the rapini and water; cook for 4 to 5 minutes, or until just tender.

2. Add the chick-peas and stock; cook for 2 to 3 minutes, or until the chick-peas are heated through.

3. Meanwhile, in a large pot of boiling water, cook the linguine for 8 to 10 minutes, or until tender. Drain and place in a large serving bowl.

4. Add the rapini mixture. Make a well in the center of the linguine; pour the vinegar into the well. Toss to mix well.

the wide world of grains

Do you have a favorite grain? Most meat eaters probably don't, but vegetarians learn early on that grains are the very foundation of their diet. Grains are excellent sources of muscle-building protein. And they're very filling, so you need never feel that meatless meals are somehow skimpy or unsatisfying.

The grain world is incredibly diverse. Choices include the familiar: rice (brown, white, wild), barley, bulgur, oats and cornmeal. But they also encompass those that you might not use very often, such as buckwheat, millet, couscous and rye. And then there are the downright exotic ones like amaranth and quinoa. But all these grains are delicious, easy to prepare and worthy of inclusion in your everyday repertoire. The recipes in this chapter can give you ideas for using grains to their best advantage.

When time is of the essence, cook the grains ahead and store them in your refrigerator. That way you'll always have a supply on hand for quick meals.

polenta with eggplant sauce

I like to make this hearty entrée on cold nights because it's so satisfying and warming. Polenta is a traditional Italian dish made from cornmeal. Some people refer to it as cornmeal mush, but that down-home name just doesn't capture the elegant possibilities of polenta—especially when it's topped with a savory sauce such as this.

Preparation time: 15 minutes
Cooking time: 55 minutes
Makes 4 servings.
Per serving: 278 calories, 5.5 g. fat (17% of calories), 9.6 g. dietary fiber, 0 mg. cholesterol, 245 mg. sodium.

2 cups boiling water	2½ cups canned low-sodium tomatoes, crushed
½ ounce dried mushrooms	
1 tablespoon olive oil	6½ cups water
2 cups cubed eggplant	1½ cups polenta or coarse yellow cornmeal
1 green pepper, cut into strips	
½ cup chopped onions	2 tablespoons chopped fresh flat-leaf parsley
1 tablespoon crushed fennel seeds	

1. In a small bowl, combine the boiling water and mushrooms. Let soak for 5 to 10 minutes, or until soft. Drain, reserving the soaking liquid.

2. In a large no-stick frying pan over medium heat, warm the oil. Add the eggplant; cook, stirring frequently, for 5 to 7 minutes, or until browned and soft. Stir in the mushrooms, peppers, onions and fennel seeds; cook, stirring constantly, for 2 minutes.

3. Pour in the tomatoes and the reserved mushroom soaking liquid; bring to a boil. Reduce the heat to low and simmer for 40 to 45 minutes, or until the sauce thickens slightly.

4. Meanwhile, to prepare the polenta, bring the 6½ cups water to a boil in a 3-quart saucepan. Slowly whisk in the polenta or cornmeal. Reduce the heat to low; cook, stirring often, for 30 to 35 minutes, or until thick and smooth.

5. Pour the polenta onto a large serving platter and keep warm until the sauce is ready. Spoon the eggplant sauce on top. Sprinkle with the parsley.

baked artichoke and pepper polenta

This is an excellent main dish to make when company's coming. Asiago cheese is an aged Italian variety that has a rich, nutty flavor. It's worth seeking out, but if you can't find any, substitute Parmesan or Romano.

Preparation time: 15 minutes
Cooking time: 10 minutes
Baking time: 35 minutes
Makes 8 servings.
Per serving: 180 calories, 4.3 g. fat (15% of calories), 5.9 g. dietary fiber, 3 mg. cholesterol, 285 mg. sodium.

1 box (9 ounces) frozen artichoke hearts, thawed and coarsely chopped	2 teaspoons dried basil
	6 cups water
	2 garlic cloves, minced
1 cup coarsely chopped spinach	¼ teaspoon freshly ground black pepper
1 cup chopped roasted sweet red peppers	2 cups polenta or coarse yellow cornmeal
¼ cup chopped fresh flat-leaf parsley	5 tablespoons grated Asiago cheese, divided
1 tablespoon olive oil	1 cup chunky tomato sauce

1. In a medium bowl, combine the artichokes, spinach, red peppers, parsley, oil and basil; set aside.

2. Preheat the oven to 350°. Coat a glass or ceramic 9" × 13" baking dish with no-stick spray; set aside.

3. In a 3-quart saucepan over high heat, bring the water, garlic and black pepper to a boil. Slowly whisk in the polenta or cornmeal. Reduce the heat to low and cook, stirring frequently, for 10 minutes, or until thick and creamy. Stir in 4 tablespoons of the Asiago.

4. Spread half of the polenta in the bottom of the prepared baking dish. Top with the tomato sauce and then the artichoke mixture. Carefully spoon the remaining polenta on top of the artichoke mixture. Sprinkle with the remaining 1 tablespoon Asiago.

5. Bake for 30 to 35 minutes, or until the polenta is golden and bubbly. Let stand for 5 minutes before serving.

creamy goat cheese risotto

This rich and creamy dish is worth all the stirring needed to make authentic risotto. You'll find that the goat cheese melts best if you shred it coarsely before incorporating it into the rice.

Preparation time: 10 minutes
Cooking time: 40 minutes
Makes 4 servings.
Per serving: 401 calories, 7.1 g. fat (16% of calories), 1.4 g. dietary fiber, 7 mg. cholesterol, 166 mg. sodium.

1	cup boiling water	1½	cups Arborio rice
½	cup sun-dried tomatoes	¼	cup chopped fresh basil
6	cups low-sodium vegetable stock	¼	teaspoon freshly ground black pepper
1	tablespoon olive oil	2	ounces goat cheese, shredded
½	cup chopped scallions		

1. In a small bowl, combine the water and tomatoes. Let stand for 2 minutes. Drain, reserving the soaking liquid. Chop the tomatoes and set aside.

2. Bring the stock to a boil in a 2-quart saucepan; reduce the heat to low and keep at a low simmer.

3. In a 3- or 4-quart saucepan over medium heat, warm the oil. Add the scallions; cook, stirring constantly, for 2 minutes, or until tender. Add the rice; stir until coated with oil.

4. Start adding the stock 1 tablespoon at a time. Allow each tablespoonful to be absorbed before adding the next, but never allow the rice to become dry. When the stock has been half used, after about 15 minutes, stir in the tomatoes, basil, pepper and 2 tablespoons of the reserved tomato soaking liquid. Continue adding stock for another 12 to 15 minutes, or until the rice is creamy and the grains are firm but not hard (you might not need all the stock).

5. Remove the pan from the heat; stir in the goat cheese until melted.

asian fried rice with bok choy

I think you'll like this different twist on the usual fried rice.

Preparation time: 20 minutes
Cooking time: 15 minutes
Makes 4 servings.
Per serving: 376 calories, 8.1 g. fat (19% of calories), 4.1 g. dietary fiber, 0 mg. cholesterol, 411 mg. sodium.

2 tablespoons peanut oil, divided	1 tablespoon soy miso
1 cup chopped scallions	3 garlic cloves, minced
½ teaspoon paprika	2 tablespoons chopped canned green chili peppers (wear plastic gloves when handling)
¼ teaspoon ground red pepper	
1 tablespoon low-sodium soy sauce	4 cups shredded bok choy
1 tablespoon chili sauce	2 cups quartered mushrooms
1 teaspoon dark brown sugar or honey	1 tablespoon grated lime peel
4 cups cold cooked white rice	½ teaspoon ground cumin
1½ tablespoons grated fresh ginger	¼ cup chopped fresh cilantro

1. Turn on the oven to a warm setting (about 150°). Place a large ovenproof platter in the oven.

2. In a wok or large frying pan over medium-high heat, warm 1 tablespoon of the oil. Add the scallions, paprika and red pepper; stir-fry for 1 minute. Stir in the soy sauce, chili sauce and sugar or honey. Add the rice and stir-fry for 2 to 3 minutes, or until the rice is coated with the scallion mixture and is heated through.

3. Spoon the rice into the center of the platter, leaving a 2" border. Return the platter to the oven.

4. Heat the remaining 1 tablespoon oil in the pan. Add the ginger, miso, garlic and chili peppers; stir-fry for 1 minute. Add the bok choy, mushrooms, lime peel and cumin; stir-fry for 5 to 7 minutes, or until the vegetables are tender.

5. Spoon the bok choy mixture around the rice on the platter. Sprinkle the rice with the cilantro.

curried brown rice and peas

This main course can also double as a side dish.

Preparation time: 10 minutes
Cooking time: 2 minutes
Baking time: 50 minutes

Makes 4 servings.
Per serving: 381 calories, 6.1 g. fat (14% of calories), 6.7 g. dietary fiber, 0 mg. cholesterol, 320 mg. sodium.

2	teaspoons peanut oil	1	box (10 ounces) frozen peas
½	cup chopped leeks (white part only)	½	cup chopped fresh cilantro
1½	teaspoons curry powder	1–2	tablespoons low-sodium soy sauce
1½	cups brown rice	¼	teaspoon hot-pepper sauce
4	cups low-sodium vegetable stock		

1. Preheat the oven to 350°.

2. In an ovenproof 3-quart saucepan over medium heat, warm the oil. Add the leeks and curry powder; cook, stirring frequently, for 2 minutes, or until the leeks are tender. Stir in the rice and mix until coated with oil.

3. Pour in the stock, peas, cilantro, soy sauce and hot-pepper sauce; bring to a boil.

4. Cover the pan and place in the oven. Bake for 40 to 50 minutes, or until the rice is tender and the liquid has been absorbed. Let stand for 10 minutes. Fluff with a fork before serving.

nutty rice burgers

I like to serve these veggie burgers in whole wheat pitas with slices of tomato and onion.

Preparation time: 15 minutes
+ standing time
Cooking time: 15 minutes
Makes 6 servings.
Per serving: 287 calories, 5.6 g. fat (17% of calories), 9.2 g. dietary fiber, 0 mg. cholesterol, 42 mg. sodium.

1½	cups water	½	cup whole wheat flour
1	cup bulgur	¼	cup finely chopped
¼	cup low-sodium		walnuts
	vegetable stock	1	teaspoon garlic powder
½	cup finely chopped onions	1	teaspoon dried rosemary,
½	cup shredded carrots		crumbled
½	cup shredded zucchini	½	teaspoon freshly ground
1	teaspoon dried thyme		black pepper
3	cups cooked brown rice	1	tablespoon canola oil
½	cup egg substitute		

1. In a large bowl, combine the water and bulgur; set aside for 30 minutes, or until the bulgur is soft. Place in a strainer and drain well, pressing out the excess water with the back of a spoon. Return the bulgur to the bowl.

2. In a large no-stick frying pan over medium heat, warm the stock. Add the onions, carrots, zucchini and thyme; cook, stirring frequently, for 4 to 5 minutes, or until the vegetables are tender and the liquid has evaporated. Add to the bulgur.

3. Stir in the rice, egg, flour, walnuts, garlic powder, rosemary and pepper; mix well. Shape into 6 patties, adding more flour if the patties are too soft.

4. Wash and dry the frying pan. Place it over medium heat and warm the oil. Add the patties and sauté for about 5 minutes per side, or until golden.

spicy cabbage and rice

Here's an unusual way to prepare cabbage. Leftovers are great cold the next day.

Preparation time: 10 minutes
Cooking time: 35 minutes

Makes 4 servings.
Per serving: 300 calories, 8.2 g. fat (24% of calories), 4.8 g. dietary fiber, 0 mg. cholesterol, 306 mg. sodium.

2½ teaspoons sesame oil, divided	1½ tablespoons peanut butter
4 cups shredded green cabbage	1½ teaspoons tahini
1 sweet red pepper, cut into strips	2 teaspoons low-sodium soy sauce
1 cup chopped scallions	2 teaspoons rice wine vinegar
2 cups water	3–4 drops hot-pepper sauce
1 cup long-grain white rice	1 can (8 ounces) bamboo shoots, drained
3 tablespoons chili sauce	1 tablespoon sesame seeds

1. In a large frying pan over medium heat, warm 2 teaspoons of the oil. Add the cabbage, peppers and scallions; cook, stirring frequently, for 4 to 5 minutes, or until just tender. Pour in the water and bring to a boil. Stir in the rice.

2. Reduce the heat to low; cover and simmer for 15 to 20 minutes, or until the rice is tender and the water has been absorbed.

3. Meanwhile, in a small bowl, combine the chili sauce, peanut butter, tahini, soy sauce, vinegar, hot-pepper sauce and the remaining ½ teaspoon oil.

4. Uncover the frying pan and cook the rice, stirring frequently, for 5 minutes. Stir in the chili sauce mixture and bamboo shoots; cook for 2 minutes longer. Sprinkle with the sesame seeds before serving.

watercress and wild rice pancakes

These easy-to-make pancakes are great served with applesauce and nonfat sour cream. Although they are terrific for dinner, you could also enjoy them as a savory breakfast or brunch dish. Reheat leftover pancakes in a toaster oven.

Preparation time: 10 minutes
Cooking time: 1¼ hours
Makes 4 servings.
Per serving: 306 calories, 7.6 g. fat (22% of calories), 1.5 g. dietary fiber, 1 mg. cholesterol, 206 mg. sodium.

2¼ cups water	½ teaspoon celery seeds
¾ cup wild rice, rinsed and drained	Pinch of freshly ground black pepper
¼ cup low-sodium vegetable stock	½ cup egg substitute
½ cup finely chopped watercress	½ cup evaporated skim milk
½ cup finely chopped shallots	2 teaspoons low-sodium soy sauce
½ cup diced celery	¾ cup all-purpose flour
1½ teaspoons dried sage	2 tablespoons oil, divided

1. In a 2-quart saucepan over high heat, bring the water and wild rice to a boil. Cover, reduce the heat to low, and simmer for 40 to 45 minutes, or until the wild rice is tender and the water has been absorbed. Fluff with a fork and transfer to a large bowl.

2. In a large no-stick frying pan over medium heat, warm the stock. Add the watercress, shallots and celery; cook, stirring frequently, for 4 to 5 minutes, or until the vegetables are tender. Stir in the sage, celery seeds and pepper. Add to the bowl with the wild rice.

3. In a small bowl, combine the egg, milk and soy sauce. Pour over the vegetables. Add the flour and mix well.

4. Clean the frying pan. Add 1 tablespoon of the oil and warm over medium heat for 1 minute. Add the batter in ¼-cup measures and flatten slightly with a spatula. Cook for 3 to 4 minutes on each side, or until golden. Remove from the pan and keep warm in an oven set at about 150°.

5. Repeat the procedure, adding the remaining 1 tablespoon oil as needed, until all the batter has been used.

bulgur-stuffed cabbage

Stuffed cabbage usually contains meat. Here I update the classic recipe with a grain filling. What I particularly like about this version is that the combination of bulgur and brown rice gives the stuffing a nutty taste— without the added fat actual nuts would contribute.

Preparation time: 10 minutes + standing time
Cooking time: 10 minutes
Baking time: 30 minutes
Makes 4 servings.
Per serving: 219 calories, 1.2 g. fat (5% of calories), 10 g. dietary fiber, 0 mg. cholesterol, 462 mg. sodium.

2	cups boiling water	1	teaspoon onion powder
1	cup bulgur	1	teaspoon paprika
12	large green cabbage leaves	1	teaspoon no-salt herb blend
1	cup cold cooked brown rice	2	cups spicy vegetable-
½	cup chopped red onions		cocktail juice, divided

1. In a large bowl, combine the water and bulgur; set aside for 30 minutes to allow the bulgur to soften. Transfer to a strainer. Drain well, pressing out any excess water with the back of a spoon. Return the bulgur to the bowl.

2. Trim any tough core areas from the cabbage. Steam the cabbage in a basket over gently simmering water for 5 to 8 minutes, or until just soft enough to bend; set aside.

3. Preheat the oven to 350°.

4. Stir the rice, onions, onion powder, paprika, herb blend and ½ cup of the juice into the bulgur. Place ¼ cup of the mixture in the center of each cabbage leaf. Fold in the sides and roll up to enclose the filling.

5. Place the rolls, seam side down, in a 9" × 13" baking dish. Pour the remaining 1½ cups juice over the rolls. Cover with foil and bake for 20 to 30 minutes, or until bubbly.

oat and bulgur loaf

This loaf is as hearty as one made with ground beef. Because there are lots of vegetables right in the loaf, a tossed salad is all you need to make a complete meal.

Preparation time: 15 minutes
+ standing time
Cooking time: 15 minutes
Baking time: 1 hour

Makes 6 servings.
Per serving: 214 calories, 4.9 g. fat (19% of calories), 8.8 g. dietary fiber, 0 mg. cholesterol, 255 mg. sodium.

Oat Loaf
1½ cups water
1 cup bulgur
4 slices rye bread, finely crumbled
1 cup coarsely chopped cooked broccoli
1 cup coarsely chopped cooked carrots
1 cup cooked oatmeal
½ cup salsa
½ cup egg substitute
¼ cup unsalted sunflower seeds

Sauce
¼ cup low-sodium vegetable stock
1 tablespoon tomato paste
1 tablespoon cider vinegar
1 tablespoon red wine vinegar
¾ teaspoon chili powder
½ teaspoon dried chives
½ teaspoon dried tarragon

1. To make the oat loaf: In a large bowl, combine the water and bulgur; set aside for 30 minutes to allow the bulgur to soften. Transfer to a strainer. Drain well, pressing out any excess water with the back of a spoon. Return the bulgur to the bowl.

2. Preheat the oven to 350°. Coat a 9" × 5" loaf pan with no-stick spray; set aside.

3. Stir the bread, broccoli, carrots, oatmeal, salsa, egg and sunflower seeds into the bulgur; mix with your fingers until well blended. Spoon into the prepared pan. Bake for 1 hour. Let stand for 10 minutes before slicing.

4. To make the sauce: In a 1-quart saucepan, combine the stock, tomato paste, cider vinegar, red wine vinegar, chili powder, chives and tarragon. Cook over medium heat, stirring frequently, for 10 to 12 minutes, or until the sauce thickens slightly. Spoon the sauce over the sliced loaf.

couscous with lentils, tomatoes and basil

To give this dish extra zip, you may use spicy vegetable-cocktail juice instead of the mild variety. Whole wheat couscous is very high in fiber. Look for it in health food and specialty stores. If you can't find any, substitute bulgur that you've soaked in boiling water for about 30 minutes, then drained well.

Preparation time: 10 minutes
Cooking time: 50 minutes
Makes 4 servings.
Per serving: 395 calories, 3.9 g. fat (9% of calories), 14 g. dietary fiber, 2 mg. cholesterol, 104 mg. sodium.

2 teaspoons margarine	1 bay leaf
½ cup chopped onions	1 cup whole wheat couscous
1½ cups water	1 medium tomato, coarsely
1 cup vegetable-cocktail juice	chopped
1 cup brown lentils, rinsed and drained	½ cup chopped fresh basil
	2 tablespoons grated Parmesan cheese

1. In a 3-quart saucepan over medium heat, melt the margarine. Stir in the onions; cook, stirring frequently, for 2 to 3 minutes, or until tender.

2. Stir in the water, juice, lentils and bay leaf; bring to a boil. Reduce the heat to low; cover and simmer for 30 to 45 minutes, or until the lentils are soft but not mushy.

3. Remove the pan from the heat and discard the bay leaf. Stir in the couscous, tomatoes, basil and Parmesan. Cover and let stand for 5 minutes, or until the couscous is soft. Uncover and fluff with a fork to separate the grains.

couscous-stuffed spaghetti squash

Excellent!!

Spaghetti squash is an unusual vegetable. When you cook it, the flesh separates into yellow spaghetti-like strands. It's an interesting alternative to regular spaghetti when you want something a little different.

Preparation time: 20 minutes
Cooking time: 1 hour
Baking time: 20 minutes
Makes 4 servings.
Per serving: 431 calories, 11.7 g. fat (24% of calories), 11.5 g. dietary fiber, 25 mg. cholesterol, 383 mg. sodium.

1 large spaghetti squash	1 teaspoon dried oregano
1 tablespoon olive oil	1 teaspoon dried mint
1½ cups julienned snow peas	1½ cups vegetable-cocktail juice
1 large zucchini, coarsely chopped	1 cup couscous
½ cup chopped scallions	4 ounces crumbled feta cheese
2 garlic cloves, minced	

1. Place the squash in a Dutch oven and add water to cover. Bring to a boil and cook, uncovered, for 30 minutes to 1 hour, or until easily pierced with a fork. Drain, halve, and set aside until cool enough to handle. Spoon out and discard the seeds. With a fork, separate the flesh into strands and place in a large bowl. Reserve the squash shells.

2. Preheat the oven to 350°.

3. In large no-stick frying pan over medium heat, warm the oil. Add the snow peas, zucchini, scallions, garlic, oregano and mint; cook, stirring frequently, for 4 to 6 minutes, or until the vegetables are tender. Stir in the juice; bring to a boil. Stir in the couscous; cover, remove from the heat, and let stand for 5 minutes, or until the couscous is soft. Fluff with a fork.

4. Add the couscous mixture and the feta to the squash. Toss to mix well. Divide between the reserved squash shells. Cover each shell with foil, place in a 9" × 13" baking dish, and bake for 15 to 20 minutes, or until heated through.

mexican-style millet

Here's a real treat for Mexican-food lovers—and a nice change of pace from the usual rice-based dishes. Thanks to the combination of millet, beans and chunky salsa, this dish is very high in fiber.

Preparation time: 15 minutes
Cooking time: 1¼ hours

Makes 4 servings.
Per serving: 471 calories, 8.9 g. fat (16% of calories), 17 g. dietary fiber, 0 mg. cholesterol, 108 mg. sodium.

1½ cups low-sodium vegetable stock
¾ cup millet
1 teaspoon ground cumin
1 tablespoon olive oil
1 red onion, chopped
1 green pepper, chopped
1 sweet red pepper, chopped
2 garlic cloves, minced
2 tablespoons chili powder
1 teaspoon paprika
1 teaspoon dried thyme
⅛ teaspoon ground red pepper
1 jar (16 ounces) chunky salsa
1 can (19 ounces) black beans, undrained
4 plum tomatoes, coarsely chopped
½ cup water
¼ cup chopped fresh flat-leaf parsley

1. In a 2-quart saucepan over medium heat, bring the stock, millet and cumin to a boil. Reduce the heat to low; cover and simmer for 35 to 40 minutes, or until the millet is tender. (Check frequently and add a few more tablespoons of water if the liquid cooks away before the millet is tender.) Remove from the heat and let stand, covered, for 10 minutes.

2. While the millet is standing, warm the oil in a 3-quart saucepan over medium heat. Add the onions, green peppers, red peppers and garlic. Cook, stirring frequently, for 4 to 5 minutes, or until the vegetables are tender. Stir in the chili powder, paprika, thyme and ground pepper; cook for 1 minute.

3. Add the salsa, beans, tomatoes, water and parsley. Fluff the millet with a fork and add to the pan; stir to combine. Partially cover and simmer for 5 to 10 minutes, or until heated through.

cheesy chick-pea and quinoa bake

This is a real favorite of mine. Quinoa is an ancient grain that's regaining some of its former popularity. Because it's higher in protein than other grains, it's an excellent addition to meatless meals. The flavor of the cheese in this dish and the crumbs that top it remind me of the macaroni and cheese I enjoyed as a kid.

Preparation time: 20 minutes
Cooking time: 5 minutes
Baking time: 1 hour 5 minutes
Makes 4 servings.
Per serving: 545 calories, 16.4 g. fat (27% of calories), 7.8 g. dietary fiber, 26 mg. cholesterol, 368 mg. sodium.

1 tablespoon margarine	1 cup canned chick-peas, rinsed and drained
1 cup coarsely chopped zucchini	1 cup shredded low-fat Cheddar cheese, divided
1 cup chopped celery	½ cup shredded low-fat Swiss cheese, divided
1 cup chopped scallions	¼ cup seasoned dry bread crumbs
4 cups water	
2 cups quinoa, rinsed and drained	

1. Preheat the oven to 350°. Coat a 2-quart casserole with no-stick spray; set aside.

2. In a large no-stick frying pan over medium heat, melt the margarine. Add the zucchini, celery and scallions; cook, stirring frequently, for 3 to 4 minutes, or until tender.

3. Stir in the water, quinoa, chick-peas, ¾ cup of the Cheddar and ¼ cup of the Swiss. Spoon into the prepared casserole. Cover and bake for 45 minutes, or until the liquid has almost been absorbed.

4. Sprinkle with the bread crumbs and the remaining ¼ cup Cheddar and ¼ cup Swiss. Bake, uncovered, for 15 to 20 minutes, or until all the liquid has been absorbed and the cheese has melted.

skillet oats and tempeh

This unusual way to cook oats helps keep the grains separate, so they don't turn into oatmeal. Here I combine the oats with tempeh, a high-protein soybean product that has a pleasant mushroomlike flavor. Look for tempeh in the freezer section of health food stores.

Preparation time: 10 minutes
Cooking time: 20 minutes
Makes 4 servings.
Per serving: 376 calories, 11.4 g. fat (26% of calories), 4.9 g. dietary fiber, 0 mg. cholesterol, 296 mg. sodium.

2	cups rolled oats	1½	cups low-sodium vegetable stock
1	cup wheat germ		
½	cup egg substitute	2½	teaspoons hoisin sauce
1	tablespoon peanut oil	1½	teaspoons low-sodium soy sauce
4	ounces tempeh, cubed		

1. In a medium bowl, stir together the oats, wheat germ and egg until the grains are well coated with the egg. Set aside.

2. In a large no-stick frying pan over medium heat, warm the oil. Add the tempeh; cook, stirring frequently, for 3 to 4 minutes, or until browned. Remove with a slotted spoon and set aside.

3. Add the oat mixture to the pan; cook, stirring constantly, for 5 to 7 minutes, or until the oats are dry and lightly browned. Stir in the stock; cook for 4 to 5 minutes, or until the liquid has been absorbed.

4. Return the tempeh to the pan. Stir in the hoisin sauce and soy sauce; cook for about 2 minutes, or until heated through.

mini kasha balls
with onion gravy

Surprise! These look like regular meatballs, but they haven't a speck of meat in them. Kasha—toasted buckwheat groats—gives them body and a meaty texture. The onion gravy is a low-fat alternative to standard gravy. Serve these mini balls over wide noodles or rice. For something entirely different, prepare the balls and simmer them in tomato sauce.

Preparation time: 20 minutes
Cooking time: 30 minutes
Makes 4 servings.
Per serving: 207 calories, 4.6 g. fat (19% of calories), 6.2 g. dietary fiber, 0 mg. cholesterol, 109 mg. sodium.

Kasha Balls
1 cup cooked kasha
¾ cup mashed cooked sweet potatoes
½ cup bran
¼ cup egg substitute
½ teaspoon onion powder
⅛ teaspoon freshly ground black pepper
⅛ teaspoon grated nutmeg
2 teaspoons sesame oil

Onion Gravy
1 cup chopped onions
1 teaspoon oil
1 tablespoon unbleached flour
1 teaspoon dried thyme
1 teaspoon dried oregano
1½ cups low-sodium vegetable stock
1½ teaspoons low-sodium teriyaki sauce

1. To make the kasha balls: In a large bowl, combine the kasha, sweet potatoes, bran, egg, onion powder, pepper and nutmeg. Mix thoroughly and divide into 16 equal portions; roll into balls.

2. In a large frying pan over medium heat, warm the oil. Add the balls; cook, stirring frequently, for 4 to 5 minutes, or until browned. Remove from the pan and keep warm.

3. To make the onion gravy: Stir the onions and oil into the pan. Cook, stirring frequently, for 2 minutes. Add the flour, thyme and oregano; cook for 1 minute. Pour in the stock; bring to a boil. Reduce the heat to low; return the balls to the pan.

4. Cover and simmer for 15 to 20 minutes, or until the sauce thickens and is reduced by half. Uncover and stir in the teriyaki sauce; cook for 2 minutes longer.

cooking grits, groats and other grains

You may cook any grain in water, but you'll get more flavor if you use stock. In general, bring the liquid to a boil and stir in the grain. Then cover the pan tightly, reduce the heat so that the liquid simmers, and cook until all the liquid has been absorbed. (Exceptions to that rule are noted below.) Turn off the heat and let the pan stand, covered, for about 5 minutes. Then fluff the grain with a fork to separate the kernels.

Amaranth. Use 3 cups liquid and 1 cup amaranth. Cook for 20 to 25 minutes. Yield: about 2½ cups.

Barley (medium pearled). Use 4 cups liquid and 1 cup barley. Cook for 45 to 50 minutes. Yield: about 4 cups.

Barley (quick cooking). Use 2 cups liquid and 1 cup barley. Cook for 10 to 15 minutes. Yield: about 3 cups.

Bulgur. Use 1¼ cups liquid and 1 cup bulgur. Cover, remove from the heat, and let stand for 15 to 20 minutes, or until the bulgur is soft. Yield: about 2½ cups.

Couscous. Use 1½ cups liquid and 1 cup couscous. Cover, remove from the heat, and let stand for about 5 minutes, or until the couscous is soft. Yield: about 3 cups.

Grits (old-fashioned). Use 5 cups liquid and 1 cup grits. Cook, whisking frequently, for 15 to 20 minutes, or until very thick. Yield: about 5 cups.

Grits (quick cooking). Use 4 cups liquid and 1 cup grits. Cook, whisking frequently, for 5 to 7 minutes, or until very thick. Yield: about 4 cups.

Kasha (buckwheat). Use 2 cups liquid and 1 cup kasha. Cook for 15 to 20 minutes. Yield: about 3 cups.

Millet. Use 2 cups liquid and 1 cup millet. Cook for 30 to 40 minutes. Yield: about 4 cups.

Quinoa. Use 2 cups liquid and 1 cup quinoa. Cook for 20 to 25 minutes. Yield: about 3 cups.

Rice (brown). Use 2½ cups water and 1 cup rice. Cook for 45 to 50 minutes. Yield: about 3 cups.

Rice (quick-cooking brown). Use 1¼ cups liquid and 1 cup rice. Cook for 10 to 15 minutes. Yield: about 2 cups.

Rice (white). Use 2 cups liquid and 1 cup rice. Cook for 20 minutes. Yield: about 3 cups.

Wild rice. Use 4 cups liquid and 1 cup wild rice. Cook for 45 to 50 minutes; drain off any excess liquid. Yield: about 4 cups.

millet-stuffed grape leaves

Here's a good side dish for the buffet table.

MAKE AHEAD

Preparation time: 20 minutes + chilling time

Makes 10 servings.
Per serving: 120 calories, 3.7 g. fat (27% of calories), 3.6 g. dietary fiber, 0 mg. cholesterol, 144 mg. sodium.

½ cup canned low-sodium tomatoes, pureed	¼ cup chopped fresh flat-leaf parsley
2 tablespoons minced red onions	¼ cup dried currants
1 tablespoon olive oil	1 tablespoon sweet pickle relish
1 tablespoon balsamic vinegar	1 jar (16 ounces) grape leaves, drained
⅛ teaspoon freshly ground black pepper	½ cup fat-free Italian dressing
2 cups cold cooked millet	
¼ cup finely chopped toasted pecans	

1. In a small bowl, combine the tomatoes, onions, oil, vinegar and pepper; set aside.

2. In a large bowl, combine the millet, pecans, parsley, currants and relish; mix well. Add the tomato mixture; toss to mix well.

3. Select 40 large grape leaves. Place each leaf, shiny side down, on a work surface. Place 1 tablespoon of the filling in the center of the leaf near the stem end. Fold the outer sides in toward the center, covering the filling; roll up to form a packet.

4. Place the packets, seam side down, in a large oval baking dish. Pour the dressing over the packets. Cover and refrigerate for at least 2 hours, or until well chilled.

brown rice egg rolls

Classic Chinese egg rolls are deep-fried, so they're high in undesirable fat. To create this version, I used superthin phyllo dough for the wrapping and brushed it with a bare minimum of margarine. Then I baked the rolls to keep the fat low. You could serve these rolls as buffet hors d'oeuvres or as appetizers before an Asian meal.

Preparation time: 25 minutes
Cooking time: 10 minutes
Baking time: 20 minutes
Makes 24 rolls.
Per roll: 50 calories, 1.6 g. fat (28% of calories), 0.4 g. dietary fiber, 0 mg. cholesterol, 33 mg. sodium.

1 tablespoon cornstarch	2 cups cold cooked brown rice
1 tablespoon rice wine vinegar	
1 tablespoon low-sodium soy sauce	1 tablespoon grated fresh ginger
1 teaspoon sesame oil	¼ cup chopped bean sprouts
2 teaspoons peanut oil	8 sheets phyllo dough (thawed, if frozen)
1 cup chopped mushrooms	
½ cup chopped scallions	1 tablespoon margarine, melted
½ cup chopped celery	

1. In a small bowl, combine the cornstarch, vinegar, soy sauce and sesame oil; set aside.

2. In a wok or large frying pan over medium-high heat, warm the peanut oil. Add the mushrooms, scallions and celery; cook, stirring constantly, for 4 to 5 minutes, or until tender. Using a slotted spoon, remove the vegetables to a large bowl.

3. Add the rice and ginger to the pan; cook, stirring constantly, for 2 to 3 minutes, or until the rice is browned. Stir in the cornstarch mixture; stir-fry until thick. Transfer the rice mixture to the bowl with the vegetables. Stir in the sprouts.

4. Preheat the oven to 350°. Coat 2 large baking sheets with no-stick spray. Cut the phyllo sheets crosswise into 3 wide strips. Stack the strips on a piece of wax paper, then cover them with plastic wrap to prevent them from drying out.

5. Place 1 strip of the phyllo on a work surface. Brush lightly with a bit of the margarine. Place 1 tablespoon of the rice filling in the center at one end of the strip. Roll the strip one-third of the way to enclose the filling. Then fold the left and right sides over the filling and continue rolling.

6. Repeat to use all the remaining strips, margarine and filling. Place the rolls on the prepared baking sheets with a little space between them. Bake for 15 to 20 minutes, or until golden.

arborio and sage timbales

These molded rice custards are ideal as side dishes for an elegant dinner or holiday meal. If you don't have Arborio rice, which is a special short-grain strain that has a creamy texture when cooked, you may substitute medium-grain white rice.

Preparation time: 10 minutes
Cooking time: 30 minutes
Baking time: 30 minutes

Makes 4 servings.
Per serving: 246 calories, 6.3 g. fat (23% of calories), 1.3 g. dietary fiber, 5 mg. cholesterol, 200 mg. sodium.

1 tablespoon olive oil	¼ cup grated Parmesan cheese
1 small red onion, finely chopped	¼ cup chopped fresh flat-leaf parsley
2 garlic cloves, minced	1½ tablespoons lemon juice
1 tablespoon dried sage	2 tablespoons poppy seed flatbread crumbs
¾ cup Arborio rice	½ cup egg substitute
2 cups low-sodium vegetable stock, divided	

1. In a 2- or 3-quart saucepan over medium heat, warm the oil. Add the onions, garlic and sage; cook, stirring frequently, for 2 minutes. Add the rice and stir for 1 minute, or until coated with the oil.

2. Pour in 1 cup of the stock. Reduce the heat to low and cook, stirring frequently, for 10 to 12 minutes, or until the stock has been absorbed.

3. Stir in the remaining 1 cup stock; cook, stirring frequently, for 10 to 12 minutes, or until the stock has been absorbed and the rice is just tender.

4. Remove the saucepan from the heat; stir in the Parmesan, parsley and lemon juice. Let cool for 10 minutes.

5. Meanwhile, preheat the oven to 350°. Coat 4 (6-ounce) custard cups with no-stick spray. Sprinkle the bottoms and sides with the crumbs. Place the cups in a baking dish large enough to hold all 4.

6. Stir the egg into the rice mixture. Divide evenly among the prepared cups. Pour enough boiling water into the baking dish to reach halfway up the outsides of the cups. Bake for 25 to 30 minutes, or until a knife inserted in the center comes out clean.

7. Remove the cups from the baking dish; let cool for 5 minutes. To unmold, invert the cups and tap the bottoms with a knife to release the timbales.

squash stuffed with bulgur and apples

This dish always reminds me of autumn, when acorn squash and the fresh new crop of apples are so abundant. Although this is a side dish, you may prepare it as a main course by using two large squash.

Preparation time: 15 minutes
Cooking time: 10 minutes
Baking time: 1½ hours
Makes 8 servings.
Per serving: 269 calories, 8.2 g. fat (25% of calories), 7 g. dietary fiber, 0 mg. cholesterol, 306 mg. sodium.

1 cup bulgur	¾ cup orange juice
3½ cups water, divided	¼ cup orange all-fruit preserves
4 medium acorn squash	
1 tablespoon margarine	1 teaspoon ground cinnamon
1 Granny Smith apple, peeled, cored and cubed	¼ teaspoon grated nutmeg
1 cup raisins	
⅔ cup coarsely chopped walnuts	

1. Place the bulgur in a large bowl. Add 2 cups of the water and set aside for about 30 minutes to soften.

2. Meanwhile, preheat the oven to 350°. Coat a 9″ × 13″ baking dish with no-stick spray.

3. Cut the squash in half and scoop out the seeds. Place, cut side down, in the prepared baking dish. Add ½ cup of the remaining water. Bake for 15 minutes.

4. In a large no-stick frying pan over medium heat, melt the margarine. Add the apples, raisins and walnuts; cook, stirring gently from time to time, for 5 minutes. Stir in the juice, preserves, cinnamon and nutmeg; cook for 2 minutes.

5. Drain any remaining water from the bulgur. Remove the frying pan from the heat and stir in the bulgur.

6. Remove the baking dish from the oven. Flip the squash so that the cut sides are up. Spoon equal amounts of the bulgur mixture into the squash cavities.

7. Pour the remaining 1 cup water into the bottom of the baking dish. Cover with foil; bake for 50 minutes to 1 hour 15 minutes, or until the squash is fork tender. Uncover and bake for 5 minutes longer.

spicy barley and sweet potatoes

The mustard and fennel seeds used in this dish really give it a lot of flavor without adding extra calories or fat. Although you could serve this as a main course for four, I prefer it as a side dish.

Preparation time: 15 minutes
Cooking time: 35 minutes

Makes 8 servings.
Per serving: 157 calories, 4.7 g. fat (26% of calories), 4.4 g. dietary fiber, 0 mg. cholesterol, 34 mg. sodium.

6	ounces firm tofu, well drained and squeezed dry between paper towels	½	cup chopped celery
1	tablespoon canola oil	1	cup quick-cooking barley
2	teaspoons mustard seeds	1½	cups low-sodium vegetable stock
2	teaspoons fennel seeds	½	cup water
1	large sweet potato, peeled and diced	½	teaspoon turmeric

1. Dice the tofu and set aside.

2. In a large saucepan over medium heat, warm the oil. Add the mustard seeds and fennel seeds; cook for 15 to 30 seconds, or until the seeds begin to pop. Stir in the sweet potatoes, celery and tofu. Cook, stirring frequently, for 10 to 15 minutes, or until the sweet potatoes are just tender.

3. Add the barley; stir and cook for 1 minute. Add the stock, water and turmeric; bring to a boil.

4. Reduce the heat to low; cover and simmer for 10 to 15 minutes, or until the barley is just tender. (Check the liquid frequently and add more water if the mixture starts to stick to the bottom of the pan.) Remove from the heat and let stand, covered, for 5 minutes.

mashed potatoes with carrots and amaranth

Amaranth is a small-seed grain resembling millet. It's high in protein, making it a good choice for meatless meals. Look for it in health food stores. This is an unusual side dish.

Preparation time: 15 minutes
Cooking time: 30 minutes
Makes 8 servings.
Per serving: 131 calories, 1 g. fat (7% of calories), 2.2 g. dietary fiber, 0 mg. cholesterol, 33 mg. sodium.

1½ cups water	2 tablespoons lemon juice
½ cup amaranth	½–1 teaspoon ground cinnamon
4 medium potatoes, peeled and quartered	½ teaspoon no-salt lemon-herb blend
4 carrots, cut into 1" pieces	⅛ teaspoon grated nutmeg
½ cup skim milk	
¼ cup nonfat sour cream	

1. In a 1-quart saucepan over high heat, bring the water and amaranth to a boil. Reduce the heat to low; cover and simmer for 25 to 30 minutes, or until the grains bind together and the water has been absorbed. Set aside.

2. Meanwhile, place the potatoes in a 3-quart saucepan and add cold water to cover. Bring to a boil over medium heat and cook for 15 minutes. Add the carrots; cook for 15 to 20 minutes, or until the vegetables are fork tender. Drain thoroughly and place in a large bowl.

3. Mash the potatoes and carrots by hand or with an electric mixer until smooth. Add the milk, sour cream, lemon juice, cinnamon, herb blend and nutmeg; blend well.

4. Gently stir in the amaranth. If needed, place the mixture in a pan and warm over low heat.

quinoa-pistachio pilaf

This pilaf gets crunch from the pistachios and a touch of sweetness from the apricots. Serve it as a side dish.

Preparation time: 15 minutes
Cooking time: 30 minutes
Makes 8 servings.
Per serving: 152 calories, 4.4 g. fat (25% of calories), 2.7 g. dietary fiber, 0 mg. cholesterol, 27 mg. sodium.

1½ teaspoons peanut oil	2 garlic cloves, minced
¼ cup shelled unsalted pistachios	2 cups low-sodium vegetable stock
1 cup chopped scallions	2–3 drops hot-pepper sauce
¾ cup coarsely chopped dried apricots	1 cup quinoa, rinsed and drained
1 tablespoon grated fresh ginger	¼ cup chopped fresh cilantro

1. In a 2-quart saucepan over medium heat, warm the oil. Add the pistachios; cook, stirring frequently, for 2 to 3 minutes, or until the nuts turn golden. With a slotted spoon, remove the nuts and place in a small bowl.

2. Add the scallions, apricots, ginger and garlic to the pan; cook, stirring constantly, for 2 minutes. Stir in the stock and hot-pepper sauce; bring to a boil.

3. Add the quinoa and cilantro; stir and reduce the heat to low. Cover and simmer for 20 to 25 minutes, or until the liquid has been absorbed. Remove from the heat and let stand for 5 minutes. Fluff the grains with a fork and stir in the pistachios.

mixed grain and pepper pilaf

This is a good recipe for times when you want to use up small amounts of different grains. I generally make this as a side dish, but you could serve it as a main course for four.

Preparation time: 15 minutes
+ standing time
Cooking time: 50 minutes
Makes 8 servings.
Per serving: 139 calories, 2.2 g. fat (14% of calories), 2 g. dietary fiber, 0 mg. cholesterol, 98 mg. sodium.

2½ cups low-sodium vegetable stock	1 sweet red pepper, chopped
½ cup basmati or other long-grain aromatic white rice	1 green pepper, chopped
⅓ cup medium pearled barley	1 cup chopped leeks (white part only)
⅓ cup wild rice, rinsed and drained	2 teaspoons low-sodium soy sauce
¼ cup amaranth	2–3 drops hot-pepper sauce
1 tablespoon margarine	

1. In a 2-quart saucepan over medium heat, bring the stock to a boil. Add the rice, barley, wild rice and amaranth; stir. Reduce the heat to medium-low. Cover and simmer for 35 to 40 minutes, or until the grains are tender. Drain thoroughly through a sieve. Spread the grains on a large baking sheet; let cool and dry for 15 minutes.

2. In a large frying pan over medium heat, melt the margarine. Add the red peppers, green peppers and leeks; cook, stirring frequently, for 4 to 5 minutes, or until tender. Stir in the grains. Stir-fry over high heat until heated through.

3. Stir in the soy sauce and hot-pepper sauce; cook for 1 minute.

cashew and pineapple barley

If you buy your cashews raw, you can easily roast them in a toaster oven or dry frying pan. Or do them in the microwave: Spread ½ cup of the nuts in a glass pie plate and microwave on high for 1 to 2 minutes, or until lightly browned. This is a side dish.

Preparation time: 10 minutes
Cooking time: 1 hour
Makes 8 servings.
Per serving: 178 calories, 6.1 g. fat (29% of calories), 5.4 g. dietary fiber, 0 mg. cholesterol, 12 mg. sodium.

1 tablespoon canola oil
1 cup shredded carrots
3 cups water
1 cup orange juice
1 cup medium pearled barley
1 tablespoon grated orange peel

1 can (8 ounces) pineapple chunks packed in juice, drained
½ cup unsalted roasted cashew halves

1. In a 3-quart saucepan over medium heat, warm the oil. Add the carrots; cook, stirring frequently, for 4 to 5 minutes, or until tender.

2. Add the water and juice; bring to a boil. Stir in the barley and orange peel. Reduce the heat to low. Cover and simmer for 45 to 50 minutes, or until the barley is tender and the liquid has been absorbed.

3. Stir in the pineapple and cashews; cook for 1 minute.

barley with bitter greens

This side dish is a good way to use leftover salad greens. If you don't have arugula and radicchio, substitute other bitter greens, such as escarole, chicory—even dandelion.

Preparation time: 15 minutes
Cooking time: 50 minutes
Makes 8 servings.
Per serving: 113 calories, 2.4 g. fat (18% of calories), 4.3 g. dietary fiber, 1 mg. cholesterol, 29 mg. sodium.

4 cups water	3 teaspoons olive oil, divided
1 cup medium pearled barley	1 cup chopped scallions
1½ tablespoons grated Parmesan cheese	1½ cups coarsely chopped arugula
1 tablespoon lemon juice	1 cup coarsely chopped radicchio
⅛ teaspoon freshly ground black pepper	

1. In a 2-quart saucepan over high heat, bring the water to a boil. Stir in the barley, reduce the heat to low, and cover the pan. Simmer for 40 to 45 minutes, or until the barley is just tender and the liquid has been absorbed. Remove from the heat and let stand, covered, for 10 minutes.

2. In a small bowl, whisk together the Parmesan, lemon juice, pepper and 2 teaspoons of the oil; set aside.

3. In a 3-quart saucepan over medium heat, warm the remaining 1 teaspoon oil. Add the scallions; cook, stirring frequently, for 2 minutes. Stir in the arugula and radicchio; cook, stirring constantly, for about 1 to 2 minutes, or until wilted.

4. Stir in the barley and the Parmesan mixture. Cook, stirring constantly, for 2 minutes to blend the flavors.

basmati tomato and ginger rice

The combination of tomato and ginger gives rice a pleasantly different flavor. Serve this as a side dish.

Preparation time: 10 minutes
Cooking time: 25 minutes
Makes 8 servings.
Per serving: 131 calories, 2.1 g. fat (14% of calories), 0.6 g. dietary fiber, 0 mg. cholesterol, 4 mg. sodium.

1	large tomato, coarsely chopped
1	tablespoon canola oil
½	cup chopped onions
2	garlic cloves, minced
2	teaspoons coriander seeds
1¼	cups basmati or other long-grain aromatic white rice
1	teaspoon powdered ginger
⅛	teaspoon red-pepper flakes

1. In a food processor, puree the tomatoes. Pour into a 4-cup glass measure. Add enough water to bring the level up to 2½ cups; set aside.

2. In a 2-quart saucepan over medium heat, warm the oil. Add the onions, garlic and coriander seeds; cook, stirring frequently, for 2 to 3 minutes, or until the onions are tender. Stir in the rice to coat with the oil.

3. Add the tomatoes and water, ginger and pepper flakes; bring to a boil. Reduce the heat to low. Cover and simmer for 30 to 35 minutes, or until the rice is tender and the liquid has been absorbed.

4. Remove from the heat and let stand, covered, for 10 minutes. Fluff with a fork.

luscious legumes

I like to think of this chapter as the best of bean cuisine. Beans are one of the oldest and most universally used foods, long ago earning the nickname "poor man's meat" because of their robust flavor, hunger-appeasing ability and cheap cost.

But beans have even more going for them than that. They're very rich sources of dietary fiber, both the insoluble form needed for healthy digestion and the soluble type that's so good at lowering cholesterol. And they're practically fat-free, so you can eat your fill with no guilt whatsoever.

I've alternated between dried beans and canned beans in these recipes just to show you how to deal with both types. Dried beans, of course, need soaking and a fairly long cooking time. But if you do this preparation ahead, you can get recipes on the table fast. Canned beans are ready to use and need only a thorough rinsing to rid them of excess sodium. Either way, you can't beat these time-honored legumes.

white herb chili

Here's a nice change of pace from the usual chili recipes featuring red kidney beans and tomatoes. If you'd like, serve the chili topped with some shredded low-fat Monterey Jack cheese and some nonfat sour cream.

MAKE
AHEAD

Preparation time: 20 minutes + soaking time
Cooking time: 2½ hours

Makes 4 servings.
Per serving: 284 calories, 6.5 g. fat (19% of calories), 10.3 g. dietary fiber, 0 mg. cholesterol, 323 mg. sodium.

2 cups dried great Northern beans, soaked overnight	4 cups low-sodium vegetable stock
1 tablespoon olive oil	½ cup chopped fresh flat-leaf parsley
2 onions, chopped	
2 cups coarsely chopped zucchini	2 tablespoons chopped fresh thyme
1 cup chopped carrots	1 tablespoon ground cumin
1 cup chopped fennel	2 teaspoons low-sodium soy sauce
1 cup chopped celery	
2 tablespoons chopped canned green chili peppers (wear plastic gloves when handling)	¼ teaspoon ground red pepper
	1 cup drained canned corn

1. Drain the beans and place them in a 2-quart saucepan. Cover with cold water. Bring to a boil over medium-high heat, then reduce the heat to medium. Simmer for 1½ to 2 hours, or until the beans are tender. Drain and set aside.

2. In a 4-quart saucepan over medium heat, warm the oil. Add the onions, zucchini, carrots, fennel and celery. Cook, stirring frequently, for 4 to 5 minutes, or until tender. Stir in the beans and chili peppers; cook for 1 minute.

3. Stir in the stock, parsley, thyme, cumin, soy sauce and red pepper; bring to a boil. Simmer for 1 hour. With the back of a wooden spoon, mash about 1 cup of the beans into a paste. Stir in the corn. Simmer for 30 minutes, or until the chili thickens.

lentil-stuffed crêpes

These crêpes make a delicious main course. For variety, you may replace the lentils in the filling with yellow split peas. You may also top the filled crêpes with spaghetti sauce. If you don't feel like taking the time to prepare crêpes, use the filling in taco shells. Unlike most other legumes, lentils don't need to be soaked before cooking.

Preparation time: 15 minutes
Cooking time: 35 minutes
Makes 4 servings.
Per serving: 344 calories, 4.3 g. fat (11% of calories), 10.2 g. dietary fiber, 1 mg. cholesterol, 119 mg. sodium.

Lentil Sauce
3 cups water
1 cup red lentils, rinsed and drained
1 cup boiling water
10 sun-dried tomatoes
1 tablespoon olive oil
1½ cups frozen mixed cauliflower, broccoli and carrots, thawed and coarsely chopped

½ cup chopped onions
1½ cups tomato sauce
1 teaspoon curry powder
½ teaspoon ground cinnamon

Crêpes
½ cup egg substitute
½ cup skim milk
¼ cup whole wheat flour

1. To make the lentil sauce: In a 2-quart saucepan, combine the 3 cups water and lentils. Bring to a boil over medium-high heat. Reduce the heat to low and simmer for 5 to 10 minutes, or until tender but not mushy. Drain and set aside.

2. In a small bowl, combine the boiling water and tomatoes. Let soak for 5 minutes. Drain and chop the tomatoes.

3. In a large no-stick frying pan over medium heat, warm the oil. Add the mixed vegetables and onions; cook, stirring frequently, for 4 to 5 minutes, or until tender. Stir in the tomato sauce, curry powder and cinnamon. Add the lentils and tomatoes. Simmer for 15 to 20 minutes, or until the sauce thickens.

4. To make the crêpes: While the lentils are cooking, whisk together the egg, milk and flour in a small bowl. Coat a medium no-stick frying pan or 9" crêpe pan with no-stick spray. Place the pan over medium-high heat and let stand for 1 minute.

5. Add about ¼ cup of the batter to the pan. Tilt the pan in all directions until the batter covers the bottom. Cook for 30 to 40 seconds, or until the top is set. Flip the crêpe and cook for 1 minute longer. Remove from the pan, place on a baking sheet, cover, and keep warm in an oven set at the lowest heat. Repeat with the remaining batter to make a total of 4 crêpes.

6. Divide the lentil mixture evenly among the crêpes; roll to enclose the filling.

moroccan fava beans

Fresh fava beans are green and are available unshelled in many markets. When buying, look for pods that aren't bulging, so you get tender young beans. You'll need to purchase about 2½ pounds of beans for this recipe. If you can't obtain fresh beans, substitute canned or cooked dried ones.

Preparation time: 25 minutes + chilling time
Cooking time: 45 minutes
Makes 4 servings.
Per serving: 363 calories, 12 g. fat (28% of calories), 9 g. dietary fiber, 0 mg. cholesterol, 10 mg. sodium.

4 cups water	½ teaspoon ground allspice
2 cups fresh fava beans	⅛ teaspoon turmeric
1 tablespoon olive oil	1 cup orange juice
1 medium onion, thinly sliced crosswise and separated into rings	1 cup pitted prunes, coarsely chopped
2 garlic cloves, minced	½ cup unsalted roasted cashews, chopped
½ teaspoon powdered ginger	

1. In a 2-quart saucepan over high heat, bring the water to a boil. Add the beans, reduce the heat to medium, and boil for 10 minutes. Drain and refrigerate until well chilled. Slip the skins from the beans. Discard the skins; set the beans aside.

2. In a large no-stick frying pan over medium heat, warm the oil. Add the onions and garlic; cook, stirring constantly, for 3 to 4 minutes, or until tender. Stir in the ginger, allspice and turmeric; cook for 1 minute.

3. Add the juice and prunes; bring to a boil. Stir in the beans. Reduce the heat to low; cover and simmer for 25 to 30 minutes, or until the beans are tender and the liquid thickens slightly. Sprinkle with the cashews.

bean quesadillas

This is one of my favorite recipes. It's something I developed from leftover beans for a light Sunday supper. Top the quesadillas with your choice of salsa, nonfat sour cream, chopped fresh cilantro or whatever Mexican garnishes you like. You may use any type of small white bean, such as pea beans or navy beans.

Preparation time: 10 minutes + soaking time
Cooking time: 2 hours
Makes 4 servings.
Per serving: 495 calories, 12.8 g. fat (23% of calories), 11.1 g. dietary fiber, 15 mg. cholesterol, 90 mg. sodium.

1 cup dried small white beans, soaked overnight	½ teaspoon garlic powder
	½ teaspoon dried basil
1 cup chopped roasted sweet red peppers	½ teaspoon dried oregano
	8 large flour tortillas
1 cup shredded low-fat Monterey Jack cheese	3 teaspoons canola oil, divided

1. Drain the beans and place in a 2-quart saucepan. Cover with cold water. Bring to a boil over high heat. Reduce the heat to low and simmer, stirring occasionally, for 1½ to 2 hours, or until the beans are tender. Drain and return the beans to the pan. Off heat, lightly mash the beans.

2. Stir in the peppers, Monterey Jack, garlic powder, basil and oregano.

3. Wrap the tortillas in a paper towel and microwave on high for about 30 seconds to soften them. Divide the bean mixture among the tortillas, spreading it to within 1" of the edges. Fold each tortilla in half.

4. In a medium no-stick frying pan over medium heat, warm about 1 teaspoon of the oil. Place 2 quesadillas in the pan. Cook for 2 to 3 minutes, or until the bottoms are golden. Flip the quesadillas and gently press on them with a spatula to help the cheese melt. Cook for another 3 to 4 minutes. Remove from the pan.

5. Continue, adding more of the remaining 2 teaspoons oil as needed, until all the quesadillas are browned.

quinoa-pistachio pilaf (p. 111)

polenta with eggplant sauce (p. 88)

pinto bean and pepper enchiladas (p. 158)

black-eyed pea and vegetable stew (p. 154)

lentil-stuffed crêpes (p. 118)

chick-peas with sun-dried tomatoes (p. 148)

anasazi beans with snow peas and tarragon (p. 151)

hoisin and black bean stir-fry (p. 137)

onion-apple soup with crumb topping (p. 177)

saffron corn chowder (p. 179)

136   split pea soup with toasted caraway croutons (p. 162)

hoisin and black bean stir-fry

Hoisin sauce is a sweet and spicy concoction of soybeans, garlic, hot peppers and spices. It's often used as a table condiment, but here I add it directly to the stir-fry. Look for it in well-stocked supermarkets, where you should also be able to find the soy sauce, rice wine vinegar and sesame oil.

Preparation time: 20 minutes
Cooking time: 15 minutes
Makes 4 servings.
Per serving: 434 calories, 8.1 g. fat (17% of calories), 8.8 g. dietary fiber, 0 mg. cholesterol, 913 mg. sodium.

¼ cup hoisin sauce	½ cup low-sodium vegetable stock
1 tablespoon low-sodium soy sauce	1 green pepper, cut into strips
1 tablespoon rice wine vinegar	1 yellow squash, thinly sliced
1 tablespoon sesame oil	1 cup snow peas
¼ teaspoon red-pepper flakes	1½ cups canned black beans, rinsed and drained
1 tablespoon peanut oil	½ cup sliced water chestnuts
2 tablespoons chopped fresh ginger	3 cups hot cooked rice
2 garlic cloves, minced	
2 cups thinly sliced carrots	

1. In a small bowl, combine the hoisin sauce, soy sauce, vinegar, sesame oil and pepper flakes; set aside.

2. In a wok or large no-stick frying pan over medium-high heat, warm the peanut oil. Add the ginger and garlic; stir-fry for 1 minute. Add the carrots; stir-fry for 3 to 4 minutes, or until just tender.

3. Pour in the stock; cook for 2 to 3 minutes, or until the liquid has evaporated.

4. Add the green peppers, squash and snow peas; stir-fry for 4 to 5 minutes, or until just tender. Stir in the beans, water chestnuts and hoisin sauce mixture; stir-fry for 2 minutes, or until heated through. Serve over the rice.

black-eyed pea soufflé

I particularly like this soufflé when it's made with black-eyed peas, but you may substitute any other variety of canned beans. This recipe calls for buttermilk. When buying it, compare labels and choose the brand that's lowest in fat.

Preparation time: 15 minutes
Cooking time: 5 minutes
Baking time: 45 minutes
Makes 4 servings.
Per serving: 259 calories, 5.3 g. fat (18% of calories), 5.4 g. dietary fiber, 9 mg. cholesterol, 380 mg. sodium.

1	teaspoon olive oil	1/3	cup yellow cornmeal
1/2	cup chopped onions	1/3	cup unbleached flour
1/2	cup chopped sweet red peppers	1 1/2	teaspoons baking powder
1	cup canned black-eyed peas, rinsed and drained	1	cup buttermilk
		1/2	cup egg substitute
1/2	cup shredded low-fat Cheddar cheese	12	Ritz crackers, crushed, or 1/3 cup dry bread crumbs
		4	large egg whites

1. In a medium no-stick frying pan over medium heat, warm the oil. Add the onions and peppers; cook, stirring constantly, for 3 to 4 minutes, or until tender. Set aside.

2. In a large mixing bowl, combine the black-eyed peas, Cheddar, cornmeal, flour and baking powder.

3. In a small bowl, whisk together the buttermilk and egg; pour over the black-eyed pea mixture. Add the onions and peppers; gently mix and set aside.

4. Preheat the oven to 375°. Coat a 2½-quart casserole or soufflé dish with no-stick spray. Sprinkle the bottom and sides of the dish with the cracker crumbs or bread crumbs. Set aside.

5. In a clean small bowl, whip the egg whites with an electric mixer until stiff but not dry. Gently fold the whites into the black-eyed pea mixture.

6. Pour the batter into the prepared dish. Bake for 40 to 45 minutes, or until puffed and golden.

cannellini and tarragon ravioli

Wonton skins are a convenient substitute for homemade pasta when making ravioli. I like to buy the tricolor ones, but you may use plain white if that's all your market carries. The duck sauce called for is also known as plum sauce and is available in the Chinese section of markets. A wonton crimper makes sealing the filled ravioli easy, but the tines of a fork work well, too.

Preparation time: 35 minutes
Cooking time: 30 minutes
Makes 4 servings.
Per serving: 350 calories, 11.7 g. fat (29% of calories), 4.3 g. dietary fiber, 0 mg. cholesterol, 846 mg. sodium.

8 ounces firm tofu, well drained and squeezed dry between paper towels	1½ teaspoons low-sodium soy sauce, divided
1 cup canned cannellini beans, rinsed and drained	¼ cup duck sauce
2 tablespoons lemon juice	1 tablespoon Dijon mustard
½ teaspoon dried tarragon	1 teaspoon hoisin sauce
¼ teaspoon dried thyme	24 wonton skins (3" × 3")
⅛ teaspoon freshly ground black pepper	1½ tablespoons canola oil, divided

1. In a food processor, combine the tofu, beans, lemon juice, tarragon, thyme, pepper and ½ teaspoon of the soy sauce. Process until smooth; set aside.

2. In a small bowl, combine the duck sauce, mustard, hoisin sauce and the remaining 1 teaspoon soy sauce; set aside.

3. Lay 1 of the wonton skins on the counter in front of you. Using a pastry brush, wet the edges with cold water. Place 2 teaspoons of the tofu filling on the bottom half of the wonton. Fold the top half over the filling. Using a wonton crimper or the tines of a fork, press the edges together to seal; set aside. Repeat with the remaining wontons and filling.

4. In a large no-stick frying pan over medium heat, warm 1 tablespoon of the oil. Working in batches, brown the ravioli for 2 to 3 minutes per side, or until golden. Add more of the remaining ½ tablespoon oil as needed. Serve with the duck sauce mixture.

braised red cabbage and beans

The smell and taste of this mixture—with its cabbage, apples and juniper berries—always reminds me of autumn.

Preparation time: 15 minutes
Cooking time: 30 minutes
Makes 4 servings.
Per serving: 177 calories, 4.8 g. fat (22% of calories), 7.9 g. dietary fiber, 0 mg. cholesterol, 582 mg. sodium.

1 tablespoon canola oil	1 cup low-sodium vegetable stock
2 carrots, diced	1 can (19 ounces) pinto beans, rinsed and drained
2 celery ribs, diced	
½ cup chopped red onions	1 tablespoon red wine vinegar
5 juniper berries	
4 cups shredded red cabbage	¼ teaspoon freshly ground black pepper
1 Granny Smith apple, diced	
2 teaspoons caraway seeds	

1. In a Dutch oven over medium heat, warm the oil. Add the carrots, celery, onions and berries. Cook, stirring frequently, for 4 to 5 minutes, or until just tender. Stir in the cabbage, apples and caraway seeds; cook for 2 minutes.

2. Add the stock. Cover and cook for 15 minutes.

3. Uncover and stir in the beans and vinegar. Cook, stirring frequently, for 5 to 7 minutes, or until most of the liquid has evaporated. Add the pepper. Remove and discard the berries.

scrambled eggs with limas and spinach

I like to make this on weeknights for a quick after-work dinner. The eggs go especially well with rye toast.

1 box (10 ounces) frozen lima beans, thawed	1½ cups egg substitute
1 tablespoon margarine	¼ cup thawed frozen chopped spinach, squeezed dry
½ cup chopped onions	
2 garlic cloves, minced	¼ cup nonfat cream cheese
Pinch of freshly ground black pepper	4 slices rye bread, toasted

Preparation time: 10 minutes
Cooking time: 10 minutes

Makes 4 servings.
Per serving: 249 calories, 4.1
g. fat (15% of calories), 5.6 g.
dietary fiber, 11 mg. cholesterol, 433 mg. sodium.

1. In a large pot of boiling water, blanch the beans for 4 minutes; drain and set aside.

2. In a medium no-stick frying pan over medium heat, melt the margarine. Add the onions and garlic; cook, stirring frequently, for 2 minutes. Stir in the beans and pepper; cook for 1 minute.

3. In a medium bowl, lightly beat together the egg, spinach and cream cheese. Pour the egg mixture into the pan; cook, stirring lightly, for 2 to 3 minutes, or until the eggs are set. Serve over the toast.

split pea and potato hash

I generally make this dish with green split peas, but you may substitute yellow split peas or even lentils.

Preparation time: 20 minutes
Cooking time: 30 minutes

Makes 4 servings.
Per serving: 303 calories, 3.9
g. fat (11% of calories), 4.3 g.
dietary fiber, 0 mg. cholesterol, 28 mg. sodium.

2½ cups water	½ teaspoon dried rosemary, crumbled
1 cup green split peas, rinsed and drained	¼ teaspoon freshly ground black pepper
1 tablespoon margarine	
1 cup finely chopped onions	6 medium red potatoes, parboiled for 10 minutes
1 cup finely chopped sweet red peppers	½ cup low-sodium vegetable stock
1 teaspoon dried thyme	

1. In a 2-quart saucepan over medium-high heat, bring the water and split peas to a boil. Reduce the heat to low; cover and simmer for 15 to 20 minutes, or until tender. Drain.

2. Meanwhile, in a 4-quart saucepan over medium heat, melt the margarine. Add the onions, red peppers, thyme, rosemary and black pepper. Cook until tender.

3. Cube the potatoes and add to the pan. Cook, stirring frequently, for 8 to 10 minutes, or until the potatoes are tender. Stir in the stock and split peas. Cook for 5 to 7 minutes.

caribbean split peas with mango salsa

Allspice has a strong flavor that I really enjoy. If you're not used to the taste, start with ¼ teaspoon and add more if you think the dish needs it. Like lentils, split peas don't need to be soaked before cooking.

Preparation time: 25 minutes
Cooking time: 45 minutes

Makes 4 servings.
Per serving: 376 calories, 6 g. fat (13% of calories), 7.9 g. dietary fiber, 0 mg. cholesterol, 134 mg. sodium.

2½ cups water	3 teaspoons olive oil, divided
1 cup yellow split peas, rinsed and drained	1 cup chopped scallions
1 medium mango, peeled and cubed	½ teaspoon powdered ginger
½ cup salsa	½ teaspoon ground allspice
½ cup drained canned pineapple chunks, coarsely chopped	¼ teaspoon ground cardamom
1 tablespoon chopped fresh cilantro	½ cup orange juice
2 teaspoons white wine vinegar	¼ cup low-sodium vegetable stock
2 teaspoons lime juice	1 teaspoon dark brown sugar or ½ teaspoon honey
½ teaspoon ground cumin	1 medium bunch kale

1. In a 2-quart saucepan over medium heat, bring the water and split peas to a boil. Reduce the heat to low. Cover the pan and simmer for 25 to 30 minutes, or until tender. Drain and set aside.

2. Meanwhile, in a medium bowl, combine the mangoes, salsa, pineapple, cilantro, vinegar, lime juice and cumin; set aside.

3. In a large no-stick frying pan, heat 2 teaspoons of the oil. Add the scallions; cook, stirring frequently, for 2 to 3 minutes, or until tender. Stir in the ginger, allspice and cardamom; cook for 1 minute.

4. Stir in the orange juice, stock and sugar or honey. Add the split peas; cook, stirring frequently, for 10 to 15 minutes, or until the mixture thickens.

5. Meanwhile, wash the kale in plenty of cold water. Remove any thick stems. If the leaves are large, coarsely chop them. Shake off some of the excess water. In a Dutch oven over medium heat, warm the remaining 1 teaspoon oil. Add the kale; cook, stirring constantly, for 4 to 5 minutes, or until the kale is wilted.

6. Line a serving platter with the kale. Top with the split pea mixture, then with the mango mixture.

cilantro beans with crisp tortilla strips

When shopping for canned beans, try various brands until you find one you like. Flavors and textures can vary significantly from brand to brand. And here's a little tip: Don't worry if the particular product you like comes in a slightly larger or smaller can size than the recipe specifies—it won't really affect the finished product.

Preparation time: 20 minutes
Cooking time: 20 minutes
Makes 4 servings.
Per serving: 297 calories, 7.3 g. fat (21% of calories), 10.4 g. dietary fiber, 0 mg. cholesterol, 366 mg. sodium.

5 teaspoons olive oil, divided	1 can (16 ounces) black beans, rinsed and drained
2 corn tortillas, cut into ½" strips	2 tablespoons tomato paste
1 cup chopped onions	1 teaspoon low-sodium Worcestershire sauce
1 sweet red pepper, cut into strips	½ teaspoon ground cumin
1 green pepper, cut into strips	2 tablespoons chopped fresh cilantro
1 cup broccoli florets	2 tablespoons lime juice
1 can (16 ounces) red kidney beans, rinsed and drained	

1. In a large no-stick frying pan over medium heat, warm 3 teaspoons of the oil. Add the tortilla strips; cook, turning the strips once, for 3 to 4 minutes, or until golden. Remove from the pan and let drain on paper towels.

2. In the same pan, heat the remaining 2 teaspoons oil. Add the onions, red peppers, green peppers and broccoli; stir-fry for 2 minutes, or until the vegetables are just tender.

3. Stir in the kidney beans, black beans, tomato paste, Worcestershire sauce and cumin; cover and simmer for 10 to 15 minutes, or until the flavors blend. Stir in the cilantro and lime juice. Sprinkle with the tortilla strips.

spaghetti squash with chunky bean sauce

If fresh shiitake mushrooms are unavailable, substitute regular white mushrooms. This bean sauce is also good tossed with cooked pasta or served on top of steamed rice.

Preparation time: 20 minutes
Cooking time: 1 hour

Makes 4 servings.
Per serving: 452 calories, 11.7 g. fat (21% of calories), 16.7 g. dietary fiber, 2 mg. cholesterol, 420 mg. sodium.

1 large spaghetti squash	1 can (16 ounces) chick-peas, rinsed and drained
2 tablespoons olive oil, divided	1 can (16 ounces) cannellini beans, rinsed and drained
8 ounces shiitake mushrooms	1 cup drained canned corn
1 red onion, thinly sliced crosswise and separated into rings	½ cup chopped fresh basil
1 yellow pepper, cut into strips	2 tablespoons grated Parmesan cheese
1 can (28 ounces) low-sodium tomatoes, drained and pureed	

1. Place the squash in a very large pot. Add water to cover. Bring to a boil and cook for 30 minutes to 1 hour, or until easily pierced with a fork. Drain, halve, and set aside until cool enough to handle. Scoop out and discard the seeds. With a fork, separate the flesh into strands and place in a large bowl. Toss with 1 tablespoon of the oil. Set aside.

2. Meanwhile, remove and discard the stems from the mushrooms. If the caps are very large, thickly slice or quarter them.

3. In a Dutch oven over medium heat, warm the remaining 1 tablespoon oil. Add the onions, peppers and mushrooms. Cook, stirring frequently, for 4 to 5 minutes, or until just tender. Stir in the tomatoes, chick-peas, beans and corn; bring to a boil. Reduce the heat to low; simmer, stirring occasionally, for 40 to 50 minutes, or until the sauce thickens.

4. Remove from the heat and stir in the basil. Pour over the squash strands and toss to mix well. Sprinkle with the Parmesan.

lentil burgers with sautéed mushrooms and onions

You'll love these "meaty," satisfying burgers. I like to make the mushroom and onion topping using Vidalia onions, which are almost sweet enough to eat like an apple. If you can't find them, choose another large sweet variety. For slightly different burgers, replace the mushroom mixture with standard burger toppers such as tomato slices, lettuce and low-fat cheese.

Preparation time: 15 minutes
Cooking time: 35 minutes
Broiling time: 10 minutes

Makes 4 servings.
Per serving: 443 calories, 13.9 g. fat (27% of calories), 10.4 g. dietary fiber, 0 mg. cholesterol, 692 mg. sodium.

1¼ cups water	1 tablespoon margarine
½ cup brown lentils, rinsed and drained	1 medium Vidalia or other sweet onion, thinly sliced crosswise and separated into rings
1 cup canned red kidney *black* beans, rinsed and drained	
½ cup wheat germ	8 ounces mushrooms, thinly sliced
⅓ cup finely chopped pecans	
¼ cup chili sauce	4 sesame-topped hamburger buns
½ teaspoon ground cumin	
¼ teaspoon garlic powder	

1. In a 2-quart saucepan over medium-high heat, bring the water and lentils to a boil. Reduce the heat to low, cover the pan, and simmer for about 25 minutes, or until tender. Drain if all the water has not been absorbed.

2. Place the lentils in a food processor. Add the beans; process until smooth.

3. Transfer to a medium bowl. Add the wheat germ, pecans, chili sauce, cumin and garlic powder; mix well. Form the mixture into 4 patties.

4. Grill or broil for about 5 minutes per side, or until golden.

5. While the burgers are cooking, melt the margarine in a large no-stick frying pan over medium heat. Add the onions and mushrooms; cook, stirring frequently, for 8 to 10 minutes, or until very tender and the mushroom liquid has evaporated.

6. To serve, place the patties in the buns and top with equal amounts of the mushroom mixture.

bruschetta with bean puree

Bruschetta is the Italian name for garlic-flavored bread slices that are grilled until golden. I like to serve this dish as a first course or even as a light supper all by itself.

MAKE
AHEAD

Preparation time: 20 minutes
Cooking time: 15 minutes
Makes 4 servings.
Per serving: 379 calories, 10.2 g. fat (24% of calories), 7 g. dietary fiber, 0 mg. cholesterol, 397 mg. sodium.

1 medium tomato, seeded and diced	¼ cup minced onions
1 cup coarsely chopped arugula	2 cups cooked white beans
1 teaspoon balsamic vinegar	½ cup water
4 garlic cloves, divided	1 tablespoon chopped fresh thyme
2 tablespoons olive oil, divided	16 slices sourdough or French bread, cut 1" thick

1. In a small bowl, combine the tomatoes, arugula and vinegar. Mince 2 of the garlic cloves and add to the bowl; set aside.

2. In a large no-stick frying pan over medium heat, warm 1 tablespoon of the oil. Add the onions; cook, stirring frequently, for 2 to 3 minutes, or until tender. Stir in the beans, water and thyme; cook, stirring frequently, for 8 to 10 minutes, or until the liquid has evaporated.

3. Transfer the bean mixture to a food processor; process until smooth. Set aside.

4. Lightly grill or toast the bread. Halve the remaining 2 garlic cloves and rub the pieces over the bread. Lightly brush the slices with the remaining 1 tablespoon oil.

5. To serve, spread the slices with the bean puree and top with the tomato mixture.

baked black beans
with crusty cheddar topping

I usually serve this tasty bean mixture over steamed white rice or broad noodles. If you'd like to save time, you may substitute about 2½ cups rinsed and drained canned beans for the dried ones.

Preparation time: 15 minutes
+ soaking time
Cooking time: 1 hour
Baking time: 1 hour 20 minutes

Makes 4 servings.
Per serving: 349 calories, 3.4 g. fat (9% of calories), 10.9 g. dietary fiber, 7 mg. cholesterol, 618 mg. sodium.

1¼ cups dried black beans, soaked overnight	¼ cup shredded low-fat Cheddar cheese
1 cup tomato sauce	¼ cup shredded low-fat Monterey Jack cheese
1 cup chopped onions	2 tablespoons seasoned dry bread crumbs
1 cup chopped celery	
1 sweet red pepper, chopped	1 tablespoon chopped fresh flat-leaf parsley
½ cup chili sauce	
1 tablespoon maple syrup	⅛ teaspoon ground red pepper
2 teaspoons chili powder	
½ teaspoon powdered ginger	

1. Drain the beans and place in a 2-quart saucepan. Add cold water to cover. Bring to a boil over high heat. Reduce the heat to low and simmer for 1 hour, or until just tender. Drain and place in a large bowl.

2. Preheat the oven to 350°. Coat a 2½-quart casserole with no-stick spray; set aside.

3. To the beans, add the tomato sauce, onions, celery, red peppers, chili sauce, maple syrup, chili powder and ginger. Mix well and spoon into the prepared casserole. Cover and bake for 1 hour, or until the beans are very tender.

4. Meanwhile, in a small bowl, mix the Cheddar, Monterey Jack, bread crumbs, parsley and ground pepper.

5. Uncover the casserole and sprinkle with the topping. Bake, uncovered, for 15 to 20 minutes, or until the cheese has melted and is bubbly.

chick-peas
with sun-dried tomatoes

This is a super-quick side dish. Sun-dried tomato bits are about the size of red-pepper flakes and are available in many markets.

MAKE AHEAD

Preparation time: 10 minutes
Cooking time: 10 minutes

Makes 4 servings.
Per serving: 227 calories, 6.4 g. fat (24% of calories), 8.9 g. dietary fiber, 0 mg. cholesterol, 24 mg. sodium.

1	tablespoon olive oil	1	medium tomato, chopped
1	small red onion, thinly sliced crosswise and separated into rings	2½	cups canned chick-peas, rinsed and drained
½	teaspoon dried rosemary, crumbled	2	tablespoons sun-dried tomato bits
½	cup low-sodium vegetable stock	1	tablespoon balsamic vinegar

1. In a large no-stick frying pan over medium-high heat, warm the oil. Add the onions and rosemary; cook, stirring frequently, for 2 to 3 minutes, or until tender.

2. Stir in the stock and chopped tomatoes. Cook for 3 to 4 minutes, or until all the liquid has evaporated.

3. Stir in the chick-peas, tomato bits and vinegar; cook for 1 to 2 minutes, or until heated through.

cannellini frittata

You'll love this unusual egg dish!

1	tablespoon margarine	½	teaspoon dried oregano
1	cup thinly sliced zucchini	3–4	drops hot-pepper sauce
1	cup chopped scallions	2	cups canned cannellini beans, rinsed and drained
2	garlic cloves, minced	1	tablespoon grated Parmesan cheese
1½	cups chopped spinach		
1½	cups egg substitute		
¼	cup skim milk		
¼	cup shredded low-fat Swiss cheese		

Preparation time: 10 minutes
Cooking time: 15 minutes
Broiling time: 2 minutes

Makes 4 servings.

Per serving: 297 calories, 5.9 g. fat (17% of calories), 11 g. dietary fiber, 6 mg. cholesterol, 225 mg. sodium.

1. In a large ovenproof frying pan over medium heat, melt the margarine. Add the zucchini, scallions and garlic; cook, stirring frequently, for 4 to 5 minutes, or until tender. Stir in the spinach; cook for 1 minute, or until wilted.

2. Meanwhile, in a medium bowl, whisk together the egg, milk, Swiss, oregano and hot-pepper sauce. Add the beans.

3. Reduce the heat under the frying pan to low. Add the egg mixture and stir gently to combine. Cover and cook for 10 minutes, or until the eggs are almost set.

4. Sprinkle with the Parmesan. Place the pan 4" to 5" from the broiler unit. Broil for 1 to 2 minutes, or until golden.

tofu hummus tacos

This dish is a cross between hummus—that creamy Middle Eastern bean dip—and tacos. It's something I can whip up quickly after work or when unexpected guests pop in.

Preparation time: 20 minutes

Makes 4 servings.

Per serving: 477 calories, 13.9 g. fat (26% of calories), 10 g. dietary fiber, 0 mg. cholesterol, 592 mg. sodium.

8	ounces firm tofu, well drained and squeezed dry between paper towels	1	teaspoon ground cumin
1	can (19 ounces) white beans, rinsed and drained	⅛	teaspoon ground red pepper
2	tablespoons tahini or creamy peanut butter	8	taco shells
2	tablespoons lemon juice	2	cups shredded lettuce
2	tablespoons lime juice	2	medium tomatoes, chopped
2	garlic cloves, minced	1	cup chopped scallions
		1	cup salsa
		2	cups hot cooked rice

1. Crumble the tofu into a food processor. Add the beans, tahini or peanut butter, lemon juice, lime juice, garlic, cumin and pepper. Process until smooth.

2. Heat the taco shells according to the package directions. Spoon ¼ cup of the bean mixture into each shell. Top with the lettuce, tomatoes, scallions and salsa. Serve with the rice.

chick-pea and cilantro pâté

I like to serve this as an appetizer with a variety of crackers and breads. If you'd like to save time, replace the dried chick-peas with about 3 cups rinsed and drained canned ones.

MAKE AHEAD

Preparation time: 10 minutes + soaking and chilling time
Cooking time: 3 hours
Baking time: 40 minutes
Makes 4 servings.
Per serving: 477 calories, 10.5 g. fat (20% of calories), 11.2 g. dietary fiber, 0 mg. cholesterol, 314 mg. sodium.

1½ cups dried chick-peas, soaked overnight
1 tablespoon olive oil
1 cup finely chopped onions
2 garlic cloves, minced
2 large plum tomatoes, finely chopped
1 green pepper, finely chopped
¾ cup fresh whole wheat bread crumbs
2 tablespoons chopped fresh cilantro
½ teaspoon ground coriander
⅛ teaspoon ground red pepper
16 slices pumpernickel cocktail bread

1. Drain the chick-peas and place in a 2-quart saucepan. Add cold water to cover. Bring to a boil over high heat. Reduce the heat to low, partially cover, and simmer for 2 to 3 hours, or until tender. If necessary, add more water as the chick-peas cook.

2. Drain and place in a large bowl. Mash until smooth.

3. In a medium no-stick frying pan over medium heat, warm the oil. Add the onions and garlic; cook, stirring frequently, for 2 to 3 minutes, or until tender. Add to the chick-peas. Stir in the tomatoes, green peppers, bread crumbs, cilantro, coriander and red pepper.

4. Preheat the oven to 350°. Line a 9" × 5" loaf pan with foil; coat the foil with no-stick spray.

5. Spoon the chick-pea mixture into the prepared pan. Bake for 35 to 40 minutes, or until golden.

6. Cool completely on a wire rack. Refrigerate for at least 4 hours, or until well chilled. Remove the foil from the pan and gently peel it off the chick-pea mixture. To serve, slice with a sharp knife and serve with the bread.

anasazi beans with snow peas and tarragon

Anasazi beans take their name from the cliff-dwelling tribes that populated the American Southwest in olden times. The beans, which have a sweet and meaty texture, have an added bonus: They're one of the least gas-producing varieties.

Preparation time: 10 minutes + soaking time
Cooking time: 2 hours
Makes 4 servings.
Per serving: 301 calories, 5 g. fat (15% of calories), 13.8 g. dietary fiber, 0 mg. cholesterol, 98 mg. sodium.

8 ounces dried Anasazi beans, soaked overnight	1 teaspoon dried tarragon
1 tablespoon canola oil	$\frac{1}{4}$ teaspoon freshly ground black pepper
1 cup chopped red onions	$\frac{1}{2}$ cup low-sodium vegetable stock
2 garlic cloves, minced	
$1\frac{1}{2}$ cups snow peas	1 tablespoon lemon juice
$1\frac{1}{2}$ cups shredded carrots	2 teaspoons Dijon mustard

1. Drain the beans and place in a 2-quart saucepan. Add cold water to cover. Bring to a boil over high heat. Reduce the heat to low, partially cover the pan, and simmer for $1\frac{1}{2}$ to 2 hours, or until tender. Drain and transfer to a large bowl.

2. Meanwhile, in a large no-stick frying pan over medium heat, warm the oil. Add the onions and garlic; cook, stirring frequently, for 2 to 3 minutes, or until tender.

3. Add the snow peas, carrots, tarragon and pepper to the pan. Cook, stirring frequently, for 4 to 5 minutes, or until the vegetables are tender.

4. In a cup, combine the stock, lemon juice and mustard; stir into the pan and cook for 1 minute to blend the flavors.

5. Gently stir in the beans. Cook for 2 to 3 minutes, or until heated through.

black-eyed pea and spinach squares

Here's a simple one-dish meal. Some recipes for black-eyed peas eliminate the soaking step— on the theory that these legumes have thinner skins than other dried beans and don't need soaking. But when I can spare the time, I soak them anyway.

Preparation time: 20 minutes + soaking time
Cooking time: 2 hours
Baking time: 50 minutes
Makes 4 servings.
Per serving: 309 calories, 1.3 g. fat (4% of calories), 14.2 g. dietary fiber, 2 mg. cholesterol, 406 mg. sodium.

8 ounces dried black-eyed peas, soaked overnight	1 teaspoon low-sodium soy sauce
3 cups finely chopped spinach	1/2 teaspoon no-salt lemon-herb blend
1 cup skim milk	1 1/2 cups nonfat yogurt, divided
1/2 cup chopped scallions	2 large egg whites
1/2 cup whole wheat flour	
1/4 cup chili sauce	

1. Drain the black-eyed peas and place in a 2-quart saucepan. Add cold water to cover. Bring to a boil over high heat. Reduce the heat to low, partially cover the pan, and simmer for 1 1/2 to 2 hours, or until tender. Drain and transfer to a large bowl.

2. Preheat the oven to 350°. Coat an 8" × 8" baking dish with no-stick spray; set aside.

3. Partially mash the black-eyed peas. Stir in the spinach, milk, scallions, flour, chili sauce, soy sauce, herb blend and 1 cup of the yogurt.

4. In a medium bowl, whip the egg whites with an electric mixer until stiff but not dry. Fold into the black-eyed pea mixture.

5. Spread in the prepared baking dish. Bake for 45 to 50 minutes, or until golden. Cut into squares and serve topped with the remaining 1/2 cup yogurt.

saving time

There's no getting around it: Dried beans need to be rehydrated by soaking them in water. (The exceptions are lentils, split peas and sometimes black-eyed peas.) And then they need to be cooked until tender. I used the overnight soaking method in these recipes, but there are other options.

First let me review the overnight method: Sort through the dried beans to remove cracked or shriveled ones and any foreign objects, such as small pebbles or little balls of dirt. Then rinse the beans well with cold water. Place them in a large bowl and cover generously with water. (Use about three times as much water as beans.) Let stand overnight, then drain in the morning. You can expect the beans to have doubled or tripled in volume. Transfer them to a pot, add fresh water, and cook according to the recipe directions. Most varieties will take $1\frac{1}{2}$ to 2 hours to become tender. A pound of dried beans yields 6 to 7 cups of cooked beans.

One quicker method involves placing the rinsed beans in a pot, covering them with plenty of water and bringing the water to a boil. Let them cook for 2 minutes, then remove the pot from the heat and let it stand for 1 hour. At the end of that time, the beans will be nice and plump. Drain and cook as usual.

A second quick method makes use of the microwave. Pick over and rinse 1 pound (about 2 cups) of dried beans. Place them in a $2\frac{1}{2}$-quart casserole and add 6 cups cold water. Microwave them on high for 15 minutes. Stir, cover the container and let stand for another 15 minutes, or until the beans have swelled. Drain and proceed with your recipe.

If you want to save actual cooking time, use a pressure cooker. *Follow the directions from the manufacturer.* For best results, don't fill the cooker more than one-third to one-half. You might also want to add a bit of oil to prevent the beans from foaming up and clogging the vent pipe. To check the beans for doneness, allow the cooker to stand for 5 minutes before opening it. That lets the pressure fall gradually.

When you're in a super hurry to prepare a legume dish, take advantage of canned beans. Empty the can into a strainer and rinse well with cold water. That washes off the thick cooking liquid the beans are packed in and also reduces the amount of sodium in the beans. A 16-ounce can will give you about 2 cups of cooked beans.

black-eyed pea and vegetable stew

This hearty dish warms me on cold nights. It's a perfect make-ahead dish because it reheats beautifully. In fact, if you have access to a microwave or stove at work, take along leftovers for a filling hot lunch.

MAKE
AHEAD

Preparation time: 15 minutes + soaking time
Cooking time: 3 hours
Makes 4 servings.
Per serving: 280 calories, 5.1 g. fat (15% of calories), 9.2 g. dietary fiber, 0 mg. cholesterol, 674 mg. sodium.

8 ounces dried black-eyed peas, soaked overnight	1 can (15 ounces) corn, drained
1 tablespoon canola oil	2 tablespoons steak sauce
1½ cups chopped onions	2 tablespoons chili sauce
4 garlic cloves, minced	1 tablespoon dark brown sugar or molasses
1 potato, peeled and cubed	
1 cup chopped turnips	1 tablespoon cider vinegar
1 cup sliced carrots	1 tablespoon cornstarch
1 can (28 ounces) low-sodium crushed tomatoes	3–4 drops hot-pepper sauce

1. Drain the black-eyed peas and place in a 2-quart saucepan. Add cold water to cover. Bring to a boil over high heat. Reduce the heat to low, partially cover the pan, and simmer for 1½ to 2 hours, or until tender. Drain and set aside.

2. In a 4-quart saucepan over medium heat, warm the oil. Add the onions and garlic; cook, stirring constantly, for 2 minutes. Stir in the potatoes, turnips and carrots; cook for 2 minutes. Stir in the tomatoes; bring to a boil. Reduce the heat to low and simmer for 10 minutes.

3. Stir in the black-eyed peas, corn, steak sauce, chili sauce, sugar or molasses, vinegar, cornstarch and hot-pepper sauce. Cover and simmer for 45 to 50 minutes, or until thick and the vegetables are tender.

tangy cuban beans

I've never been to Cuba, but this is the kind of dish I'd expect to find on menus there. It's a very hearty meal, and I especially enjoy it on cold winter nights. These beans can be made ahead and reheated—add a little stock or water to the pan to make heating easier. For a change, substitute pinto and cranberry beans for the black and kidney beans.

MAKE
AHEAD

Preparation time: 10 minutes + soaking time
Cooking time: 2 hours 10 minutes

Makes 8 servings.
Per serving: 352 calories, 3.9 g. fat (10% of calories), 10.1 g. dietary fiber, 0 mg. cholesterol, 9 mg. sodium.

8 ounces dried black beans, soaked overnight	1½ tablespoons canola oil
8 ounces dried red kidney beans, soaked overnight	1 medium tomato, coarsely chopped
1 medium onion, finely chopped	2 garlic cloves, minced
¼ teaspoon ground cloves	¼ cup red wine vinegar
2 bay leaves	1 tablespoon tomato paste
2 green peppers, finely chopped and divided	1 teaspoon dark brown sugar or ½ teaspoon honey

1. Drain the black beans and kidney beans. Place in a 4-quart saucepan. Add the onions, cloves, bay leaves, half of the peppers and cold water to cover. Bring to a boil over high heat. Reduce the heat to low, partially cover the pan, and simmer for 1½ to 2 hours, or until the beans are tender and most of the liquid has been absorbed. Drain any remaining liquid and discard the bay leaves.

2. Remove 1 cup of the beans and mash them to make a thick paste. Return them to the pan.

3. Meanwhile, in a large no-stick frying pan over medium-high heat, warm the oil. Add the tomatoes, garlic and the remaining peppers. Cook, stirring frequently, for 3 to 4 minutes, or until the peppers are tender.

4. Stir the tomato mixture into the bean mixture. Add the vinegar, tomato paste and sugar or honey. Simmer, stirring often, for 10 minutes, or until thick.

black bean pizza

I like to make this pizza with the soft lavash bread that's available in many Middle Eastern markets. It's not the same as the hard crackers of the same name that many supermarkets carry. If you can't find lavash, a large prebaked pizza shell or Boboli bread will do as well. Or use individual pitas. To save time on weeknights, cook the beans ahead. Or use rinsed and well-drained canned beans (you'll need about 2 cups).

Preparation time: 20 minutes
+ soaking time
Cooking time: 2 hours
Baking time: 7 minutes
Broiling time: 8 minutes
Makes 4 servings.
Per serving: 625 calories, 11 g. fat (16% of calories), 10.3 g. dietary fiber, 32 mg. cholesterol, 853 mg. sodium.

1 cup dried black beans, soaked overnight	1 large tomato, diced
3 small Japanese eggplants, thinly sliced lengthwise	$\frac{1}{2}$ cup chopped scallions
$\frac{1}{2}$ teaspoon garlic powder	2 ounces shredded nonfat or part-skim mozzarella cheese
$\frac{1}{4}$ teaspoon freshly ground black pepper	2 tablespoons grated Parmesan cheese
1 large lavash bread (about 15 ounces)	1 teaspoon olive oil
3 ounces goat cheese, at room temperature	

1. Drain the beans and place in a 2-quart saucepan. Add cold water to cover. Bring to a boil over high heat. Reduce the heat to low, partially cover the pan, and simmer for 1½ to 2 hours, or until tender. Drain well.

2. Meanwhile, preheat the broiler. Coat a large baking sheet with no-stick spray. Place the eggplant slices in a single layer on the sheet. Sprinkle with the garlic powder and pepper. Broil for 3 minutes. Flip the pieces and broil for 4 minutes, or until the eggplant is tender and the edges begin to brown.

3. Preheat the oven to 475°. Place the lavash on another large baking sheet or a pizza pan.

4. Crumble the goat cheese and sprinkle it evenly over the lavash. Top with the eggplant, tomatoes, scallions and beans. Sprinkle with the mozzarella and Parmesan. Drizzle with the oil.

5. Bake for 6 to 8 minutes, or until the cheese is golden and has lightly melted. Let stand for 5 minutes before slicing.

spicy curried lentils and peppers

This curry is medium spicy, which is just the way I like it. For a milder dish, use only 1 tablespoon of the chili peppers and reduce the red pepper to a mere pinch. Serve the lentils over rice.

Preparation time: 10 minutes
Cooking time: 30 minutes

Makes 4 servings.
Per serving: 200 calories, 4.3 g. fat (18% of calories), 5.3 g. dietary fiber, 0 mg. cholesterol, 235 mg. sodium.

1¾ cups water
¾ cup red lentils, rinsed and drained
1 tablespoon olive oil
1 cup chopped scallions
1 green pepper, diced
2 tablespoons chopped canned green chili peppers (wear plastic gloves when handling)
1 tablespoon unbleached flour
2 teaspoons curry powder
⅛ teaspoon ground red pepper
¾ cup low-sodium vegetable stock
1 teaspoon low-sodium soy sauce
1 teaspoon rice wine vinegar
1 tablespoon chopped fresh cilantro
2 tablespoons chopped mango chutney

1. In a 2-quart saucepan, combine the water and lentils; bring to a boil over medium-high heat. Reduce the heat to low. Cover the pan and simmer for 25 to 30 minutes, or until the lentils are tender; drain.

2. Meanwhile, in a large no-stick frying pan over medium heat, warm the oil. Add the scallions, green peppers and chili peppers. Cook, stirring frequently, for 2 to 3 minutes, or until tender. Stir in the flour, curry powder and red pepper; cook for 1 minute.

3. Whisk in the stock, soy sauce and vinegar. Add the lentils; cook for 1 to 2 minutes, or until heated through and slightly thick. Sprinkle with the cilantro. Top each serving with a dollop of the chutney.

pinto bean and pepper enchiladas

This is my version of a Mexican favorite. For variety, you may add leftover cooked vegetables to the bean filling.

**Preparation time: 20 minutes
+ soaking time
Cooking time: 2 hours
Baking time: 20 minutes**

Makes 6 servings.
Per serving: 433 calories, 8.9 g. fat (18% of calories), 10.6 g. dietary fiber, 10 mg. cholesterol, 369 mg. sodium.

8 ounces dried pinto beans, soaked overnight	1 cup chunky salsa
1 cup nonfat or part-skim ricotta cheese	¼ cup tomato paste
½ teaspoon chili powder	¼ teaspoon finely chopped jalapeño peppers (wear plastic gloves when handling)
1 cup shredded low-fat Cheddar cheese, divided	
1 tablespoon olive oil	¼ cup chopped fresh cilantro
1 cup chopped scallions	1 tablespoon red wine vinegar
2 garlic cloves, minced	12 flour tortillas

1. Drain the beans and place in a 2-quart saucepan. Add cold water to cover. Bring to a boil over high heat. Reduce the heat to low, partially cover the pan, and simmer for 1½ to 2 hours, or until tender.

2. Drain the beans and transfer to a large bowl. Stir in the ricotta, chili powder and ¾ cup of the Cheddar. Set aside.

3. Preheat the oven to 350°. Coat two 9" × 13" baking dishes with no-stick spray; set aside.

4. In a large no-stick frying pan over medium heat, warm the oil. Add the scallions and garlic; cook, stirring frequently, for 2 to 3 minutes, or until tender. Stir in the salsa, tomato paste, peppers and cilantro; bring to a boil.

5. Reduce the heat to low; simmer for 5 to 10 minutes, or until the sauce thickens slightly. Stir in the vinegar.

6. Briefly dip each tortilla into the sauce to coat and soften it. Place 2 rounded tablespoons of the bean filling on each tortilla; roll to enclose the filling. Place, seam side down, in 1 of the prepared baking dishes. Repeat to use the remaining tortillas. Spoon the remaining sauce evenly over the enchiladas. Sprinkle with the remaining ¼ cup Cheddar.

7. Cover the pans with foil and bake for 15 to 20 minutes, or until the cheese has melted and the sauce is bubbly.

thyme and lima gratin

This creamy side dish is a perfect accompaniment for any meal.

Preparation time: 10 minutes + soaking time
Cooking time: 2 hours
Broiling time: 8 minutes

Makes 4 servings.
Per serving: 257 calories, 7.1 g. fat (25% of calories), 10.2 g. dietary fiber, 21 mg. cholesterol, 308 mg. sodium.

8 ounces dried lima beans, soaked overnight
1 teaspoon olive oil
2 garlic cloves, minced
2 teaspoons chopped fresh thyme
½ cup buttermilk
4 ounces feta cheese, crumbled
⅛ teaspoon grated nutmeg
2 tablespoons seasoned dry bread crumbs
1 tablespoon shredded provolone cheese
½ teaspoon paprika

1. Drain the beans and place in a 2-quart saucepan. Add cold water to cover. Bring to a boil over high heat. Reduce the heat to low, partially cover the pan, and simmer for 1½ to 2 hours, or until tender. Drain.

2. In a medium no-stick frying pan over medium heat, warm the oil. Add the garlic and thyme; cook, stirring constantly, for 1 minute. Stir in the beans; cook for 2 minutes longer.

3. Preheat the broiler. Coat a 1-quart casserole dish with no-stick spray; set aside.

4. Transfer the bean mixture to a food processor; add the buttermilk, feta and nutmeg. Process until smooth. Spoon into the prepared casserole. Sprinkle with the bread crumbs, provolone and paprika. Broil about 5" from the heat for 8 minutes, or until golden.

hearty soups

Here's a collection of my favorite soups. They range from cold-weather warm-ups to refreshing summer coolers. Soups are a natural for vegetarians. It's easy to prepare hearty meatless soups that can serve as dinner entrées. Those containing beans, pasta, grains or winter vegetables are particularly filling.

If you're a vegan, or if you're a vegetarian for ethical reasons, you'll want to use vegetable stock as the basis for your soups. I've included a recipe for it on page 171, so you can prepare a large batch to keep on hand. If you have no objections to chicken stock, you may certainly substitute it.

Soup is a perfect make-ahead dish. Just keep a few things in mind when reheating it. Warm very thick soups or dairy-based potages over low heat to keep them from scorching or curdling. Also, pasta and bean soups often thicken as they stand, so add a little extra water or stock as you reheat them.

pumpkin soup

This smooth soup is rich in fiber and beta-carotene, both nutrients essential for good health. I like to serve pumpkin soup on Thanksgiving and garnish it with extra chopped peanuts. But you needn't reserve this bisquelike blend for special occasions.

MAKE AHEAD

Preparation time: 10 minutes
Cooking time: 25 minutes

Makes 4 servings.
Per serving: 246 calories, 8.7 g. fat (30% of calories), 4.5 g. dietary fiber, 4 mg. cholesterol, 236 mg. sodium.

2 medium baking potatoes, peeled and cut into 2" pieces	2 cups low-sodium vegetable stock
1 cup buttermilk	1½ cups skim milk
1 tablespoon margarine	¼ teaspoon ground cinnamon
2 cups canned pumpkin	⅛ teaspoon grated nutmeg
2 tablespoons chunky peanut butter	2 teaspoons lemon juice

1. Place the potatoes in a 2-quart saucepan; add cold water to cover. Bring to a boil over medium-high heat. Reduce the heat to low; cover and simmer for 15 to 20 minutes, or until fork tender. Drain well.

2. Transfer the potatoes to a blender. Add the buttermilk and process until smooth.

3. In a 3-quart saucepan over medium heat, melt the margarine. Stir in the potato mixture, pumpkin and peanut butter; mix until smooth. Stir in the stock, milk, cinnamon and nutmeg; cook, stirring frequently, for 4 to 5 minutes, or until heated through. Remove from the heat and stir in the lemon juice.

split pea soup with toasted caraway croutons

This soup has such a rich flavor that you'll never miss the ham bone typically called for in split pea soup. Feel free to substitute other vegetables for the parsnips and carrots. I particularly like fennel and celery.

MAKE
AHEAD

Preparation time: 15 minutes
Cooking time: 2 hours

Makes 4 servings.
Per serving: 525 calories, 5.8 g. fat (10% of calories), 11.5 g. dietary fiber, 1 mg. cholesterol, 146 mg. sodium.

7 cups water	1 tablespoon olive oil
1 pound green split peas, rinsed and drained	2 slices rye bread, cubed
1 cup chopped onions	1 tablespoon caraway seeds, crushed
1 cup diced parsnips	½ teaspoon dry mustard
½ cup diced carrots	1 cup skim milk
1 teaspoon celery flakes	
½ teaspoon dried rosemary, crumbled	

1. In a 3-quart saucepan, combine the water, split peas, onions, parsnips, carrots, celery flakes and rosemary; bring to a boil over high heat. Reduce the heat to low; simmer, stirring occasionally, for 1½ to 2 hours, or until thick and the water has been absorbed.

2. Meanwhile, in a large no-stick frying pan over medium heat, warm the oil. Add the bread, caraway seeds and mustard; sauté for 5 minutes, or until the croutons are golden. Set aside.

3. Stir the milk into the split pea mixture. Simmer for 5 to 10 minutes, or until heated through. Serve sprinkled with the croutons.

gremolata rice soup

Gremolata is a garnish made from minced herbs, citrus peels and garlic. It's often sprinkled over osso buco (veal shanks), but it's just as good on soups like this and even stirred into plain rice. My version of gremolata calls for the peel and juice of both a lemon and a lime. You'll find it easier to remove the peel if you do so before juicing the fruit. If you can't obtain the Swiss chard called for in the soup, substitute fresh spinach.

MAKE
AHEAD

Preparation time: 20 minutes
Cooking time: 25 minutes

Makes 4 servings.
Per serving: 211 calories, 4.3 g. fat (18% of calories), 2.3 g. dietary fiber, 0 mg. cholesterol, 201 mg. sodium.

Gremolata	Soup
1 tablespoon finely chopped fresh basil	½ tablespoon olive oil
1 tablespoon finely chopped fresh flat-leaf parsley	1½ cups chopped fennel
1 teaspoon finely grated lemon peel	½ cup chopped shallots
1 teaspoon finely grated lime peel	1 teaspoon dried thyme
2 teaspoons lemon juice	⅔ cup long-grain white rice
1 teaspoon lime juice	4 cups low-sodium vegetable stock
1 garlic clove, minced	4 cups water
Pinch of ground red pepper	3 cups coarsely chopped Swiss chard leaves

1. To make the gremolata: In a small bowl, mix the basil, parsley, lemon peel, lime peel, lemon juice, lime juice, garlic and pepper. Set aside.

2. To make the soup: In a 4-quart saucepan over medium heat, warm the oil. Add the fennel, shallots and thyme; cook, stirring frequently, for 4 to 5 minutes, or until tender.

3. Add the rice and stir to coat it evenly with the oil. Add the stock and water; bring to a boil. Reduce the heat to low. Partially cover and simmer for 15 to 20 minutes, or until the rice is tender.

4. Stir in the Swiss chard; cook for 1 to 2 minutes, or until wilted. Stir in the gremolata.

roasted red pepper soup

I always have jars of roasted red peppers or pimentos and some frozen corn on hand. They give me endless possibilities when preparing meals. What I especially like about this soup is the way the robust flavor of the pimentos complements the sweetness of the corn.

MAKE AHEAD

Preparation time: 15 minutes
Cooking time: 15 minutes

Makes 4 servings.
Per serving: 170 calories, 4 g. fat (9% of calories), 2.5 g. dietary fiber, 1 mg. cholesterol, 178 mg. sodium.

½ cup nonfat yogurt	1 cup spicy vegetable-cocktail juice
2 tablespoons finely chopped scallions	2 cups frozen corn
2 tablespoons finely chopped fresh cilantro	½ teaspoon ground cumin
2 teaspoons lime juice	3 cups low-sodium vegetable stock
1 tablespoon margarine	1½ cups chopped roasted sweet red peppers
1 onion, chopped	
2 garlic cloves, minced	1 tablespoon chili sauce

1. In a small bowl, combine the yogurt, scallions, cilantro and lime juice. Set aside.

2. In a 2-quart saucepan over medium heat, melt the margarine. Add the onions and garlic; cook, stirring frequently, for 3 to 4 minutes, or until tender. Stir in the vegetable juice, corn and cumin; simmer for 5 minutes.

3. Transfer to a food processor; process with on/off turns until the mixture is coarsely chopped (bits of corn should still be visible). Return the mixture to the pan. Stir in the stock, peppers and chili sauce. Simmer for 5 to 7 minutes to blend the flavors.

4. Serve topped with dollops of the yogurt mixture.

black bean and spinach soup

The pureed beans give this soup an unusual color. I like to top the soup with dollops of non-fat sour cream.

MAKE AHEAD

Preparation time: 10 minutes + soaking time
Cooking time: 1 hour 40 minutes

Makes 4 servings.
Per serving: 290 calories, 5.6 g. fat (17% of calories), 10 g. dietary fiber, 0 mg. cholesterol, 199 mg. sodium.

1	cup dried black beans, soaked overnight	2	tablespoons cider vinegar
8	cups low-sodium vegetable stock	1	teaspoon brown sugar or ½ teaspoon honey
1	cup chopped leeks (white part only)	½	teaspoon dry mustard
2	bay leaves	1	box (10 ounces) frozen chopped spinach, thawed and squeezed dry
1	tablespoon margarine	1	cup seeded and chopped tomatoes
1	tablespoon unbleached flour		

1. Drain the beans and place them in a 3-quart saucepan. Add the stock, leeks and bay leaves. Bring to a boil over medium-high heat, then reduce the heat to medium-low. Simmer for 1½ to 2 hours, or until the beans are tender. Discard the bay leaves.

2. Working in batches, transfer the mixture to a blender and process until smooth. Return the mixture to the pan.

3. In a 1-quart saucepan over medium heat, melt the margarine. Stir in the flour and cook for 1 minute. Add the vinegar, sugar or honey and mustard. Scrape the mixture into the pan with the beans. Cook, stirring frequently, for 4 to 5 minutes, or until the soup thickens slightly.

4. Stir in the spinach. Cook for 1 to 2 minutes to heat through. Serve sprinkled with the tomatoes.

dried-tomato and barley soup

This soup goes very well with a simple arugula salad. For variety, you may replace the barley with rice.

MAKE AHEAD

Preparation time: 10 minutes
Cooking time: 40 minutes

Makes 4 servings.
Per serving: 210 calories, 5.1 g. fat (21% of calories), 5.9 g. dietary fiber, 0 mg. cholesterol, 179 mg. sodium.

1 tablespoon margarine	½ cup medium pearled barley
1 cup chopped celery	2 teaspoons dried basil
½ cup chopped onions	¼ cup sun-dried tomato bits
2 garlic cloves, minced	1 tablespoon red wine vinegar
5 cups low-sodium vegetable stock	2 tablespoons chopped fresh flat-leaf parsley
1 cup low-sodium tomato juice	

1. In a 3-quart saucepan over medium heat, melt the margarine. Add the celery, onions and garlic; cook, stirring frequently, for 3 to 4 minutes, or until tender. Stir in the stock, juice, barley and basil; bring to a boil. Reduce the heat to low; cover and simmer for 30 minutes.

2. Stir in the tomato bits and vinegar; simmer for 5 minutes, or until heated through. Sprinkle with the parsley.

curried zucchini soup

You decide whether this soup is better hot or cold. I think it's terrific both ways.

2 teaspoons olive oil	2 tablespoons chopped fresh cilantro
3 cups sliced zucchini	½ cup evaporated skim milk
1 cup chopped celery	
1 cup thinly sliced onions	3–4 drops hot-pepper sauce
1 tablespoon curry powder	¼ cup nonfat sour cream
4 cups low-sodium vegetable stock	

Preparation time: 15 minutes
Cooking time: 30 minutes

Makes 4 servings.
Per serving: 130 calories, 4.2
g. fat (28% of calories), 3.1 g.
dietary fiber, 1 mg. cholesterol, 160 mg. sodium.

1. In a 3-quart saucepan over medium heat, warm the oil. Add the zucchini, celery and onions; cook, stirring frequently, for 8 to 10 minutes, or until tender. Stir in the curry powder; cook, stirring constantly, for 2 minutes.

2. Stir in the stock and cilantro; simmer for 15 minutes. Reduce the heat to very low. Stir in the milk and hot-pepper sauce; simmer for 5 minutes longer.

3. Working in batches, transfer the mixture to a blender and process until smooth. Serve immediately or refrigerate until chilled. Serve topped with dollops of the sour cream.

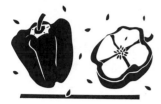

lentil and pasta soup

This hearty soup contains some of my all-time favorite foods: lentils, spaghetti and a variety of vegetables.

Preparation time: 15 minutes
Cooking time: 45 minutes

Makes 4 servings.
Per serving: 433 calories, 8.2
g. fat (16% of calories), 9.4 g.
dietary fiber, 2 mg. cholesterol, 470 mg. sodium.

1 tablespoon olive oil	1 cup red lentils, rinsed and drained
2 celery ribs, diced	4 ounces spaghetti, broken into 2" pieces
1 carrot, diced	
1 green pepper, diced	1 box (10 ounces) frozen chopped spinach, thawed and squeezed dry
½ cup chopped scallions	
2 garlic cloves, minced	
7 cups low-sodium vegetable stock	2 tablespoons grated Parmesan cheese
2 cups canned low-sodium tomatoes with juice	

1. In a 3-quart saucepan over medium heat, warm the oil. Add the celery, carrots, peppers, scallions and garlic; cook, stirring frequently, for 4 to 5 minutes, or until tender. Add the stock and tomatoes (with their liquid); bring to a boil.

2. Reduce the heat to low and stir in the lentils; simmer, partially covered, for 20 to 25 minutes.

3. Add the spaghetti and spinach; simmer for 10 to 12 minutes. Sprinkle with the Parmesan.

minestrone with cheese dumplings

As I worked on this chapter, this soup emerged as my very favorite. Although it requires a little advance planning, I think it's well worth it. If you are really short on time, you can make the soup without the dumplings.

MAKE AHEAD

Preparation time: 40 minutes + chilling time
Cooking time: 45 minutes

Makes 4 servings.
Per serving: 232 calories, 8.5 g. fat (31% of calories), 3.9 g. dietary fiber, 6 mg. cholesterol, 226 mg. sodium.

Dumplings
1	cup skim milk
1½	tablespoons margarine
½	cup quick-cooking cream of farina
2	tablespoons shredded provolone cheese
1	tablespoon finely chopped fresh flat-leaf parsley
⅛	teaspoon freshly ground black pepper
¼	cup egg substitute

Soup
2	teaspoons olive oil
1	cup thinly sliced leeks (white part only)
¼	cup chopped celery
¼	cup chopped carrots
2	garlic cloves, minced
4	large tomatoes, peeled, seeded and diced
2	cups low-sodium vegetable stock
1½	cups vegetable-cocktail juice
2	cups water
¼	cup chopped fresh basil
1	cup chopped kale
¼	cup orzo

1. To make the dumplings: In a 2-quart saucepan over medium heat, bring the milk and margarine just to the boiling point. Reduce the heat to low and whisk in the farina. Then whisk in the provolone, parsley and pepper; cook, stirring constantly, for 1 to 2 minutes, or until thick. Remove from the heat and stir in the egg. Transfer the mixture to a medium bowl and refrigerate for at least 2 hours.

2. Form the dumpling dough into ½″ balls (approximately 24); cover and set aside.

3. To make the soup: In a 3-quart saucepan over medium heat, warm the oil. Add the leeks, celery, carrots and garlic; cook, stirring frequently, for 4 to 5 minutes, or until the vegetables are just tender. Add the tomatoes, stock, juice, water and basil; bring to a boil. Reduce the heat to low and simmer for 15 minutes. Stir in the kale and orzo; simmer for 10 minutes longer.

4. Return the soup to a full boil; drop the dumplings into the pan. Partially cover and simmer for 15 minutes, or until the dumplings are firm.

tortellini and bean soup

Pesto—that sublime mixture of basil, garlic, Parmesan and olive oil— adds a flavor boost to most any dish, including most types of soup.

MAKE AHEAD

Preparation time: 10 minutes
Cooking time: 15 minutes

Makes 4 servings.
Per serving: 374 calories, 10.5 g. fat (25% of calories), 5.3 g. dietary fiber, 35 mg. cholesterol, 655 mg. sodium.

4 cups low-sodium vegetable stock	1 teaspoon dried rosemary, crumbled
1 can (15 ounces) cannellini beans, undrained	1/2 teaspoon dried oregano
1 1/2 cups cheese tortellini	1 box (10 ounces) frozen green beans
2 teaspoons olive oil	1 1/2 tablespoons prepared pesto sauce
2 carrots, diced	
2 celery ribs, diced	1/4 teaspoon freshly ground black pepper
2 garlic cloves, minced	

1. In a 3-quart saucepan, combine the stock and canellini beans (with their liquid). Bring to a boil over medium-high heat. Reduce the heat to medium and add the tortellini; cook, stirring frequently, for 5 minutes.

2. Meanwhile, in a large no-stick frying pan over medium heat, warm the oil. Add the carrots, celery, garlic, rosemary and oregano; cook, stirring constantly, for 4 minutes, or until the vegetables are just tender.

3. Add the vegetables to the pan containing the tortellini. Stir in the green beans and pesto. Reduce the heat to low. Simmer for about 5 minutes. Sprinkle with the pepper.

french-style vegetable barley soup

I admit that this soup has quite a few ingredients, but the end result is well worth some extra measuring and chopping. I always serve this soup as you would classic French onion soup—with golden pieces of cheese-flavored bread floating on top.

MAKE
AHEAD

Preparation time: 25 minutes
Cooking time: 35 minutes
Broiling time: 5 minutes

Makes 4 servings.
Per serving: 445 calories, 7.8 g. fat (15% of calories), 8.6 g. dietary fiber, 2 mg. cholesterol, 559 mg. sodium.

4 cups low-sodium vegetable stock	1 teaspoon dried thyme
4 cups water	4 slices Italian bread
4 small red potatoes, chopped	1 tablespoon olive oil
1 cup shredded green cabbage	1 tablespoon grated Parmesan cheese
1 cup chopped leeks (white part only)	½ cup nonfat yogurt
	½ cup skim milk
1 carrot, diced	2 tablespoons Dijon mustard
1 cup cut (1" pieces) green beans	2 teaspoons no-salt herb blend
1 cup quick-cooking barley	1 teaspoon low-sodium soy sauce
¾ cup old-fashioned rolled oats	¼ teaspoon freshly ground black pepper
2 tablespoons chopped fresh flat-leaf parsley	

1. In a 4-quart saucepan, combine the stock, water, potatoes, cabbage, leeks, carrots and beans. Bring to a boil over medium-high heat. Reduce the heat to medium-low and simmer for 15 to 20 minutes, or until the vegetables are just tender.

2. Stir in the barley, oats, parsley and thyme. Bring back to a boil, then reduce the heat again, partially cover, and simmer for 10 to 12 minutes, or until the barley is tender.

3. Meanwhile, preheat the broiler. Brush the top of each bread slice with the oil. Place on a baking sheet. Sprinkle evenly with the Parmesan. Broil about 5" from the heat for 3 to 5 minutes, or until golden. Set aside.

4. Remove the soup from the heat. Slowly stir in the yogurt, milk, mustard, herb blend, soy sauce and pepper.

5. Serve topped with the bread slices.

taking stock

You'll notice that most recipes in this chapter—and many others through-out the book—call for vegetable stock. You can buy canned varieties, or you can make your own. The simple recipe that follows gives my favorite mix of vegetables. You may certainly substitute others to suit your own taste.

You'll need to strain the stock well after it's simmered. Most recipes call for a few layers of cheesecloth. But if you don't have any, use this trick: Line your strainer with a clean dishcloth—one that's a little too tattered for regular use.

This recipe makes about 3½ quarts of stock. Freeze whatever you won't be using within a few days. I put most of it in 1-pint containers, but I reserve some to fill an ice cube tray or two. When the cubes are solid, I pop them from the trays and store them in a plastic bag.

linda's vegetable stock

1 teaspoon canola oil	1 cup chopped fennel
1 cup chopped onions	½ cup chopped carrots
4 garlic cloves, minced	1 tablespoon low-sodium soy sauce
4 quarts water	1 tablespoon black peppercorns
2 cups chopped celery	2 teaspoons dried thyme
2 medium tomatoes, quartered	2 teaspoons dark brown sugar
1 cup shredded cabbage	or 1 teaspoon honey

1. In a 6-quart pot over medium heat, warm the oil. Add the onions and gar-lic; cook, stirring frequently, for 3 to 4 minutes, or until tender.

2. Add the water, celery, tomatoes, cabbage, fennel, carrots, soy sauce, pep-percorns, thyme and sugar or honey.

3. Bring to a boil, then reduce the heat to medium-low. Partially cover and simmer for 2 hours. Strain through 2 thicknesses of cheesecloth. Chill.

4. If there are any globules of oil floating on the top, skim them off. Freeze whatever stock you won't use within 4 days; keep the remainder, covered, in the refrigerator.

MAKE AHEAD

Preparation time: 20 minutes. Cooking time: 2 hours.
Makes about 3½ quarts.

creamy mushroom soup

I like the flavor of ginger so much that I often double the amount called for in this recipe. Dried mushrooms can be found in most grocery stores, often in the Oriental section. You may use any type you like—some really delicious, albeit expensive, ones include morel, porcini and chanterelle.

MAKE AHEAD

Preparation time: 20 minutes
Cooking time: 50 minutes
Makes 4 servings.
Per serving: 180 calories, 3.2 g. fat (15% of calories), 1.9 g. dietary fiber, 1 mg. cholesterol, 98 mg. sodium.

1½ cups water	2 tablespoons chopped fresh tarragon or 1 teaspoon dried
½ cup wild rice, rinsed and drained	
1 cup boiling water	2 cups low-sodium vegetable stock
½ ounce dried mushrooms	
1 tablespoon margarine	1 large sweet potato, peeled and cubed
1 cup thinly sliced white mushrooms	
	1½ cups skim milk
1 cup chopped scallions	⅛ teaspoon powdered ginger
½ cup chopped fresh flat-leaf parsley	
	⅛ teaspoon grated nutmeg

1. In a 1-quart saucepan, combine the 1½ cups water and wild rice. Bring to a boil over medium-high heat. Reduce the heat to medium-low, cover, and simmer for 45 to 50 minutes, or until tender and the water has been absorbed. Set aside.

2. Meanwhile, in a small bowl, combine the boiling water and dried mushrooms. Let stand for 15 minutes, or until soft. Drain, reserving the soaking liquid. If necessary, chop the mushrooms into bite-size pieces.

3. In a 2-quart saucepan over medium heat, melt the margarine. Add the white mushrooms and softened dried mushrooms. Cook, stirring frequently, for 4 to 5 minutes, or until golden. Stir in the scallions, parsley and tarragon; cook for 2 to 3 minutes, or until tender. Scrape into a small bowl and set aside.

4. In the same pan, combine the stock, sweet potatoes and the reserved mushroom soaking liquid; cover and simmer for 15 to 20 minutes, or until the potatoes are tender. Transfer to a blender and process until smooth.

5. Return the mixture to the pan. Stir in the milk, ginger, nutmeg, wild rice and mushroom mixture. Heat for 2 minutes.

chili cheese soup

I like to serve this soup with tortilla chips. It can accompany a Mexican entrée or be a light meal by itself. If you're making this soup ahead, wait until you reheat it to add the cheese.

MAKE AHEAD

Preparation time: 15 minutes
Cooking time: 25 minutes

Makes 4 servings.
Per serving: 263 calories, 9.2 g. fat (30% of calories), 1.6 g. dietary fiber, 17 mg. cholesterol, 429 mg. sodium.

1 tablespoon margarine	1 cup evaporated skim milk
1 cup chopped sweet red peppers	1 cup drained canned corn
2 tablespoons chopped canned green chili peppers (wear plastic gloves when handling)	1 medium tomato, seeded and diced
	½ teaspoon chili powder
	¼ teaspoon ground cumin
2 tablespoons unbleached flour	1 cup shredded low-fat Cheddar cheese
1½ tablespoons cornstarch	½ teaspoon low-sodium Worcestershire sauce
1 cup water	
4½ cups low-sodium vegetable stock	

1. In a medium no-stick frying pan over medium heat, melt the margarine. Add the red peppers and chili peppers; cook, stirring frequently, for 3 to 4 minutes, or until the peppers are tender. Set aside.

2. In a small bowl, whisk together the flour and cornstarch. Gradually add the water and whisk until smooth. Set aside.

3. In a 3-quart saucepan over medium-high heat, bring the stock to a boil. Whisk in the flour mixture and milk. Bring back to a boil, whisking constantly.

4. Reduce the heat to medium-low. Add the corn, tomatoes, chili powder, cumin and peppers. Simmer for 5 to 10 minutes to blend the flavors. Stir in the Cheddar and Worcestershire sauce; cook, stirring constantly, until the Cheddar has melted.

watercress and squash soup

You can use most any winter squash for this recipe. Acorn is particularly good. But it's hard to peel before cooking, so I steam, bake or microwave cut halves and then scoop out the flesh. You'll notice that I call for a combination of regular skim milk and evaporated skim. That's because the evaporated milk gives the soup extra-creamy body. If you like, you can use all evaporated milk.

MAKE
AHEAD

Preparation time: 20 minutes
Cooking time: 20 minutes

Makes 4 servings.
Per serving: 162 calories, 4.2 g. fat (22% of calories), 3.1 g. dietary fiber, 2 mg. cholesterol, 155 mg. sodium.

3 cups low-sodium vegetable stock	¾ cup chopped watercress leaves
1¼ pounds butternut squash, peeled and cubed	½ cup chopped fresh basil
1 tablespoon margarine	1 tablespoon cider vinegar
1 cup chopped scallions	½ cup skim milk
2 garlic cloves, minced	½ cup evaporated skim milk

1. In a 3-quart saucepan over medium-high heat, bring the stock and squash to a boil. Reduce the heat to low; partially cover and simmer for 15 to 20 minutes, or until tender.

2. Meanwhile, in a large no-stick frying pan over medium heat, melt the margarine. Add the scallions and garlic; cook, stirring frequently, for 2 to 3 minutes, or until tender. Add the watercress; cook for 5 minutes.

3. Transfer to the pan with the squash. Stir in the basil and vinegar.

4. Working in batches, transfer the mixture to a blender and process until smooth. Return the soup to the saucepan; stir in the skim milk and evaporated milk. Rewarm over low heat, but do not boil.

creamy broccoli and carrot soup with pepper relish

The crunchy pepper relish provides an interesting counterpoint to the creamy soup. I used canned cream of mushroom soup as a shortcut in this recipe. Sometimes, for variety, I use cream of celery soup instead. No matter which type you use, look for brands low in fat and sodium.

MAKE AHEAD

Preparation time: 15 minutes
Cooking time: 15 minutes

Makes 4 servings.
Per serving: 123 calories, 2.5 g. fat (18% of calories), 4.6 g. dietary fiber, 12 mg. cholesterol, 418 mg. sodium.

1 medium tomato, diced	4 ounces carrots, cut into 1" pieces
½ cup finely chopped roasted sweet red peppers	1 can (10¾ ounces) condensed low-fat cream of mushroom soup
¼ cup finely chopped red onions	1 cup low-sodium vegetable stock
¼ cup minced fresh basil	¼ teaspoon curry powder
¼ teaspoon freshly ground black pepper	½ cup nonfat yogurt
1 small head broccoli, separated into florets	

1. In a small bowl, combine the tomatoes, red peppers, onions, basil and black pepper; set aside.

2. Steam the broccoli and carrots for about 10 minutes, or until tender. Transfer to a food processor. Add the soup, stock and curry powder. Process until smooth.

3. Transfer to a 2-quart saucepan. Place over medium heat and stir constantly until bubbly. Remove from the heat and whisk in the yogurt. Serve topped with the pepper relish.

meghan's noodle soup

Meghan is my niece, and I can tell you that she just loves this soup. You will, too—especially since the recipe is so simple.

MAKE AHEAD

Preparation time: 15 minutes
Cooking time: 20 minutes

Makes 4 servings.
Per serving: 219 calories, 6.2 g. fat (25% of calories), 3.7 g. dietary fiber, 29 mg. cholesterol, 294 mg. sodium.

1 tablespoon margarine	4 ounces no-yolk fine egg noodles
2 medium carrots, diced	
2 celery ribs, diced	1 cup thinly sliced yellow squash
½ cup chopped scallions	
3 cups low-sodium vegetable stock	½ cup thinly sliced zucchini
2 cups water	2 tablespoons grated Parmesan cheese
¼ cup chopped fresh basil	
1 tablespoon chopped fresh tarragon or 1 teaspoon dried	1 teaspoon low-sodium teriyaki sauce
	½ cup herb-flavored croutons

1. In a 3-quart saucepan over medium heat, melt the margarine. Add the carrots, celery and scallions; cook, stirring frequently, for 4 to 5 minutes, or until tender. Stir in the stock, water, basil and tarragon; bring to a boil.

2. Reduce the heat to low. Stir in the noodles, squash, zucchini, Parmesan and teriyaki sauce; simmer for 10 to 12 minutes, or until the vegetables and noodles are tender. Serve topped with the croutons.

onion-apple soup with crumb topping

I find that the sweetness of apple juice helps mellow out the strong flavor of the onions in this soup. To prepare a more traditional French onion soup, replace the crumb topping with shredded low-fat cheese (Swiss is good). Broil for a few minutes to melt the cheese.

MAKE AHEAD

Preparation time: 15 minutes
Cooking time: 20 minutes
Makes 4 servings.
Per serving: 169 calories, 5.6 g. fat (29% of calories), 2.1 g. dietary fiber, 0 mg. cholesterol, 223 mg. sodium.

2 teaspoons margarine	1 tablespoon chopped fresh thyme or 1 teaspoon dried
1 cup fresh bread crumbs	
1 tablespoon pine nuts, chopped	2 teaspoons dark brown sugar or 1 teaspoon honey
1 teaspoon grated Parmesan cheese	1 tablespoon unbleached flour
½ teaspoon dry mustard	2 garlic cloves, minced
1 teaspoon olive oil	1 cup water
1¾ cups low-sodium vegetable stock, divided	1 cup apple juice
2 medium onions, thinly sliced crosswise and separated into rings	2 teaspoons low-sodium soy sauce

1. In a 1-quart saucepan over medium heat, melt the margarine. Stir in the bread crumbs, pine nuts, Parmesan and mustard; cook for 2 to 3 minutes, or until the nuts and crumbs are golden. Set aside.

2. In a 2-quart saucepan over medium heat, warm the oil and ¼ cup of the stock. Add the onions and thyme; cook, stirring frequently, for 8 to 10 minutes, or until the onions are tender.

3. Stir in the sugar or honey; cook, stirring constantly, for 2 minutes. Add the flour and garlic; stir for 1 minute.

4. Whisk in the water, juice, soy sauce and the remaining 1½ cups stock; bring to a boil. Reduce the heat to low and simmer for 2 minutes.

5. Serve sprinkled with the crumb mixture.

orange borscht

The orange gives a novel twist to traditional beet soup. I like to swirl a little nonfat yogurt or sour cream into each bowl as I serve the borscht.

MAKE
AHEAD

Preparation time: 15 minutes + chilling time
Cooking time: 30 minutes
Makes 4 servings.
Per serving: 142 calories, 0.8 g. fat (5% of calories), 3.6 g. dietary fiber, 0 mg. cholesterol, 67 mg. sodium.

3	cups water	2	tablespoons coarsely chopped fresh ginger
2	cups orange juice	1	small orange, peeled and sectioned
4	beets, peeled and sliced ½" thick		
1	cup cherry tomatoes	¼	cup fresh mint leaves
1	yellow pepper, sliced	2	teaspoons honey

1. In a 3-quart saucepan, mix the water, juice, beets, tomatoes, peppers and ginger. Bring to a boil over medium-high heat. Reduce the heat to low; cover and simmer for 25 to 30 minutes, or until tender.

2. Place the oranges in a food processor or blender; process with on/off turns until smooth. Add the mint and honey; mix well. Working in batches, add the beet mixture and process until smooth.

3. Transfer to a large bowl. Cover and refrigerate for at least 2 hours.

caraway cabbage soup

Here's a simple soup that's full of flavor. It's great to serve on St. Patrick's Day.

2	medium potatoes, peeled and chopped	1	cup chopped leeks (white part only)
2	cups low-sodium vegetable stock	1	tablespoon caraway seeds
2	cups water	½	teaspoon paprika
4	cups shredded green cabbage	½	cup skim milk
		1	teaspoon white wine vinegar

1. In a 3-quart saucepan over medium-high heat, bring the potatoes, stock and water to a boil. Reduce the heat to low; cover and simmer for 15 minutes, or until the potatoes are tender.

2. Stir in the cabbage, leeks, caraway seeds and paprika; cover and simmer for 20 to 25 minutes, or until the vegetables are completely tender. Remove from the heat and stir in the milk and vinegar.

3. Working in batches, transfer the soup to a blender and process until smooth. Return to the pan and place over low heat until warmed through.

Preparation time: 15 minutes
Cooking time: 40 minutes
Makes 4 servings.
Per serving: 122 calories, 1.3 g. fat (9% of calories), 3.3 g. dietary fiber, 1 mg. cholesterol, 79 mg. sodium.

saffron corn chowder

Saffron is a distinctive spice that is actually the dried stigmas of a certain crocus. It lends a rich, almost indescribable flavor and a deep yellow color to this soup.

1	tablespoon canola oil	1½ cups frozen corn
½	cup chopped onions	1 cup frozen lima beans
1	sweet red pepper, diced	⅛ teaspoon saffron threads, crushed
1	cup sliced mushrooms	
2	tablespoons unbleached flour	⅛ teaspoon freshly ground black pepper
2	cups skim milk	
1½	cups low-sodium vegetable stock	

Preparation time: 10 minutes
Cooking time: 10 minutes
Makes 4 servings.
Per serving: 209 calories, 4.6 g. fat (19% of calories), 4.3 g. dietary fiber, 2 mg. cholesterol, 121 mg. sodium.

1. In a 2-quart saucepan over medium heat, warm the oil. Add the onions, red peppers and mushrooms; cook, stirring frequently, for 3 to 4 minutes, or until tender.

2. Stir in the flour; cook for 1 minute. Whisk in the milk and stock; cook, whisking constantly, until the soup thickens slightly.

3. Stir in the corn, beans, saffron and black pepper; simmer for 4 to 5 minutes, or until the frozen vegetables are thawed and heated through.

summer salsa soup

Make this chilled soup when summer tomatoes are at their peak. (And freeze some to serve warm in winter.) If you'd like, you may omit the cheese.

MAKE AHEAD

Preparation time: 20 minutes + chilling time
Cooking time: 25 minutes
Makes 4 servings.
Per serving: 140 calories, 5.2 g. fat (30% of calories), 5.3 g. dietary fiber, 5 mg. cholesterol, 140 mg. sodium.

2 teaspoons olive oil	¼ cup chopped fresh flat-leaf parsley
½ cup chopped scallions	1½ tablespoons tomato paste
2 garlic cloves, minced	2 tablespoons balsamic vinegar
1 cup low-sodium vegetable stock	2 teaspoons coarse Dijon mustard
1 cup low-sodium tomato juice	½ cup shredded low-fat Monterey Jack cheese
6 tomatoes, seeded and chopped	
2 small cucumbers, peeled, seeded and chopped	

1. In a 2-quart saucepan over medium heat, warm the oil. Add the scallions and garlic; cook, stirring frequently, for 4 to 5 minutes, or until tender. Stir in the stock, juice, tomatoes, cucumbers, parsley and tomato paste; bring to a boil. Reduce the heat to low and simmer for 20 minutes.

2. Working in batches, transfer to a blender and process until smooth. Place in a large bowl and refrigerate for at least 2 hours. Stir in the vinegar and mustard.

3. Serve topped with the Monterey Jack.

chilled peach and nectarine soup

This chilled summer soup can also be served as a light dessert. In fact, it's so full of flavor that my friends couldn't believe it's got hardly any fat and very few calories. For best results, be sure to use the season's freshest, ripest fruits. You can prepare the soup with just peaches, but I like the extra dimension nectarines add.

MAKE AHEAD

Preparation time: 15 minutes
+ chilling time
Cooking time: 5 minutes

Makes 4 servings.
Per serving: 95 calories, 0.3 g. fat (2% of calories), 1.3 g. dietary fiber, 0 mg. cholesterol, 14 mg. sodium.

1 cup thinly sliced peeled peaches	1 cup apple juice
1 cup thinly sliced peeled nectarines	1 cinnamon stick
2 tablespoons lemon juice	1 whole nutmeg
1 tablespoon honey	2 whole cloves
1 cup low-calorie cranberry juice cocktail	¼ cup nonfat sour cream

1. Place the peaches and nectarines in a food processor; process until smooth. Pour into a large bowl. Stir in the lemon juice and honey; cover and refrigerate.

2. In a 1-quart saucepan over medium-high heat, bring the cranberry juice, apple juice, cinnamon, nutmeg and cloves to a boil. Reduce the heat to low and simmer for 5 minutes. Strain and discard the spices. Set aside to cool completely.

3. When cool, stir the juice mixture into the puree. Cover and refrigerate for at least 2 hours. Serve topped with the sour cream.

chilled avocado-asparagus soup with jícama salsa

Jícama (pronounced *HEE-kah-mah*) is a popular Latin American vegetable. It's essentially a large tuber covered with thick brown skin that you remove with a paring knife. Inside is crisp white flesh that looks like an apple or potato. If your market doesn't carry jícama, use canned water chestnuts. Although avocados are high in fat, the fat is mostly the monounsaturated variety that is good for you.

MAKE
AHEAD

Preparation time: 25 minutes + chilling time
Makes 4 servings.
Per serving: 180 calories, 8.8 g. fat (44% of calories), 4.8 g. dietary fiber, 2 mg. cholesterol, 169 mg. sodium.

1 cup diced jícama	2 cups low-sodium vegetable stock
1/2 cup seeded and diced tomatoes	20 asparagus spears, cooked and coarsely chopped
1/4 cup chopped scallions	1 cup skim milk
1/4 cup drained canned corn	1/2 cup nonfat yogurt
1/4 cup chopped fresh cilantro	1 teaspoon Dijon mustard
2 garlic cloves, minced	1/8 teaspoon ground red pepper
4 tablespoons lime juice, divided	
1 medium avocado, coarsely chopped	

1. In a medium bowl, combine the jícama, tomatoes, scallions, corn, cilantro, garlic and 2 tablespoons of the lime juice. Set aside.

2. In a medium bowl, combine the avocados and the remaining 2 tablespoons lime juice.

3. Bring the stock to a boil in a 1-quart saucepan. Pour it over the avocados and mix well. Let cool for about 5 minutes.

4. Transfer the avocado mixture to a blender. Add the asparagus and process until smooth. Add the milk, yogurt, mustard and pepper; process until blended.

5. Refrigerate for at least 2 hours. Serve topped with the jícama salsa.

miso bean soup

This soup is very soothing. I find it's just the thing to settle my stomach when I'm a little under the weather. Miso is also known as bean paste and is a staple in Japanese cooking. Don't boil soup after adding miso because it might turn bitter. Tempeh is a high-protein "cake" made from soybeans. It has a whitish covering like Brie. Look for it in the freezer section of health food stores. You may also substitute tofu.

3 cups low-sodium vegetable stock	1 cup thinly sliced sweet red peppers
3 cups water	1 teaspoon minced fresh ginger
1 cup cubed tempeh	1 tablespoon toasted sesame seeds
1 tablespoon miso	
1 cup cut (1" pieces) green beans	
1 cup coarsely chopped spinach	

1. In a 3-quart saucepan over medium-high heat, bring the stock and water to a boil. Add the tempeh; cook for 2 minutes.

2. Ladle out about ¼ cup of the liquid and place in a cup. Add the miso and mix well to dissolve it. Set aside.

3. Reduce the heat to medium. Stir in the beans, spinach, peppers and ginger. Cook for 5 minutes, or until the vegetables are just tender.

4. Just before serving, add the miso mixture. Simmer for 2 minutes. Serve sprinkled with the sesame seeds.

MAKE
AHEAD

Preparation time: 15 minutes
Cooking time: 10 minutes

Makes 4 servings.
Per serving: 148 calories, 5.8 g. fat (33% of calories), 1.8 g. dietary fiber, 0 mg. cholesterol, 322 mg. sodium.

arugula gazpacho

I really like the slightly bitter, piquant flavor of arugula (also known as rocket or roquette). Maybe that's why this is one of my favorite summer soups. Arugula is making its way into mainstream supermarkets, but if you can't find any, substitute watercress. If you like your soup a little more spicy, use a small chili pepper in place of the red pepper.

1	bunch scallions, coarsely chopped	½	cup chopped fresh basil or flat-leaf parsley
2	large cucumbers, peeled, seeded and coarsely chopped	1	cup nonfat plain yogurt
		1	cup nonfat vanilla yogurt
1	sweet red pepper, coarsely chopped	¼	cup herb vinegar
		1	tablespoon olive oil
2	cups chopped arugula	4–5	drops hot-pepper sauce

1. In a food processor, combine the scallions, cucumbers, peppers, arugula and basil or parsley. Mix with a few on/off turns. Add the plain yogurt, vanilla yogurt, vinegar, oil and hot-pepper sauce; process with on/off turns until the vegetables are finely chopped but not pureed.

2. Cover and refrigerate for at least 4 hours. Stir well before serving.

MAKE
AHEAD

Preparation time: 15 minutes + chilling time
Makes 4 servings.
Per serving: 140 calories, 3.9 g. fat (23% of calories), 2.3 g. dietary fiber, 2 mg. cholesterol, 91 mg. sodium.

miso bean soup (p. 183)

tricolor rotelle and cucumber salad (p. 204)

roasted vegetable and cheese salad (p. 214)

black bean citrus salad (p. 212)

cherry tomato gazpacho salad (p. 211)

curried fruit and rice salad (p. 205)

mozzarella and bread salad (p. 207)

peanut butter raisin bread (p. 240)   **193**

194   rosemary hash browns (p. 248) and red pepper frittata (p. 243)

196   cheese blintzes with raspberry sauce (p. 236)

breakfast granola (p. 230)

substantial salads

Like soups, salads come in infinite variety. And they're no longer just side dishes. You can prepare quite substantial salads that can serve as main courses. Those featuring grains, low-fat dairy products or beans, for example, have lots of protein and can stand on their own. With crusty bread and perhaps some soup, they make a filling meal.

For those times when you want a first course or a luncheon entrée, opt for the lighter salads in this chapter, such as Bitter Greens with Tangy Dressing or Watercress Salad with Scallion Dressing.

Before I came to realize how diverse salads can be, I used to eat great quantities of the mixed greens variety during the summer and practically forget about salads during the winter. Now I see that I can enjoy them all year long.

I tried to give you versatile dressings in the recipes that follow. Mix and match them with other ingredients to create your own favorites.

crunchy lentil salad

What makes this salad crunchy is the addition of jícama, a delicious root vegetable that has a sweet, nutty flavor. If your market doesn't carry jícama, substitute canned chopped water chestnuts. Sometimes, when I want a salad that's a little more filling, I toss the warm lentils with steamed spaghetti squash or some cooked pasta.

3 cups water	2 tablespoons lime juice
1 cup brown lentils, rinsed and drained	1 teaspoon prepared horseradish
2 teaspoons olive oil	½ teaspoon ground cumin
½ cup chopped red onions	1 cup frozen corn, thawed
2 celery ribs, chopped	½ cup chopped jícama
2 garlic cloves, minced	2 tablespoons chopped fresh flat-leaf parsley
1 cup salsa	

1. In a 2-quart saucepan over high heat, bring the water and lentils to a boil. Reduce the heat to low; partially cover and simmer for 30 to 40 minutes, or until the lentils are tender. Drain and transfer to a large bowl.

2. Meanwhile, in a large no-stick frying pan over medium heat, warm the oil. Add the onions, celery and garlic; cook, stirring frequently, for 2 minutes. Stir in the salsa, lime juice, horseradish and cumin; simmer for 2 minutes.

3. Pour over the lentils. Add the corn, jícama and parsley; gently toss to mix well. Serve warm or chilled.

MAKE AHEAD

Preparation time: 10 minutes
Cooking time: 40 minutes

Makes 4 servings.
Per serving: 259 calories, 4.3 g. fat (14% of calories), 7.1 g. dietary fiber, 0 mg. cholesterol, 263 mg. sodium.

cannellini salad

Although I call this cannellini salad, you may substitute any other canned beans. One of my favorite variations is a mixture of cannellinis and chick-peas. No matter what type of beans you use, be sure to rinse and drain them well. That removes excess sodium and the thick liquid the beans are packed in.

MAKE
AHEAD

Preparation time: 10 minutes
Cooking time: 5 minutes

Makes 4 servings.
Per serving: 282 calories, 4.2 g. fat (13% of calories), 1.2 g. dietary fiber, 0 mg. cholesterol, 30 mg. sodium.

10	sun-dried tomatoes	½	teaspoon dried sage
½	cup boiling water	¼	teaspoon freshly ground
1	tablespoon olive oil		black pepper
½	cup chopped red onions	2	cans (19 ounces each)
2	garlic cloves, minced		cannellini beans, rinsed
1	tablespoon balsamic vinegar		and drained
1	tablespoon chopped fresh		Spinach leaves
	flat-leaf parsley		

1. In a small bowl, combine the tomatoes and water. Let stand for 5 minutes. Drain, reserving the soaking liquid. Chop the tomatoes and set aside.

2. In a 1-quart saucepan over medium heat, warm the oil. Add the onions and garlic; cook, stirring frequently, for 2 minutes. Stir in the vinegar, parsley, sage, pepper, tomatoes and the reserved tomato soaking liquid. Bring to a boil and cook for 2 minutes to reduce the liquid slightly.

3. Place the beans in a large bowl. Add the tomato mixture; toss gently to mix. Serve warm or chilled on the spinach.

tricolor rotelle and cucumber salad

The creamy buttermilk dressing that I use for this salad goes very nicely with virtually any tossed salad. The fresh herbs impart such a fresh and light taste that it's worth seeking them out when they're not in season. For a more tangy dressing, use less mayonnaise and more yogurt.

MAKE
AHEAD

Preparation time: 15 minutes + chilling time
Cooking time: 10 minutes

Makes 4 servings.
Per serving: 295 calories, 5.5 g. fat (17% of calories), 1.9 g. dietary fiber, 6 mg. cholesterol, 58 mg. sodium.

½ cup chopped fresh dill	¼ cup nonfat yogurt
½ cup chopped fresh flat-leaf parsley	8 ounces tricolor rotelle
¼ cup chopped fresh basil	1 sweet red pepper, thinly sliced
2 scallions, coarsely chopped	½ cucumber, peeled, seeded and chopped
½ cup buttermilk	
¼ cup light mayonnaise	1 tablespoon lemon juice

1. In a food processor, combine the dill, parsley, basil and scallions; process with on/off turns until finely chopped. Add the buttermilk, mayonnaise and yogurt; process until smooth.

2. In a large pot of boiling water, cook the rotelle for 8 to 10 minutes, or until just tender. Drain and rinse with cold water. Transfer to a medium bowl.

3. Add the peppers and cucumbers. Pour on the dressing and toss to mix well. Cover and refrigerate for at least 1 hour. Just before serving, sprinkle with the lemon juice and toss lightly.

curried fruit and rice salad

Curry, fruit and rice are a classic combination for a light luncheon salad. The small amount of chutney in the recipe really helps perk up the flavor of the other ingredients. My favorite brand is Major Grey, but there are others available. Look for chutney in supermarkets among the condiments or in the ethnic foods section.

MAKE AHEAD

Preparation time: 10 minutes + chilling time
Cooking time: 20 minutes

Makes 4 servings.
Per serving: 335 calories, 7.5 g. fat (20% of calories), 2.7 g. dietary fiber, <1 mg. cholesterol, 29 mg. sodium.

2½ cups water	1 cup green seedless grapes, halved
1 cup long-grain white rice	½ cup chopped dried apricots
2 tablespoons peanut oil	½ cup nonfat yogurt
1½ tablespoons red wine vinegar	2 tablespoons mango chutney
1 teaspoon curry powder	1 tablespoon chopped fresh cilantro
½ teaspoon dry mustard	
¼ teaspoon freshly ground black pepper	
1 cup red seedless grapes, halved	

1. In a 2-quart saucepan over high heat, bring the water to a boil. Stir in the rice. Reduce the heat to medium-low, cover, and simmer for 20 minutes. Remove from the heat and let stand for 5 minutes, or until all the water has been absorbed. Fluff the rice with a fork and transfer to a large bowl.

2. In a small bowl, whisk together the oil, vinegar, curry powder, mustard and pepper. Pour over the rice and toss to mix well. Add the red grapes, green grapes and apricots; toss lightly.

3. In the same small bowl, mix the yogurt, chutney and cilantro. Add to the salad; toss to mix well. Cover and refrigerate for at least 1 hour.

bitter greens with tangy dressing

This is a wonderful salad to start a meal.

MAKE
AHEAD

Preparation time: 10 minutes
Makes 4 servings.
Per serving: 53 calories, 1.8 g. fat (28% of calories), 1.4 g. dietary fiber, 6 mg. cholesterol, 547 mg. sodium.

8 ounces escarole, coarsely torn	¼ cup lemon juice
1 bunch watercress, coarsely torn	3 tablespoons chili sauce
	1 teaspoon coarse-grain mustard
1 cup drained canned baby corn, cut into 1" pieces	⅛ teaspoon ground red pepper
8 radishes, thinly sliced	1 ounce peppercorn-flavored feta cheese

1. In a large bowl, combine the escarole, watercress, corn and radishes.

2. In a small bowl, whisk together the lemon juice, chili sauce, mustard and pepper. Pour over the salad; toss to mix well. Crumble the feta over the top.

corn and barley salad

Make sure to rinse the black beans well before mixing them with the rest of the ingredients, so they don't discolor the salad.

2¾ cups water	2 tablespoons minced fresh basil
¾ cup medium pearled barley	
1 can (16 ounces) black beans, rinsed and drained	2 tablespoons low-sodium vegetable stock
2 cups frozen corn, thawed	1 tablespoon canola oil
1 cup frozen peas, thawed	2 tablespoons grated Parmesan cheese
3 tablespoons balsamic vinegar	

Preparation time: 10 minutes
Cooking time: 35 minutes

Makes 4 servings.
Per serving: 390 calories, 5.4
g. fat (12% of calories), 12.4 g.
dietary fiber, 2 mg. cholesterol, 105 mg. sodium.

1. In a 2-quart saucepan over high heat, bring the water and barley to a boil. Reduce the heat to medium-low; partially cover and simmer for 30 to 35 minutes, or until tender. Drain off any remaining water. Transfer the barley to a large bowl.

2. Add the beans, corn and peas.

3. In a small bowl, whisk together the vinegar, basil, stock and oil. Pour over the salad; toss to mix well. Sprinkle with the Parmesan. Serve warm or chilled.

mozzarella and bread salad

The concept of a bread salad comes from Europe, where it's a way to use up stale pieces. The bread absorbs liquid from the dressing and becomes soft.

6 cups stale bread cubes	6 ounces nonfat or part-skim mozzarella cheese, cubed
2 medium tomatoes, seeded and chopped	
¼ teaspoon freshly ground black pepper	¼ cup balsamic vinegar
	1½ tablespoons olive oil
2 cups coarsely chopped spinach	2 teaspoons capers, rinsed, drained and finely chopped
1 sweet red pepper, diced	
1 medium zucchini, diced	1 garlic clove, minced

Preparation time: 20 minutes
+ standing time

Makes 4 servings.
Per serving: 208 calories, 7.2
g. fat (24% of calories), 3.1 g.
dietary fiber, 7 mg. cholesterol, 631 mg. sodium.

1. In a large bowl, toss together the bread, tomatoes and black pepper. Add the spinach, red peppers, zucchini and mozzarella. Toss lightly.

2. In a small bowl, mix the vinegar, oil, capers and garlic. Pour over the salad and toss well. Let stand for at least 15 minutes for the bread to soften.

fruited coleslaw

No picnic would be complete without coleslaw. This delicious version adds apples, pears and raisins to the standard cabbage mixture. It's sort of a cross between coleslaw and Waldorf salad. For something a little more unusual, replace the apples and pears with melon balls.

MAKE AHEAD

Preparation time: 20 minutes + chilling time

Makes 4 servings.
Per serving: 181 calories, 3.1 g. fat (14% of calories), 6 g. dietary fiber, 3 mg. cholesterol, 194 mg. sodium.

3	cups shredded red cabbage	½	cup nonfat yogurt
3	cups shredded green cabbage	2	tablespoons light or nonfat mayonnaise
1	medium Granny Smith apple, diced	1½	tablespoons Dijon mustard
1	medium pear, diced	1½	tablespoons red wine vinegar
1	green pepper, diced	½	teaspoon celery seeds
½	cup chopped celery	⅛	teaspoon freshly ground black pepper
½	cup raisins		

1. In a large bowl, combine the red cabbage, green cabbage, apples, pears, green peppers, celery and raisins.

2. In a small bowl, whisk together the yogurt, mayonnaise, mustard, vinegar, celery seeds and black pepper. Pour over the salad; toss to mix well. Cover and refrigerate for at least 2 hours. Toss again before serving.

roasted vegetable salad with basil vinaigrette

Serve this salad either at room temperature or chilled.

MAKE AHEAD

Preparation time: 15 minutes
Cooking time: 30 minutes

Makes 4 servings.
Per serving: 243 calories, 7.1 g. fat (25% of calories), 1.4 g. dietary fiber, 0 mg. cholesterol, 70 mg. sodium.

1½	pounds small red potatoes, halved (quartered if large)	2	garlic cloves
12	ounces green beans, cut into 1" pieces	2	tablespoons red wine vinegar
2	sweet red peppers, thinly sliced	1½	tablespoons olive oil
1	red onion, thinly sliced crosswise and separated into rings	½	teaspoon dried basil
		¼	teaspoon freshly ground black pepper
½	cup low-sodium vegetable stock	8	kalamata olives, pitted and sliced
		1–2	tablespoons lemon juice

1. Preheat the oven to 425°.

2. Coat a 9" × 13" baking dish with no-stick spray. Add the potatoes, beans, red peppers, onions, stock and garlic. Mix well. Roast, stirring every 10 minutes, for 20 to 30 minutes, or until the vegetables are tender; set aside.

3. Transfer the garlic to a small bowl and mash. Whisk in the vinegar, oil, basil and black pepper.

4. Place the vegetables in a large bowl. Add the dressing and olives. Toss to mix well. Serve warm or chilled. Sprinkle with the lemon juice just before serving.

blue cheese and mushroom salad

You may prepare this salad using regular white button mushrooms, but you'll get a more exotic flavor with chanterelle, enoki, shiitake or other unusual types.

Preparation time: 10 minutes
Makes 4 servings.
Per serving: 115 calories, 4 g. fat (30% of calories), 2.7 g. dietary fiber, 3 mg. cholesterol, 199 mg. sodium.

8 ounces mushrooms, thinly sliced	1 teaspoon Dijon mustard
1½ cups julienned snow peas	⅛ teaspoon freshly ground black pepper
2 cups arugula leaves	1½ teaspoons peanut oil
1 cup coarsely chopped red leaf lettuce	2 cups seasoned croutons
3 tablespoons white wine vinegar	2 tablespoons crumbled blue cheese
2 teaspoons coarse-grain mustard	

1. In a large bowl, toss together the mushrooms, snow peas, arugula and lettuce.

2. In a small bowl, whisk together the vinegar, coarse-grain mustard, Dijon mustard and pepper; whisk in the oil. Pour over the salad. Toss to mix well. Sprinkle with the croutons and blue cheese.

cherry tomato gazpacho salad

This is a cross between a tomato salad and gazpacho, that wonderful cold soup from Spain. It's best made with the summer's freshest produce. If you have access to yellow cherry tomatoes, add them for some extra color.

MAKE AHEAD

Preparation time: 15 minutes + chilling time

Makes 4 servings.
Per serving: 79 calories, 2.7 g. fat (28% of calories), 2.3 g. dietary fiber, 0 mg. cholesterol, 103 mg. sodium.

1 pint cherry tomatoes, quartered	2 teaspoons olive oil
½ cup peeled, seeded and diced cucumbers	1 tablespoon lime juice
	1 tablespoon minced shallots
½ cup diced zucchini	1 garlic clove, minced
½ cup diced sweet red peppers	¼ teaspoon finely minced jalapeño peppers (wear plastic gloves when handling)
¼ cup chopped Vidalia or other sweet onions	¼ teaspoon no-salt lemon herb blend
2 tablespoons red wine vinegar	1 cup garlic-flavored croutons

1. In a large bowl, mix the tomatoes, cucumbers, zucchini, red peppers and onions.

2. In a small bowl, combine the vinegar, oil, lime juice, shallots, garlic, jalapeño peppers and herb blend. Pour over the salad; toss to mix well. Cover and refrigerate for at least 2 hours. Sprinkle with the croutons.

black bean citrus salad

You might never have thought of this combination, but oranges and beans go really well together. Actually, I came up with the combo almost by accident. When first thinking about how this recipe could be different from other bean salads, I looked in the refrigerator for inspiration. The only thing that sparked my interest was an orange. I'm glad it did.

MAKE
AHEAD

Preparation time: 20 minutes + chilling time
Makes 4 servings.
Per serving: 312 calories, 7.9 g. fat (22% of calories), 11.5 g. dietary fiber, 0 mg. cholesterol, 293 mg. sodium.

3	navel oranges, peeled, sectioned and chopped	½ cup chopped red onions
1	can (16 ounces) black beans, rinsed and drained	2 tablespoons canola oil
1	can (16 ounces) red kidney beans, rinsed and drained	2 tablespoons lemon juice
2	medium cucumbers, peeled, seeded and coarsely chopped	1 tablespoon minced fresh cilantro
		¼ teaspoon freshly ground black pepper

1. In a large bowl, combine the oranges, black beans, kidney beans, cucumbers and onions.
2. In a small bowl, whisk together the oil, lemon juice, cilantro and pepper. Pour over the salad; toss to mix well. Cover and chill.

thai tofu salad

I'm confident you'll like this Asian salad even if you're not a big tofu fan. Make sure to use freshly squeezed lime juice; bottled brands are too acidic and will change the taste of this dish.

MAKE
AHEAD

Preparation time: 15 minutes
Cooking time: 10 minutes
Makes 4 servings.
Per serving: 275 calories, 9.6 g. fat (30% of calories), 4 g. dietary fiber, 0 mg. cholesterol, 114 mg. sodium.

8 ounces firm tofu, well drained and squeezed dry between paper towels
3 teaspoons canola oil, divided
¼ cup lime juice
2 tablespoons chopped fresh mint
2 tablespoons chopped fresh cilantro
1½ tablespoons chopped canned green chili peppers (wear plastic gloves when handling)
1 teaspoon low-sodium soy sauce
½ teaspoon brown sugar or honey
2½ cups cooked brown rice
1 medium cucumber, peeled, seeded and chopped
½ cup chopped red onions
Romaine lettuce leaves

1. Cut the tofu into cubes.

2. In a large no-stick frying pan over medium heat, warm 1 teaspoon of the oil. Add the tofu; cook, turning frequently, for 5 to 7 minutes, or until golden. Set aside.

3. In a large bowl, combine the remaining 2 teaspoons oil, lime juice, mint, cilantro, peppers, soy sauce and sugar or honey. Add the tofu, rice, cucumbers and onions; toss to coat well. Serve on plates lined with the lettuce.

roasted vegetable and cheese salad

Roasting the vegetables really brings out their individual flavors. I like to use small mozzarella balls because they add visual interest to the salad. But if they're not available in your area, cut regular nonfat or part-skim mozzarella into ½" cubes.

MAKE AHEAD

Preparation time: 20 minutes
Cooking time: 30 minutes
Makes 4 servings.
Per serving: 211 calories, 10.2 g. fat (31% of calories), 4.7 g. dietary fiber, 33 mg. cholesterol, 857 mg. sodium.

2	red onions, quartered and the layers separated
2	medium zucchini, cubed
1	small eggplant, cubed
2	sweet red peppers, thinly sliced
1	large tomato, cut into ½" wedges
1	teaspoon olive oil
1	teaspoon dried basil
½	teaspoon fennel seeds, crushed
¼	teaspoon freshly ground black pepper
1	package (9 ounces) small nonfat mozzarella cheese balls, drained and halved
4	ounces provolone cheese, diced
3	tablespoons balsamic vinegar
2	tablespoons grated Parmesan cheese

1. Preheat the oven to 450°.

2. Coat a 9" × 13" baking dish with no-stick spray. Add the onions, zucchini, eggplant, red peppers, tomatoes, oil, basil, fennel seeds and black pepper. Toss to mix well. Roast, stirring occasionally, for 20 to 30 minutes, or until the vegetables are tender.

3. Transfer to a large bowl. Add the mozzarella, provolone, vinegar and Parmesan; toss to mix well.

white bean and asparagus salad

When asparagus is out of season, I use broccoli florets or green beans. If you don't have any small red potatoes, you may use regular baking potatoes—but the salad won't look as pretty.

MAKE AHEAD

Preparation time: 15 minutes
Cooking time: 20 minutes
Makes 4 servings.
Per serving: 245 calories, 4.2 g. fat (15% of calories), 2.9 g. dietary fiber, 0 mg. cholesterol, 75 mg. sodium.

1 pound small red potatoes, cut into ¼" slices	2 tablespoons apple juice
12 thin asparagus spears, cut into 2" pieces	1 tablespoon olive oil
1 can (16 ounces) cannellini beans, rinsed and drained	2 teaspoons Dijon mustard
1 small red onion, chopped	2 teaspoons grated lemon peel
2 tablespoons minced scallions	1 teaspoon tarragon vinegar
2 tablespoons chopped fresh tarragon or 1 teaspoon dried	¼ teaspoon freshly ground black pepper

1. Place the potatoes in a 3-quart saucepan. Add cold water to cover. Bring to a boil and cook for 10 minutes. Add the asparagus; cook for 5 to 7 minutes, or until the vegetables are tender. Drain and rinse gently with cold water. Transfer to a large bowl.

2. Add the beans, onions, scallions and tarragon. Mix lightly.

3. In a small bowl, whisk together the juice, oil, mustard, lemon peel, vinegar and pepper. Pour over the vegetables; toss to mix well.

watercress salad with scallion dressing

This simple tossed salad is a perfect addition to any menu. And the creamy dressing complements most any greens, so I like to keep some on hand.

MAKE AHEAD

Preparation time: 20 minutes
Makes 4 servings.
Per serving: 55 calories, 1.4 g. fat (23% of calories), 1 g. dietary fiber, 1 mg. cholesterol, 79 mg. sodium.

2½	cups packed watercress leaves	¾	cup nonfat yogurt
1½	cups torn Bibb lettuce	⅓	cup minced scallions
3	heads Belgian endive, cut into 1" pieces	1	garlic clove, minced
1	cup fresh bread crumbs	1	teaspoon cider vinegar
½	cup halved cherry tomatoes	1	teaspoon Dijon mustard
1	tablespoon finely ground pecans	1	teaspoon grated lemon peel
		⅛	teaspoon freshly ground black pepper

1. In a large bowl, combine the watercress, lettuce, endive, bread crumbs, tomatoes and pecans.

2. In a small bowl, combine the yogurt, scallions, garlic, vinegar, mustard, lemon peel and pepper. Pour over the salad; toss to mix well.

creamy cucumber mint salad

This simple, refreshing salad is perfect for hot summer days. The fresh mint really makes this dish, so try to locate some.

3	medium cucumbers, thinly sliced	1	tablespoon chopped fresh dill
¾	cup nonfat yogurt	1	tablespoon white wine vinegar
1	small red onion, chopped		
¼	cup golden raisins	¼	teaspoon freshly ground black pepper
¼	cup dark raisins		Red leaf lettuce
2	tablespoons chopped fresh mint	¼	cup toasted pine nuts

Preparation time: 15 minutes
Makes 4 servings.
Per serving: 174 calories, 5.6
g. fat (26% of calories), 5.3 g.
dietary fiber, 1 mg. cholesterol, 42 mg. sodium.

1. In a large bowl, combine the cucumbers, yogurt, onions, golden raisins, dark raisins, mint, dill, vinegar and pepper. Toss to mix well.

2. Serve on the lettuce and sprinkle with the pine nuts.

mango spinach salad

To me, fruit and greens are a natural combination and a pleasant change from traditional tossed green salads. If you can't get a mango, try using strawberries instead. I sometimes serve this salad garnished with avocado slices.

6 cups torn spinach	1½ teaspoons coarse-grain
3 cups torn Boston lettuce	mustard
1 cup cubed mangoes	Pinch of freshly ground
1 tablespoon poppy seeds	black pepper
2 tablespoons balsamic vinegar	Pinch of ground
2 tablespoons rice wine vinegar	cardamom
1 tablespoon honey	

1. In a large bowl, combine the spinach, lettuce, mangoes and poppy seeds.

2. In a small bowl, whisk together the balsamic vinegar, rice wine vinegar, honey, mustard, pepper and cardamom. Pour over the salad; toss to mix well.

Preparation time: 15 minutes
Makes 4 servings.
Per serving: 90 calories, 1.6 g. fat (16% of calories), 3.7 g. dietary fiber, 0 mg. cholesterol, 104 mg. sodium.

five-bean chili salad

Feel free to vary the beans to your own taste. Don't be concerned about the amount of chili powder; it does not add too much heat to the dish.

MAKE AHEAD

Preparation time: 15 minutes
Cooking time: 10 minutes
Makes 4 servings.
Per serving: 462 calories, 7.2 g. fat (13% of calories), 20.9 g. dietary fiber, 0 mg. cholesterol, 683 mg. sodium.

8	ounces green beans, cut into 1" pieces	½	teaspoon ground cumin
1	box (10 ounces) frozen lima beans, thawed	1	can (19 ounces) red kidney beans, rinsed and drained
1½	tablespoons canola oil	1	can (19 ounces) black-eyed peas, rinsed and drained
1	cup chopped scallions		
2	garlic cloves, minced	1	can (19 ounces) black beans, rinsed and drained
1	tablespoon chili powder		
¼	cup red wine vinegar	1	yellow pepper, chopped
1	teaspoon brown sugar or ½ teaspoon honey	¼	cup chopped fresh flat-leaf parsley

1. Place the green beans in a 3-quart saucepan and add cold water to cover. Bring to a boil over high heat, then reduce the heat to low. Cover and simmer for 5 minutes. Add the lima beans. Cover and simmer for 5 minutes, or until both beans are crisp-tender. Drain and place in a large bowl.

2. Meanwhile, in a small no-stick frying pan over medium heat, warm the oil. Add the scallions and garlic; cook, stirring frequently, for 2 minutes. Stir in the chili powder; cook for 1 minute. Remove from the heat and stir in the vinegar, sugar or honey and cumin.

3. Pour over the beans in the bowl. Add the kidney beans, black-eyed peas, black beans, peppers and parsley; mix well.

fat-free salad dressings

When is a salad a dieter's demise? When it's buried under a fatty dressing. According to one study, the use of full-fat dressings was a major factor in determining a woman's total fat intake. Women with the highest fat intakes ate regular salad dressing more frequently and in larger helpings than women with the lowest fat intakes.

Fortunately, there are a variety of fat-free dressings on the market that can help you eat salads often without overdoing your calorie or fat limit. For those times when you want a homemade dressing, here are a couple of ways to avoid the fat trap.

For a creamy dressing . . .

Puree nonfat cottage cheese in a food processor until smooth. Stir in some mustard, Worcestershire sauce, garlic, horseradish—in whatever combination and quantity you choose—until you get just the flavor you want. Mince some fresh herbs and add them to help boost the flavor. For an extra bit of richness, add some finely minced sun-dried tomatoes. For variety, replace the pureed cottage cheese with some nonfat yogurt; lightly whisk it with the other ingredients.

For a no-oil vinaigrette . . .

Tracy Ritter, chef-owner of Stamina Cuisine, in San Diego, has this suggestion: Let mustard give the dressing body. Mustard is a natural emulsifier that helps hold the other ingredients together and gives them the thickness needed to cling to your greens. One of Ritter's favorite dressings combines a strong-flavored vinegar (such as sherry) with lots of mustard, fresh herbs and some stock. Just whisk the dressing together in a small bowl. When you want a dressing that's a little sweeter, replace the stock with apple juice. The sweet version is terrific with cabbage, cauliflower and carrot salads.

couscous and tomato salad

This is my twist on the popular tabbouleh salad. Couscous and zucchini replace the typical bulgur and cucumbers. Try it for a light lunch salad. When I have a nice chunk of aged provolone on hand, I like to shave off thin "curls" and sprinkle them on the salad.

MAKE
AHEAD

Preparation time: 25 minutes
+ chilling time
Cooking time: 5 minutes

Makes 4 servings.
Per serving: 368 calories, 6.3 g. fat (15% of calories), 14.5 g. dietary fiber, 0 mg. cholesterol, 33 mg. sodium.

1¼ cups water	½ cup chopped Vidalia or other sweet onions
¾ cup low-sodium vegetable stock	½ cup chopped fresh basil
½ cup lemon juice, divided	¼ cup chopped fresh mint
1½ cups whole wheat or white couscous	1½ tablespoons olive oil
2 large zucchini, diced	¼ teaspoon freshly ground black pepper
6 plum tomatoes, chopped	

1. In a 2-quart saucepan over high heat, bring the water, stock and ¼ cup of the lemon juice to a boil. Stir in the couscous. Remove from the heat; cover and let stand for 5 minutes. Fluff with fork and cool completely.

2. Meanwhile, in a large bowl, combine the zucchini, tomatoes, onions, basil, mint, oil, pepper and the remaining ¼ cup lemon juice. Mix well. Let stand for 10 minutes.

3. Stir in the couscous; toss to mix well. Cover and refrigerate for at least 1 hour.

crunchy oriental salad

I like to serve this salad at a summer barbecue with grilled vegetables, especially corn.

MAKE AHEAD

Preparation time: 20 minutes + chilling time
Cooking time: 5 minutes
Makes 4 servings.
Per serving: 58 calories, 2.1 g. fat (30% of calories), 2.3 g. dietary fiber, 0 mg. cholesterol, 111 mg. sodium.

1½	cups shredded red cabbage	
1½	cups shredded napa cabbage	
4	ounces snow peas, julienned	
1	sweet red pepper, thinly sliced	
½	cup thinly sliced radishes	
½	cup low-sodium vegetable stock	
3	tablespoons lemon juice	
1	tablespoon low-sodium teriyaki sauce	
¾	teaspoon sesame oil	
1	teaspoon cornstarch	
1	tablespoon grated fresh ginger	
2	teaspoons sesame seeds	
¼	teaspoon red-pepper flakes	

1. In a large bowl, combine the red cabbage, napa cabbage, snow peas, red peppers and radishes; set aside.

2. In a small saucepan, mix the stock, lemon juice, teriyaki sauce, oil and cornstarch until the cornstarch is dissolved. Bring to a boil over medium heat, stirring frequently, and cook until slightly thick. Remove from the heat and stir in the ginger, sesame seeds and pepper flakes.

3. Pour over the vegetables; toss to mix well. Cover and refrigerate for at least 1 hour.

german potato salad with cornichons

This is a low-fat version of a German favorite. The cornichons (another name for gherkin pickles) add characteristic tang to the salad. For variety, you might like to sprinkle some finely chopped eggs over the top. This salad is best served at room temperature shortly after preparation.

Preparation time: 20 minutes
Cooking time: 30 minutes
Makes 4 servings.
Per serving: 154 calories, 0.2 g. fat (1% of calories), 3.5 g. dietary fiber, 0 mg. cholesterol, 134 mg. sodium.

4 medium baking potatoes	2 tablespoons cider vinegar
½ cup finely shredded onions	1 tablespoon honey
¼ cup coarsely chopped cornichons	¼ teaspoon freshly ground black pepper
1 tablespoon chopped fresh dill	

1. Place the potatoes in a 3-quart saucepan. Add cold water to cover them by about 2". Bring to a boil over high heat. Reduce the heat to medium and cook for 25 to 30 minutes, or until tender. Drain and cool for 10 minutes. Peel and cut into ½" cubes.

2. Place in a large bowl. Add the onions, cornichons and dill.

3. In a cup, stir together the vinegar, honey and pepper. Pour over the salad; toss to mix well.

fennel raisin salad

Warm or chilled, this salad is a real treat. For variety, you may replace the apples with pears and use dried apricots for the raisins. For a pretty presentation, serve the salad on large lettuce leaves.

MAKE AHEAD

Preparation time: 15 minutes
Cooking time: 5 minutes
Makes 4 servings.
Per serving: 141 calories, 3.8 g. fat (22% of calories), 0.9 g. dietary fiber, 0 mg. cholesterol, 51 mg. sodium.

1 small fennel bulb	1 tablespoon orange juice
1 large red apple, chopped	1 tablespoon lemon juice
½ cup golden raisins	1 tablespoon canola oil
2 tablespoons chopped fresh cilantro	1 tablespoon honey
2 tablespoons chopped fresh flat-leaf parsley	½ teaspoon celery seeds
	½ teaspoon Dijon mustard

1. Trim the feathery leaves from the fennel and discard or reserve for another use. Peel off any blemished outer stalks and discard. Cut the remaining bulb in half lengthwise and coarsely chop. Place in a large bowl.

2. Add the apples, raisins, cilantro and parsley.

3. In a 1-quart saucepan, combine the orange juice, lemon juice, oil, honey, celery seeds and mustard. Bring to a simmer over medium heat; cook for 2 minutes. Pour over the fennel mixture. Toss to combine. Serve warm or chilled.

orzo salad
with carrot dressing

I came up with this recipe, which is based on a vegetable puree, while I was searching for a way to make a thick low-fat dressing. I often use this type of dressing with other grain-based salads.

MAKE
AHEAD

Preparation time: 15 minutes + chilling time
Cooking time: 20 minutes
Makes 4 servings.
Per serving: 358 calories, 7 g. fat (17% of calories), 6.2 g. dietary fiber, 2 mg. cholesterol, 127 mg. sodium.

8 ounces orzo	¼ cup herb vinegar or white wine vinegar
2 cups cut (1½" pieces) green beans	3 tablespoons chopped fresh dill
1 yellow or sweet red pepper, diced	Pinch of freshly ground black pepper
4 teaspoons olive oil, divided	2 tablespoons grated Parmesan cheese
6 large carrots, thinly sliced	
1 cup low-sodium vegetable stock	

1. In a large pot of boiling water, cook the orzo for 5 minutes. Add the beans; cook for 5 to 7 minutes, or until the beans and pasta are tender. Drain and place in a large bowl. Add the yellow or red peppers. Sprinkle with 1 teaspoon of the oil; toss well and set aside.

2. Meanwhile, in a 3-quart saucepan, combine the carrots, stock, vinegar, dill, black pepper and the remaining 3 teaspoons oil. Bring to a boil over medium-high heat. Reduce the heat to low; simmer for 15 to 20 minutes, or until the carrots are very tender. Transfer to a food processor; process until very smooth.

3. Pour the carrot dressing over the orzo mixture. Sprinkle with the Parmesan and toss to mix well. Cover and refrigerate for at least 2 hours. Mix well before serving.

basic breakfasts

I f you were once the ham-and-eggs type, you probably thought you couldn't have satisfying morning meals without meat. Now you know better. But you might be slightly at a loss when it comes to creating interesting breakfast dishes that are a step above plain cereal, simple scrambled eggs or toast and coffee.

The recipes in this chapter run the gamut from those that you can make ahead and eat on the run to those more suited to a leisurely brunch. Brown Rice Breakfast Parfaits, for example, can be readied the night before and eaten quickly. Strawberry Whole-Grain Waffles, on the other hand, are probably something you'd reserve for when you're not rushed.

I've included both sweet and savory dishes, so you can tailor your breakfasts to your early morning appetite. Then you won't have any excuse to skip this all-important meal.

mushroom-tomato brunch bake

I like to double this recipe and serve it to a large crowd for brunch. You may substitute any other bread for the whole wheat and use whatever variety of vegetables you have on hand.

Preparation time: 15 minutes
Cooking time: 55 minutes

Makes 6 servings.
Per serving: 192 calories, 5.1 g. fat (24% of calories), 3.3 g. dietary fiber, 11 mg. cholesterol, 306 mg. sodium.

6 slices light-textured whole wheat bread, lightly toasted and torn into 1" pieces	1 tablespoon grated Parmesan cheese
1 tomato, seeded and diced	½ teaspoon dried basil
1 small red onion, chopped	1½ cups egg substitute
1 cup thinly sliced mushrooms	1½ cups skim milk
4 ounces low-fat Cheddar cheese, shredded	1 tablespoon Dijon mustard
	¼ teaspoon freshly ground black pepper

1. Preheat the oven to 325°.

2. Coat a 9" × 9" baking dish with no-stick spray. Place half of the bread in the baking dish, evenly covering the bottom. Sprinkle the tomatoes, onions, mushrooms, Cheddar, Parmesan and basil over the bread. Top with the remaining bread.

3. In a medium bowl, whisk together the egg, milk, mustard and pepper. Pour over the bread.

4. Bake for 45 to 55 minutes, or until the egg is set and the cheese is bubbly. Let stand for 5 minutes before cutting.

fried polenta with cranberry-maple topping

As I was working on this chapter, this emerged as one of my favorite recipes. I particularly like to have it on Sunday mornings. You may prepare both the polenta and the cranberry topping ahead; reheat the topping just before serving.

MAKE AHEAD

Preparation time: 10 minutes + chilling time
Cooking time: 40 minutes

Makes 4 servings.
Per serving: 390 calories, 9.5 g. fat (19% of calories), 3.4 g. dietary fiber, 1 mg. cholesterol, 68 mg. sodium.

2 cups water	½ cup golden raisins
1 cup skim milk	½ cup apple juice
1 teaspoon honey	¼ cup maple syrup
2 tablespoons margarine, divided	2 tablespoons grated orange peel
1 cup yellow cornmeal	¼ teaspoon ground cinnamon
½ cup walnut halves	
1 cup fresh cranberries	

1. In a 3-quart saucepan over medium heat, bring the water, milk, honey and 1 tablespoon of the margarine to a simmer. Slowly whisk in the cornmeal. Reduce the heat to low and cook, stirring constantly with a wooden spoon, for 10 to 15 minutes, or until the mixture is very stiff and thick and pulls away from the sides of the pan.

2. Line an 8" × 4" loaf pan with plastic wrap. Spoon the cornmeal mixture into the pan. Cover and refrigerate for at least 2 hours.

3. About 30 minutes before serving, place the walnuts in a 2-quart saucepan over medium heat. Toast, stirring frequently, for 3 to 4 minutes, or until the nuts are fragrant. Remove from the pan and set aside.

4. To the pan, add the cranberries, raisins, juice, maple syrup, orange peel and cinnamon; bring to a boil. Reduce the heat to low and simmer for 10 to 15 minutes, or until the cranberries begin to pop. Stir in the walnuts; keep warm over low heat.

5. Unmold the polenta and cut it into ½" slices. In a large no-stick frying pan over medium heat, melt the remaining 1 tablespoon margarine. Add the slices; cook, turning once, until golden on both sides. Serve topped with the cranberry mixture.

toasted bagels with roasted red pepper spread

This spread is good for more than just breakfast. You can turn it into a dip by thinning it with skim milk. Serve the dip with crudités and crackers.

MAKE
AHEAD

Preparation time: 10 minutes + chilling time

Makes 4 servings.
Per serving: 232 calories, 4.5 g. fat (15% of calories), 1.6 g. dietary fiber, 1 mg. cholesterol, 240 mg. sodium.

8 ounces soft tofu, well drained and squeezed dry between paper towels	¼ cup chopped roasted sweet red peppers
1 tablespoon skim milk	2 tablespoons minced scallions
1 tablespoon rice wine vinegar	1 tablespoon sweet pickle relish
1 teaspoon honey	4 bagels, split in half
⅛ teaspoon freshly ground black pepper	8 tomato slices

1. Crumble the tofu into a food processor. Add the milk, vinegar, honey and black pepper; process until smooth. Transfer to a small bowl.

2. Stir in the red peppers, scallions and relish. Cover and refrigerate for at least 1 hour.

3. To serve, toast the bagels. Spread with the red pepper mixture; top each half with a tomato slice.

strawberry whole-grain waffles

I love waffles but hardly ever make them because it means hunting for the waffle iron. However, when the search and preparations are complete, the results are definitely worth the trouble. Needless to say, I save this recipe for weekends. (And I freeze leftover waffles for quick breakfasts other times.)

MAKE
AHEAD

Preparation time: 10 minutes
Cooking time: 20 minutes

Makes 4 servings.
Per serving: 452 calories, 6.8 g. fat (13% of calories), 10.6 g. dietary fiber, <1 mg. cholesterol, 330 mg. sodium.

1 cup whole wheat flour	¼ teaspoon baking soda
1 cup unbleached flour	1½ cups water
½ cup yellow cornmeal	¾ cup orange juice
½ cup quick-cooking oats	2 teaspoons canola oil
¼ cup rye flour	¾ cup finely chopped strawberries
¼ cup nonfat dry milk powder	
1 tablespoon baking powder	
½ teaspoon ground cinnamon	

1. Preheat the waffle iron according to the manufacturer's directions.

2. In a large bowl, mix the whole wheat flour, unbleached flour, cornmeal, oats, rye flour, milk powder, baking powder, cinnamon and baking soda. Stir in the water, juice and oil. Fold in the strawberries. (If the batter is too stiff, thin it with a little skim milk or water.)

3. Ladle enough batter into the waffle iron to come within 1" of the edges. Cover and bake according to the manufacturer's directions.

4. Repeat until all the batter has been used.

breakfast granola

Granola is great served with skim milk or yogurt. And you needn't reserve it for breakfast—take some along to work for an afternoon snack.

MAKE AHEAD

Preparation time: 15 minutes
Baking time: 25 minutes
Makes 12 servings.
Per serving: 327 calories, 8.8 g. fat (22% of calories), 6.8 g. dietary fiber, 0 mg. cholesterol, 21 mg. sodium.

3 cups quick-cooking rolled oats	¼ cup maple syrup
½ cup coarsely chopped unsalted peanuts	¼ cup thawed frozen apple juice concentrate
¼ cup plain or honey-flavored wheat germ	2 tablespoons honey
¼ cup sesame seeds	1½ teaspoons pumpkin pie spice
2 tablespoons grated lemon peel	1 cup dried currants
2 tablespoons smooth peanut butter	1 cup coarsely chopped mixed dried fruit

1. Preheat the oven to 350°.

2. Coat a jelly-roll pan with no-stick spray. Add the oats, peanuts, wheat germ, sesame seeds and lemon peel to the pan; toss to combine.

3. Place the peanut butter in a small bowl. Microwave on high for 1 minute to melt. Stir in the maple syrup, juice concentrate and honey. Drizzle over the oat mixture. Mix well, then spread evenly in the pan.

4. Bake for 20 minutes, stirring twice during that time to prevent burning. Sprinkle with the pumpkin pie spice and toss to mix well. Bake for an additional 5 minutes, or until golden.

5. Transfer to a large sealable bowl. Stir in the currants and fruit. Cool completely. Store tightly sealed in the refrigerator.

cornmeal pancakes

I like to make these pancakes and freeze them. They are great to reheat for a last-minute brunch. Serve them with nonfat sour cream. Or arrange them on a platter, sprinkle with low-fat cheese, and broil until the cheese has melted and the pancakes are heated through.

Preparation time: 10 minutes
Cooking time: 20 minutes
Makes 4 servings.
Per serving: 366 calories, 7.2 g. fat (18% of calories), 2.3 g. dietary fiber, 4 mg. cholesterol, 398 mg. sodium.

1½ cups unbleached flour	1½ cups skim milk
⅓ cup yellow cornmeal	½ cup egg substitute
2 tablespoons grated Parmesan cheese	1½ tablespoons canola oil
2 teaspoons baking powder	1½ tablespoons honey
⅛ teaspoon freshly ground black pepper	½ teaspoon low-sodium soy sauce
	¾ cup drained canned corn

1. In a large bowl, combine the flour, cornmeal, Parmesan, baking powder and pepper.

2. In a medium bowl, whisk together the milk, egg, oil, honey and soy sauce. Stir into the flour mixture until smooth. Gently stir in the corn.

3. Coat a large no-stick frying pan or griddle with no-stick spray. Warm over medium heat for 2 minutes. Ladle in ¼ cup of the batter for each pancake, making a few at a time. Cook until the tops are bubbly and the pancakes are dry around the edges. Flip and cook for 2 to 3 minutes, or until golden on both sides. Place on a platter and keep warm.

4. Repeat until all the batter has been used; use more no-stick spray as needed.

peanut butter french toast

I think there's nothing more indulgent than peanut butter French toast. It certainly makes a very special breakfast—one that's even fairly low in fat!

Preparation time: 10 minutes
Cooking time: 10 minutes
Makes 4 servings.
Per serving: 256 calories, 8.6 g. fat (24% of calories), 1.9 g. dietary fiber, <1 mg. cholesterol, 221 mg. sodium.

½ cup egg substitute
½ cup skim milk
3 tablespoons chunky peanut butter, at room temperature
1 teaspoon ground cinnamon

1 teaspoon honey
4 thick slices French bread
1 tablespoon margarine
½ cup unsweetened applesauce
¼ cup maple syrup

1. In a shallow bowl or pie plate, whisk together the egg, milk, peanut butter, cinnamon and honey until smooth. Add the bread and soak on both sides.

2. Coat a large no-stick frying pan with no-stick spray. Place over medium heat and melt the margarine. Add the bread and cook for 3 to 4 minutes per side, or until golden. Serve topped with the applesauce and maple syrup.

couscous breakfast cereal

This cereal is high in fiber, thanks to the dried fruit. I like this best when made with apple juice, but you may use other juices. Serve the cereal warm or cold.

1¼ cups apple juice
¼ cup chopped dried apricots
¼ cup chopped prunes
¼ teaspoon ground cinnamon

¾ cup couscous
¼ cup chopped walnuts
¼ cup nonfat yogurt

1. In a 2-quart saucepan over medium-high heat, bring the juice, apricots, prunes and cinnamon to a boil. Stir in the couscous and walnuts. Remove from the heat.

2. Cover and let stand for 5 minutes, or until the couscous is soft. Fluff with a fork. Serve topped with the yogurt.

Preparation time: 15 minutes
Makes 4 servings.
Per serving: 248 calories, 3.3 g. fat (12% of calories), 7.2 g. dietary fiber, <1 mg. cholesterol, 18 mg. sodium.

nutty peach cereal

This is an easy alternative to boxed cold cereals. I like to serve this cereal sprinkled with fresh raspberries or another fruit.

2	bananas, thinly sliced	½	cup golden raisins or chopped dates
2	peaches, coarsely chopped	2	teaspoons maple syrup
¼	cup unsalted cashew halves	⅛	teaspoon ground cinnamon
2	tablespoons unsweetened shredded coconut		Pinch of ground allspice
1	tablespoon sesame seeds	2	cups skim milk or nonfat yogurt

Preparation time: 10 minutes
Makes 4 servings.
Per serving: 263 calories, 6.7 g. fat (21% of calories), 3.4 g. dietary fiber, 2 mg. cholesterol, 76 mg. sodium.

1. In a medium bowl, combine the bananas and peaches.

2. In a food processor, combine the cashews, coconut and sesame seeds. Process with on/off turns until coarsely ground; do not overprocess or the mixture will become a paste. Sprinkle over the fruit.

3. Stir in the raisins or dates, maple syrup, cinnamon and allspice. Serve topped with the milk or yogurt.

great shakes

You know you *should* eat breakfast. But what if you can't face solid food so early in the day? Try drinking your morning meal. These shakes are easy to make and easy to consume. You can even take them along to work to sip on the commute or at your desk.

pineapple-banana breakfast shake

2 cups drained canned crushed pineapple	2 medium bananas, coarsely chopped
1½ cups ice cubes	½ cup apricot nectar
1⅓ cups nonfat yogurt	¼ cup toasted wheat germ
	1 kiwifruit, peeled and sliced

1. In a blender, combine the pineapple, ice cubes, yogurt, bananas, apricot nectar and wheat germ. Blend until smooth.

2. Serve in tall glasses; garnish with the kiwi slices.

MAKE AHEAD

Preparation time: 10 minutes.
Makes 4 servings.
Per serving: 189 calories, 1.4 g. fat (6% of calories), 3.6 g. dietary fiber, 1 mg. cholesterol, 62 mg. sodium.

banana fruit shake

2 cups nonfat vanilla yogurt	1 tablespoon honey
2 cups low-calorie cranberry juice	¼ teaspoon ground cinnamon
1 cup frozen banana slices	2 ice cubes
1 cup coarsely chopped peaches	

1. In a blender, combine the yogurt, juice, bananas, peaches, honey, cinnamon and ice cubes. Blend on high speed until smooth and creamy.

MAKE AHEAD

Preparation time: 5 minutes.
Makes 4 servings.
Per serving: 185 calories, 0.3 g. fat (1% of calories), 1.5 g. dietary fiber, 3 mg. cholesterol, 76 mg. sodium.

raisin-barley pudding

This is perfect for busy mornings because you prepare the dish ahead. You could even take the pudding with you to eat at work. For variety, replace the barley with quick-cooking brown rice.

MAKE
AHEAD

Preparation time: 10 minutes
Cooking time: 15 minutes
Makes 4 servings.
Per serving: 192 calories, 0.6 g. fat (3% of calories), 3.4 g. dietary fiber, 1 mg. cholesterol, 50 mg. sodium.

1	cup water	½	cup nonfat vanilla yogurt
½	cup quick-cooking barley	¼	cup nonfat sour cream
¼	cup golden raisins	1	tablespoon orange all-fruit preserves
½	teaspoon ground cinnamon	2	teaspoons honey
¼	teaspoon vanilla		

1. In a 1-quart saucepan over medium-high heat, bring the water to a boil. Stir in the barley. Cover, reduce the heat to low, and simmer for 10 to 12 minutes, or until the barley is tender and the liquid has been absorbed. Remove from heat and let stand, covered, for 5 minutes. Cool completely.

2. In a medium bowl, combine the barley, raisins, cinnamon and vanilla. Gently stir in the yogurt, sour cream and preserves.

3. Divide among individual custard or dessert dishes. Cover and refrigerate overnight. Serve drizzled with the honey.

cheese blintzes with raspberry sauce

Blintzes are ultrathin pancakes, like crêpes, that can hold most any type of sweet or savory filling. I particularly like these cottage cheese blintzes. Although this recipe looks complicated, you can make all the parts ahead. The unfilled blintzes keep in the refrigerator for a week or in the freezer for three months. The filling and raspberry sauce can be made a day ahead. Warm the sauce over low heat before serving.

MAKE
AHEAD

Filling
- 1 cup nonfat cottage cheese
- 2 teaspoons grated orange peel
- 1 teaspoon honey
- ½ teaspoon vanilla

Blintzes
- ½ cup unbleached flour
- ½ teaspoon baking powder
- ½ cup skim milk
- ¼ cup egg substitute

- 1 tablespoon honey
- 1 tablespoon margarine, melted

Raspberry Sauce
- 1 cup fresh raspberries
- ⅔ cup apple juice
- 1 tablespoon cornstarch
- 2 tablespoons water
- 1 teaspoon grated lemon peel

1. To make the filling: In a food processor, combine the cottage cheese, orange peel, honey and vanilla. Process until smooth. Cover and refrigerate until needed.

2. To make the blintzes: In a medium bowl, stir together the flour and baking powder.

3. In a small bowl, whisk together the milk, egg and honey. Pour over the flour and mix well. (The batter should be the consistency of heavy cream; if it is too thick, thin with a little additional milk.)

4. Coat an 8" crêpe pan or medium no-stick frying pan with no-stick spray. Warm over medium heat for 2 minutes. Ladle about 2 tablespoons of the batter into the pan, swirling the pan to evenly coat the bottom. Cook for 1 minute, or until the top is set and the bottom is lightly browned. Flip the blintz and cook for 10 to 15 seconds longer. Transfer to a wire rack to cool.

5. Repeat until all the batter has been used. (For storage, separate the blintzes with squares of wax paper, wrap tightly in plastic, and refrigerate or freeze.)

6. Preheat the oven to 350°. Coat a baking sheet with no-stick spray.

Preparation time: 30 minutes
Cooking time: 20 minutes
Baking time: 10 minutes

Makes 4 servings.
Per serving: 201 calories, 3.9 g. fat (17% of calories), 1.9 g. dietary fiber, 3 mg. cholesterol, 327 mg. sodium.

7. To assemble the blintzes, place a blintz on a flat surface. Put 2 tablespoons of the filling 1" from the lower edge. Turn up the bottom edge and fold in the sides; roll to enclose the filling. Place, seam side down, on the prepared baking sheet. Repeat to fill all the blintzes.

8. Brush the tops with the margarine. Bake for about 10 minutes to heat through.

9. To make the raspberry sauce: While the blintzes are baking, combine the raspberries and juice in a 1-quart saucepan. Bring to a boil over medium heat. Reduce the heat to low and simmer for 5 minutes.

10. In a cup, dissolve the cornstarch in the water. Add to the pan, along with the lemon peel. Cook, stirring constantly, for 1 to 2 minutes, or until slightly thick. Serve spooned over the blintzes.

brown rice breakfast parfaits

This is an excellent way to use up leftover rice.

MAKE

AHEAD

Preparation time: 10 minutes + chilling time

Makes 4 servings.
Per serving: 302 calories, 7.2 g. fat (20% of calories), 3.4 g. dietary fiber, 3 mg. cholesterol, 126 mg. sodium.

2 cups nonfat vanilla or lemon yogurt	¼ teaspoon almond extract
1 cup cooked brown rice	2 cups blueberries
1 cup drained canned crushed pineapple	¼ cup Grape-Nuts cereal
½ cup coarsely chopped walnuts	2 tablespoons unsweetened shredded coconut

1. In a medium bowl, combine the yogurt, rice, pineapple, walnuts and almond extract. Cover and refrigerate for at least 8 hours.

2. To serve, layer the rice mixture and blueberries in 4 parfait glasses. Sprinkle with the cereal and coconut.

cornmeal and oat bran muffins

When oat bran became so popular a few years ago, I tried a lot of muffin recipes calling for it. Most of them were disappointing. That's when I developed this recipe, which uses a fair amount of oat bran but isn't heavy like so many others. For a change of pace, I sometimes sprinkle the filling on top of the muffins instead of putting it in the middle. To avoid overbrowning the coconut and oats, I just barely toast them first.

MAKE
AHEAD

Preparation time: 10 minutes
Cooking time: 25 minutes

Makes 12 muffins.
Per muffin: 185 calories, 6.2 g. fat (28% of calories), 3 g. dietary fiber, <1 mg. cholesterol, 85 mg. sodium.

Oat Filling
½ cup quick-cooking rolled oats
2 tablespoons unsweetened shredded coconut
1 tablespoon brown sugar
Muffins
1 cup yellow cornmeal
1 cup oat bran
2 tablespoons brown sugar

2 tablespoons grated orange peel
2½ teaspoons baking powder
½ teaspoon ground cinnamon
1 cup skim milk
¼ cup canola oil
¼ cup egg substitute
¼ cup orange juice
¾ cup golden raisins

1. To make the oat filling: In a medium no-stick frying pan over medium heat, toast the oats and coconut, stirring constantly, until golden. Transfer to a small bowl. Stir in the sugar; set aside.

2. To make the muffins: Preheat the oven to 425°. Coat 12 muffin cups with no-stick spray.

3. In a large bowl, combine the cornmeal, oat bran, sugar, orange peel, baking powder and cinnamon.

4. In a small bowl, whisk together the milk, oil, egg and juice. Stir in the raisins. Pour over the cornmeal mixture. Mix until the dry ingredients are moistened.

5. Divide half of the batter among the prepared muffin cups. Sprinkle evenly with the oat mixture. Cover with the remaining batter.

6. Bake for 20 to 25 minutes, or until a cake tester inserted in the center comes out clean. Cool in the pan for 10 minutes. Transfer to a wire rack.

apple-bran muffins

These fiber-filled muffins get sweetness from the shredded apples and applesauce. To make this a really apple-intensive breakfast treat, serve them with apple butter.

MAKE AHEAD

Preparation time: 15 minutes
Baking time: 25 minutes
Makes 12 muffins.
Per muffin: 145 calories, 3 g. fat (17% of calories), 2.8 g. dietary fiber, <1 mg. cholesterol, 128 mg. sodium.

1	cup bran flakes cereal	1	cup shredded Granny Smith apples
½	cup buttermilk	½	cup brown sugar
1	teaspoon baking soda	½	cup chopped walnuts
¼	cup unsweetened applesauce	½	teaspoon ground cinnamon
2	egg whites		
2	tablespoons maple syrup		
1	cup unbleached or oat-blend flour		

1. Preheat the oven to 375°. Coat 12 muffin cups with no-stick spray.

2. In a small bowl, combine the cereal, buttermilk and baking soda.

3. In a large bowl, mix the applesauce, egg whites and maple syrup. Stir in the buttermilk mixture, flour, apples, sugar, walnuts and cinnamon. Do not overmix.

4. Divide among the prepared muffin cups. Bake for 18 to 25 minutes, or until a cake tester inserted in the center of a muffin comes out clean. Cool in the pan for 10 minutes. Transfer to a wire rack.

peanut butter raisin bread

This bread freezes well. I sometimes make several loaves at a time around the holidays and freeze them for gifts. Then I give the bread with a jar of homemade preserves. If you'd like, you can add some chopped peanuts to the batter before baking.

MAKE AHEAD

Preparation time: 15 minutes
Baking time: 1 hour
Makes 1 loaf; 10 slices.
Per slice: 213 calories, 7.9 g. fat (31% of calories), 4 g. dietary fiber, <1 mg. cholesterol, 119 mg. sodium.

2	cups whole wheat flour	3	tablespoons canola oil
2	tablespoons brown sugar	1	teaspoon vanilla
2	teaspoons baking powder	1½	cups skim milk
½	teaspoon ground cinnamon	½	cup golden raisins
¼	cup smooth peanut butter, at room temperature		

1. Preheat the oven to 350°. Coat a 9" × 5" loaf pan with no-stick spray.

2. In a large bowl, combine the flour, sugar, baking powder and cinnamon.

3. In a medium bowl, whisk together the peanut butter, oil and vanilla until smooth. Stir in the milk. Pour over the flour mixture. Stir until just combined. Gently stir in the raisins.

4. Spoon the batter into the prepared pan. Bake for 50 minutes to 1 hour, or until a cake tester inserted in the center comes out clean.

5. Cool in the pan for 10 minutes. Unmold onto a wire rack to cool.

red and yellow pepper omelets

These whites-only omelets are a good way to cut unwanted cholesterol from your breakfasts. You can easily double this recipe to serve four. I like to accompany this dish with salsa and toasted English muffins.

Preparation time: 5 minutes
Cooking time: 10 minutes
Makes 2 servings.
Per serving: 85 calories, 3 g. fat (32% of calories), 1.2 g. dietary fiber, 2 mg. cholesterol, 151 mg. sodium.

1	teaspoon olive oil	½	teaspoon dried basil
1	sweet red pepper, thinly sliced	¼	teaspoon freshly ground black pepper
1	yellow pepper, thinly sliced	2	teaspoons grated Parmesan cheese, divided
4	egg whites		

1. In a large no-stick frying pan over medium heat, warm the oil. Add the red peppers and yellow peppers; cook, stirring frequently, for 4 to 5 minutes, or until just tender. Keep warm over low heat.

2. In a small bowl, lightly whisk together the egg whites, basil and black pepper.

3. Coat a small no-stick frying pan with no-stick spray. Warm over medium-high heat for 1 minute. Add half of the egg mixture, swirling the pan to evenly coat the bottom. Cook for 30 seconds or until the eggs are set. Carefully loosen and flip; cook for 1 minute, or until firm.

4. Sprinkle half of the peppers over the eggs. Fold to enclose the filling. Transfer to a plate. Sprinkle with 1 teaspoon of the Parmesan.

5. Repeat with the remaining egg mixture, peppers and 1 teaspoon Parmesan.

vidalia onion omelets

Vidalia onions are a sweet variety grown in Georgia. They appear in grocery stores in the spring. If they are unavailable, substitute another type of sweet onion.

Preparation time: 10 minutes
Cooking time: 20 minutes
Makes 4 servings.
Per serving: 106 calories, 3.4 g. fat (29% of calories), 1 g. dietary fiber, 8 mg. cholesterol, 122 mg. sodium.

1 teaspoon olive oil	½ teaspoon dried marjoram
1 medium Vidalia or other sweet onion, diced	¼ teaspoon freshly ground black pepper
1 cup chopped zucchini	2 tablespoons minced fresh flat-leaf parsley
4 egg whites	
1 cup egg substitute	4 tablespoons shredded Fontina cheese, divided
¼ cup skim milk	

1. In a medium no-stick frying pan over medium heat, warm the oil. Add the onions and zucchini; cook, stirring frequently, for 4 to 5 minutes, or until tender. Transfer to a small bowl and set aside. Do not wash the pan.

2. In a medium bowl, whisk together the egg whites, egg substitute, milk, marjoram and pepper. Stir in the parsley.

3. Coat the pan with no-stick spray. Place over medium heat for 2 minutes. Add one-quarter of the egg mixture and swirl the pan to coat the bottom. As soon as the bottom of the omelet is set, lift the edges with a small spatula and tilt the pan to let the uncooked egg run underneath. Cook for 30 seconds longer.

4. Sprinkle one-quarter of the vegetables and 1 tablespoon of the Fontina over the eggs. Fold to enclose the filling. Transfer to a plate.

5. Wipe out the pan with a paper towel. Coat with more no-stick spray. Make 3 more omelets, using the remaining egg mixture, vegetables and 3 tablespoons Fontina.

red pepper frittata

A frittata is an open-faced Italian omelet. It's great to serve for brunch or even a light dinner. This egg white version is full of flavor. If your friends are like mine, they won't miss the egg yolks (or the cholesterol in them).

Preparation time: 10 minutes
Cooking time: 10 minutes
Broiling time: 2 minutes
Makes 4 servings.
Per serving: 77 calories, 2.8 g. fat (33% of calories), 0.8 g. dietary fiber, 1 mg. cholesterol, 153 mg. sodium.

2 teaspoons olive oil, divided	2 tablespoons chopped fresh flat-leaf parsley
½ cup chopped sweet red peppers	½ teaspoon dried oregano
½ cup chopped celery	⅛ teaspoon freshly ground black pepper
½ cup chopped onions	1 tablespoon grated Parmesan cheese
2 garlic cloves, minced	
8 egg whites	

1. In a large ovenproof frying pan over medium heat, warm 1 teaspoon of the oil. Add the red peppers, celery, onions and garlic; cook, stirring frequently, for 4 to 5 minutes, or until tender. Remove from the heat and set aside.

2. In a large bowl, lightly whisk together the egg whites, parsley, oregano and black pepper. Stir in the vegetable mixture.

3. In the same frying pan over medium heat, warm the remaining 1 teaspoon oil. Add the egg mixture and cook until it begins to brown around the edges. Cover the pan and reduce the heat to low. Cook for 3 to 4 minutes longer, or until the eggs are set.

4. Meanwhile, preheat the broiler. Sprinkle the frittata with the Parmesan. Place the pan about 5" from the heat and broil for 1 to 2 minutes, or until golden brown. Serve cut into wedges.

potato and tofu scramble

I call this a scramble even though it's got no eggs. Although the mixture can stand on its own as a breakfast dish, I have also used it as an omelet filling.

Preparation time: 10 minutes
Cooking time: 12 minutes
Makes 4 servings.
Per serving: 222 calories, 6.9 g. fat (28% of calories), 1.1 g. dietary fiber, 0 mg. cholesterol, 95 mg. sodium.

1 teaspoon peanut oil	8 ounces firm tofu, well drained and squeezed dry between paper towels
1½ cups diced cooked potatoes	
1 cup chopped sweet red peppers	1 teaspoon low-sodium soy sauce
½ cup chopped scallions	½ teaspoon turmeric
2 garlic cloves, minced	¼ teaspoon powdered ginger
⅛ teaspoon freshly ground black pepper	¼ cup salsa

1. In a large no-stick frying pan over medium heat, warm the oil. Add the potatoes, red peppers, scallions, garlic and black pepper. Cook, stirring frequently, for 4 to 5 minutes, or until the potatoes are golden.

2. Cut the tofu into cubes; add to the pan. Add the soy sauce, turmeric and ginger; cook, carefully turning the mixture with a spatula, for 4 to 5 minutes, or until the tofu is golden. Add the salsa; cook for 1 minute to blend the flavors.

scrambled eggs and greens

Fennel is a strong herb, but it really gives a flavor boost to this egg dish. If fennel is not one of your favorites, use basil or oregano. You may also replace the spinach and collards with watercress.

Preparation time: 10 minutes
Cooking time: 15 minutes
Makes 4 servings.
Per serving: 119 calories, 3.7 g. fat (27% of calories), 1 g. dietary fiber, 6 mg. cholesterol, 141 mg. sodium.

½	cup chopped red onions	1	teaspoon Dijon mustard
2	garlic cloves, minced	¼	teaspoon fennel seeds, crushed
1	cup coarsely chopped spinach	⅛	teaspoon freshly ground black pepper
1	cup coarsely chopped collard greens	1	teaspoon canola oil
3	tablespoons water, divided	¼	cup shredded low-fat Monterey Jack cheese
2	cups egg substitute		

1. Coat a large no-stick frying pan with no-stick spray. Warm over medium heat for 1 minute. Add the onions and garlic. Cook, stirring frequently, for 2 to 3 minutes, or until tender. Add the spinach, collards and 1 tablespoon of the water. Cook, stirring frequently, for 5 minutes, or until the greens are wilted and the water has evaporated. Transfer to a bowl and set aside. Wipe out the pan.

2. In a medium bowl, whisk together the egg, mustard, fennel seeds, pepper and the remaining 2 tablespoons water.

3. Using the same pan, warm the oil over medium heat. Add the egg mixture; cook, stirring with a spatula, for 3 minutes, or until soft. Stir in the greens and Monterey Jack. Cook for 30 seconds, or until the cheese begins to melt and the eggs are firm.

south of the border scrambled eggs

This dish has a little more fat than what I usually serve for breakfast. But that's okay because it contains avocado, a fruit high in heart-healthy monounsaturated fat. I like to serve these eggs on toasted English muffins or stuffed into pitas.

Preparation time: 10 minutes
Cooking time: 10 minutes
Makes 4 servings.
Per serving: 179 calories, 11.7 g. fat (56% of calories), 2 g. dietary fiber, 7 mg. cholesterol, 72 mg. sodium.

1 small avocado	½ cup shredded low-fat Cheddar cheese
2 teaspoons lemon juice	¼ cup chopped tomatoes
1 cup egg substitute	2 tablespoons chopped fresh cilantro
½ cup skim milk	¼ teaspoon freshly ground black pepper
Pinch of ground red pepper	
1 tablespoon margarine	

1. Peel, seed and chop the avocado. Place in a small bowl, sprinkle with the lemon juice, and toss well to coat. Set aside.

2. In another small bowl, whisk together the egg, milk and red pepper.

3. In a large no-stick frying pan over medium heat, melt the margarine. Add the egg mixture; cook, stirring frequently, for 4 to 5 minutes, or until the eggs thicken but are not set.

4. Stir in the Cheddar; continue cooking and stirring until the eggs are no longer runny. Stir in the avocados and tomatoes; cook for 1 minute. Sprinkle with the cilantro and black pepper.

apple pancakes

The possibilities are endless when making pancakes. You can reserve them for a relaxing weekend brunch or serve them as a hearty weekday breakfast when you have a little extra time in the morning. I always serve these pancakes with maple syrup or fruit syrup.

Preparation time: 10 minutes
Cooking time: 20 minutes
Makes 4 servings.
Per serving: 273 calories, 7.5 g. fat (25% of calories), 1.7 g. dietary fiber, 1 mg. cholesterol, 208 mg. sodium.

1¼	cups unbleached flour	1	small apple, diced
2	teaspoons baking powder	1⅓	cups skim milk
½	teaspoon ground cinnamon	¼	cup egg substitute
⅛	teaspoon grated nutmeg	2	tablespoons canola oil
		1	tablespoon honey

1. In a large bowl, mix the flour, baking powder, cinnamon and nutmeg. Stir in the apples.

2. In a small bowl, mix the milk, egg, oil and honey. Pour over the flour mixture and mix well.

3. Coat a large no-stick frying pan or griddle with no-stick spray. Warm over medium heat for 2 minutes. Ladle in ¼ cup of the batter for each pancake, making a few at a time. Cook until the tops are bubbly and the pancakes are dry around the edges. Flip and cook for 2 to 3 minutes, or until golden on both sides. Place on a platter and keep warm.

4. Repeat until all the batter has been used; use more no-stick spray as needed.

breakfast fried rice

This sweet fried rice can be made savory by substituting scallions, garlic and peppers for the apricots, cinnamon and syrup.

MAKE AHEAD

Preparation time: 5 minutes
Cooking time: 10 minutes
Makes 4 servings.
Per serving: 251 calories, 6.5 g. fat (22% of calories), 1.6 g. dietary fiber, 0 mg. cholesterol, 44 mg. sodium.

1	tablespoon margarine	½	cup coarsely chopped dried apricots
2	cups cooked brown rice	¼	cup chopped walnuts
1	cup egg substitute	1	tablespoon maple syrup
2	tablespoons skim milk		
½	teaspoon ground cinnamon		

1. In a wok or large no-stick frying pan over medium heat, melt the margarine. Add the rice; cook, stirring constantly, for 3 to 4 minutes, or until lightly browned.

2. In a medium bowl, whisk together the egg, milk and cinnamon. Stir in the apricots and walnuts. Add to the pan. Cook, stirring constantly, for 2 to 3 minutes, or until the mixture is set and golden. Drizzle with the maple syrup. Serve warm or chilled.

rosemary hash browns

Hash browns are my absolute favorite. This recipe is similar to one that my grandmother used to make in her treasured cast-iron pan.

2	baking potatoes, shredded and patted dry	½	teaspoon dried thyme
1	onion, shredded	1	tablespoon olive oil
1	teaspoon dried rosemary, crushed	¼	cup skim milk
		¼	teaspoon freshly ground black pepper

Preparation time: 10 minutes
Cooking time: 30 minutes

Makes 4 servings.
Per serving: 143 calories, 3.6 g. fat (23% of calories), 1.6 g. dietary fiber, 0 mg. cholesterol, 14 mg. sodium.

1. In a medium bowl, toss together the potatoes, onions, rosemary and thyme.

2. In a large no-stick frying pan over medium heat, warm the oil. Add the potato mixture. Press down firmly with a spatula to make a uniform layer. Cook for 10 to 20 minutes, or until the bottom and edges are browned.

3. Using the spatula, cut the potatoes into quarters. Carefully flip each quarter. Pour the milk evenly over the potatoes; sprinkle with the pepper.

4. Cook for 8 to 10 minutes longer, or until the potatoes are crisp and browned on the bottom.

oat and fruit pudding

Here's a different twist on oatmeal that I use when I'm in a hurry. Feel free to add any seasonal fruit to the mixture.

Preparation time: 10 minutes
Cooking time: 5 minutes

Makes 4 servings.
Per serving: 234 calories, 2.4 g. fat (9% of calories), 5.4 g. dietary fiber, 1 mg. cholesterol, 49 mg. sodium.

1 cup water	½	cup cinnamon-flavored applesauce
½ cup apple juice	½	cup nonfat yogurt
¾ cup quick-cooking rolled oats	1	banana, thinly sliced
¼ cup nonfat dry milk powder	½	teaspoon ground cinnamon
¼ cup raisins	⅛	teaspoon grated nutmeg
2 teaspoons vanilla		

1. In a 2-quart saucepan, combine the water, juice, oats, milk powder, raisins and vanilla. Bring to a boil over medium heat. Reduce the heat to low and cook, stirring, for 1 minute.

2. Remove from the heat. Stir in the applesauce, yogurt, bananas, cinnamon and nutmeg. Return to the heat and cook for 1 minute.

the weekday cook

These are the recipes to turn to when you need super-quick weekday dinners for your family. All the entrées in this chapter can be ready—start to finish—in 45 minutes or less.

The key to fast dinner preparation is organization—and a well-stocked pantry. Items such as canned beans, stock, canned tomatoes, sun-dried tomatoes and dried herbs should always be on hand. So should different shapes and sizes of pasta, quick-cooking legumes such as lentils, tofu (look for the packages that don't need refrigeration) and quick-cooking rice and other grains. Frozen vegetables and long-keeping fresh varieties, such as onions, celery, carrots and potatoes, are also a must.

To tell the truth, I created many of the recipes in this section on the spur of the moment out of ingredients I had on hand. You can turn these dishes into complete meals by adding a steamed vegetable, bread and maybe a tossed salad.

creamy walnut-stuffed zucchini

I often serve these stuffed zucchini with nonfat sour cream. If you want to save time, make them ahead and reheat them in the microwave.

MAKE AHEAD

Preparation time: 10 minutes
Cooking time: 5 minutes
Baking time: 25 minutes

Makes 4 servings.
Per serving: 215 calories, 6.7 g. fat (27% of calories), 6.9 g. dietary fiber, 7 mg. cholesterol, 329 mg. sodium.

4 large zucchini	¼ cup shredded low-fat Cheddar cheese
2 teaspoons canola oil	¼ cup seasoned dry bread crumbs
1 cup shredded carrots	
½ cup chopped scallions	
¼ cup finely chopped walnuts	1 teaspoon low-sodium Worcestershire sauce
1 cup nonfat cottage cheese	½ teaspoon dried basil
½ cup egg substitute	

1. Slice the zucchini in half lengthwise. Scoop out the pulp, leaving ¼" shells; set aside. Coarsely chop the pulp.

2. Preheat the oven to 375°. Coat a 9" × 13" baking dish with no-stick spray.

3. In a large no-stick frying pan over medium-high heat, warm the oil. Add the carrots and chopped zucchini; cook, stirring frequently, for 2 minutes. Add the scallions and walnuts; cook for 2 minutes longer. Set aside.

4. In a large bowl, mix the cottage cheese, egg, Cheddar, bread crumbs, Worcestershire sauce and basil. Stir in the zucchini mixture.

5. Evenly divide the mixture among the zucchini shells. Place in the prepared baking dish. Bake for 20 to 25 minutes, or until heated through and bubbly.

bean sprout pancake with stir-fried vegetables

This pancake reminds me of the very thin ones served as appetizers in Chinese restaurants.

Preparation time: 10 minutes
Cooking time: 15 minutes
Makes 4 servings.
Per serving: 81 calories, 2.6 g. fat (27% of calories), 1.7 g. dietary fiber, 0 mg. cholesterol, 234 mg. sodium.

1 cup egg substitute	2 teaspoons peanut oil, divided
1/4 teaspoon ground coriander	1 cup snow peas
1/4 teaspoon freshly ground black pepper	1 cup sweet red pepper strips
1 cup drained canned or fresh bean sprouts	1 cup thinly sliced mushrooms
2 tablespoons minced scallions	1 tablespoon low-sodium soy sauce
1 teaspoon minced fresh ginger	2 garlic cloves, minced

1. In a medium bowl, whisk together the egg, coriander and black pepper. Stir in the sprouts, scallions and ginger; set aside.

2. In a large no-stick frying pan over medium-high heat, warm 1 teaspoon of the oil. Add the snow peas, red peppers, mushrooms, soy sauce and garlic. Cook, stirring frequently, for 4 to 5 minutes, or until the vegetables are tender. Remove from the pan and set aside. Wipe out the pan with a paper towel.

3. Preheat the broiler.

4. Add the remaining 1 teaspoon oil to the frying pan and warm over medium heat. Add the egg mixture. Swirl the pan to coat the bottom evenly. Cook for 4 to 5 minutes, or until the bottom is golden and the top is almost set.

5. Sprinkle the top of the pancake with the vegetable mixture. Broil about 5" from the heat for 2 minutes, or until the egg is completely set. Cut into wedges to serve.

ginger couscous primavera

I like to make this a day ahead and serve it cold. All sorts of unusual dried fruits are available these days. Try substituting different varieties, such as cranberries, blueberries or chopped strawberries, for the cherries.

MAKE AHEAD

Preparation time: 10 minutes
Cooking time: 10 minutes
Makes 4 servings.
Per serving: 297 calories, 4.7 g. fat (14% of calories), 11.1 g. dietary fiber, 0 mg. cholesterol, 84 mg. sodium.

3 teaspoons olive oil, divided	1 medium yellow squash, thinly sliced
1 medium Vidalia or other sweet onion, thinly sliced crosswise and separated into rings	2 tablespoons minced fresh ginger
1 sweet red pepper, cut into thin strips	1½ teaspoons low-sodium soy sauce
1 yellow pepper, cut into thin strips	1¼ cups water
	½ cup chopped dried cherries
1 medium zucchini, thinly sliced	2 tablespoons lemon juice
	1 cup couscous

1. In a large no-stick frying pan over medium-high heat, warm 2 teaspoons of the oil. Add the onions; cook, stirring frequently, for 2 minutes. Add the red peppers, yellow peppers, zucchini, squash, ginger and soy sauce; cook, stirring frequently, for 6 to 7 minutes, or until the vegetables are just tender.

2. Meanwhile, in a 2-quart saucepan over medium-high heat, bring the water, cherries and lemon juice to a boil. Stir in the couscous and the remaining 1 teaspoon oil. Remove from the heat. Cover and let stand for 5 minutes, or until the couscous is soft.

3. Fluff the couscous with a fork and place in a large bowl. Add the vegetables and toss well.

vegetable fajitas with papaya salsa

I discovered an easy way to warm and soften tortillas before filling them—I microwave them. This papaya salsa is an interesting change from regular salsa. It's also delicious served over baked sweet potatoes.

Preparation time: 15 minutes
Cooking time: 20 minutes
Makes 4 servings.
Per serving: 330 calories, 7.8 g. fat (20% of calories), 6.8 g. dietary fiber, 5 mg. cholesterol, 256 mg. sodium.

Papaya Salsa
1   ripe papaya, diced
½   cup drained canned crushed pineapple
¼   cup chopped scallions
2   tablespoons chopped fresh cilantro
1   tablespoon lime juice
1   teaspoon honey
1   teaspoon chopped canned green chili peppers (wear plastic gloves when handling)

Fajitas
1   tablespoon canola oil
1   cup chopped scallions
1   cup thinly sliced carrots
8   ounces red potatoes, cubed
1   green pepper, cut into thin strips
2   garlic cloves, minced
¼   cup low-sodium vegetable stock
¼   cup tomato sauce
2   tablespoons chopped fresh cilantro
8   large corn or flour tortillas
½   cup shredded low-fat Cheddar cheese
¼   cup nonfat sour cream

1. To make the papaya salsa: In a medium bowl, combine the papaya, pineapple, scallions, cilantro, lime juice, honey and peppers. Mix well and set aside.

2. To make the fajitas: In a large no-stick frying pan over medium-high heat, warm the oil. Add the scallions, carrots, potatoes, peppers and garlic. Cook, stirring frequently, for 4 to 5 minutes, or until tender. Add the stock, tomato sauce and cilantro; bring to a boil.

3. Reduce the heat to low. Simmer, stirring frequently, for 8 to 10 minutes, or until the vegetables are tender and the liquid has evaporated.

4. Wrap the tortillas in a paper towel and microwave on

high for 40 seconds, or until warm and pliable. (Or wrap in foil and bake at 350° for 5 minutes.)

5. To assemble the fajitas, divide the vegetable mixture evenly among the tortillas. Top each with the salsa, Cheddar and sour cream. Fold in the sides of each tortilla and roll it up to enclose the filling.

mashed potato gratin

I like to make this dish whenever I have leftover mashed potatoes. Sometimes I even purposely make extra so I can have this gratin. Here I top the potatoes with spinach and tomatoes, but you can use virtually any vegetables.

MAKE AHEAD

Preparation time: 10 minutes
Baking time: 25 minutes

Makes 4 servings.
Per serving: 218 calories, 3 g. fat (12% of calories), 6.9 g. dietary fiber, 5 mg. cholesterol, 484 mg. sodium.

2 cups mashed potatoes	1 teaspoon prepared horseradish
1 cup canned cannellini beans, rinsed and drained	2 cups thawed frozen chopped spinach, squeezed dry
1 cup nonfat cottage cheese	1 medium tomato, thinly sliced
3 ounces feta cheese, crumbled	
1 teaspoon coarse Dijon mustard	

1. Preheat the oven to 400°. Coat a 2-quart casserole with no-stick spray; set aside.

2. In a food processor, combine the potatoes, beans, cottage cheese, feta, mustard and horseradish; process until well mixed. Spoon into the prepared casserole.

3. Evenly spread the spinach over the potato mixture. Top with the tomatoes. Bake for 15 to 20 minutes, or until heated through.

spaghetti niçoise

Potatoes and pasta are two of my favorite foods. Together they make a great weeknight dish, full of flavor. I named this *spaghetti niçoise* because it contains so many of the foods popular in the cooking of Nice: olive oil, tomatoes, olives, garlic, pesto and potatoes.

Preparation time: 10 minutes
Cooking time: 25 minutes
Makes 4 servings.
Per serving: 551 calories, 12.7 g. fat (20% of calories), 0.9 g. dietary fiber, 4 mg. cholesterol, 348 mg. sodium.

14 sun-dried tomatoes	¼ cup chopped fresh flat-leaf parsley
1 cup boiling water	
3 teaspoons olive oil, divided	20 kalamata olives, pitted and coarsely chopped
4 medium red potatoes, chopped	4 garlic cloves, minced
½ cup chopped scallions	¾ cup low-sodium vegetable stock
¼ teaspoon freshly ground black pepper	12 ounces whole wheat spaghetti
¼ cup prepared pesto sauce	

1. In a small bowl, combine the tomatoes and water. Let stand for 2 minutes. Drain and chop the tomatoes. Set aside.

2. In a large no-stick frying pan over medium-high heat, warm 2 teaspoons of the oil. Add the potatoes, scallions and pepper; cook, stirring frequently, for 8 to 10 minutes, or until the potatoes are just tender.

3. Stir in the pesto, parsley, olives, garlic and tomatoes. Add the stock. Reduce the heat to low. Simmer, stirring frequently, for 10 to 15 minutes, or until the potatoes are tender.

4. Meanwhile, in a large pot of boiling water, cook the spaghetti for 8 to 10 minutes, or until just tender. Drain and place in large serving bowl. Toss with the remaining 1 teaspoon oil. Add the potato mixture. Toss to mix well.

chick-peas and brown rice

Quick-cooking brown rice is a real time-saver for weeknight dinners. And I love the nutty flavor it gives to dishes like this. If you don't have chick-peas on hand, substitute any other type of canned beans.

Preparation time: 10 minutes
Cooking time: 25 minutes
Makes 4 servings.
Per serving: 461 calories, 6.1 g. fat (12% of calories), 7.6 g. dietary fiber, 0 mg. cholesterol, 553 mg. sodium.

1½ cups water	2 cups canned chick-peas, rinsed and drained
2 cups quick-cooking brown rice	2 tablespoons red wine vinegar
1 tablespoon olive oil	½ teaspoon dried rosemary, crushed
½ cup chopped red onions	½ teaspoon dried thyme
2 garlic cloves, minced	1 cup canned black beans, rinsed and drained
1 sweet red pepper, cut into strips	2 tablespoons chopped fresh flat-leaf parsley
1 green pepper, cut into strips	
2 cups chopped tomatoes	

1. In a 2-quart saucepan over medium-high heat, bring the water to a boil. Add the rice. Cover, reduce the heat to medium-low, and simmer for 5 minutes. Remove from the heat and let stand for 5 minutes, or until all the liquid has been absorbed. Fluff with a fork and keep warm.

2. Meanwhile, in a large no-stick frying pan over medium-high heat, warm the oil. Add the onions and garlic; cook, stirring frequently, for 2 minutes, or until tender. Add the red peppers and green peppers; cook for 2 minutes.

3. Stir in the tomatoes, chick-peas, vinegar, rosemary and thyme. Reduce the heat to low and simmer for 8 to 10 minutes, or until the liquid released from the tomatoes is reduced slightly. Stir in the beans; cook for 2 minutes, or until heated through.

4. To serve, line a platter with the rice. Top with the chick-pea mixture. Sprinkle with the parsley.

cellophane noodle chow mein

Stir-fries are great for weeknight dinners. Be daring and try different combinations. I like to use up all my leftovers and make a completely different dish every time. Look for cellophane noodles, also called bean threads, in the Chinese section of your supermarket. They're very thin and white. When cooked, they turn translucent.

Preparation time: 10 minutes
Cooking time: 15 minutes
Makes 4 servings.
Per serving: 233 calories, 7.5 g. fat (28% of calories), 5.3 g. dietary fiber, 0 mg. cholesterol, 886 mg. sodium.

1 package (3½ ounces) cellophane noodles	1½ tablespoons low-sodium soy sauce
2 tablespoons peanut oil	2 teaspoons hoisin sauce
2 garlic cloves, minced	2 teaspoons finely chopped fresh ginger
1 cup diagonally sliced celery	1 teaspoon brown sugar or ½ teaspoon honey
1 cup snow peas	
1 cup chopped onions	1 cup baby corn, rinsed and cut in half lengthwise
1 cup quartered mushrooms	
½ cup sliced water chestnuts	2 tablespoons chopped fresh cilantro
¼ cup low-sodium vegetable stock	

1. In a medium pot of boiling water, cook the noodles for 5 minutes, or until translucent and tender; drain and rinse with cold water. Drain well and set aside.

2. Meanwhile, in a large no-stick frying pan or wok over medium-high heat, warm the oil. Add the garlic; stir-fry for 30 seconds. Add the celery, snow peas, onions, mushrooms and water chestnuts; stir-fry for 5 minutes. Add the noodles; stir-fry for 1 minute.

3. In a small bowl, combine the stock, soy sauce, hoisin sauce, ginger and sugar or honey. Add to the pan; stir-fry for 2 minutes. Add the corn and cilantro; stir-fry for 2 to 3 minutes, or until heated through.

pinto bean jambalaya

This dish is so full of flavor that you won't miss the shrimp and sausage found in traditional jambalaya. The best part of this updated version is the shorter cooking time—due in part to the use of bulgur instead of rice and the omission of a time-consuming flour and oil roux.

Preparation time: 15 minutes
Cooking time: 25 minutes
Makes 4 servings.
Per serving: 320 calories, 6.2 g. fat (16% of calories), 12.9 g. dietary fiber, 0 mg. cholesterol, 596 mg. sodium.

1 tablespoon canola oil	½ teaspoon dried thyme
1 cup chopped onions	¼ teaspoon ground red pepper
½ cup chopped celery	½ cup low-sodium vegetable stock, divided
½ cup chopped green peppers	1 can (19 ounces) pinto beans, rinsed and drained
2 garlic cloves, minced	1 cup drained canned corn
1 cup salsa	
1 cup tomato sauce	
1 cup bulgur	

1. In a large no-stick frying pan over medium-high heat, warm the oil. Add the onions, celery, green peppers and garlic; cook, stirring frequently, for 4 to 5 minutes, or until just tender.

2. Stir in the salsa, tomato sauce, bulgur, thyme, red pepper and ¼ cup of the stock. Bring to a boil. Reduce the heat to low; cover and simmer for 10 minutes.

3. Stir in the beans, corn and the remaining ¼ cup stock. Cover and simmer for 5 to 10 minutes longer, or until the bulgur is cooked.

cauliflower and raisin curry

If you want a little more protein in this dish, stir in some drained canned chick-peas. I often serve this curry with couscous, which cooks very quickly. But you could also spoon it over rice or toss it with pasta.

Preparation time: 15 minutes
Cooking time: 20 minutes
Makes 4 servings.
Per serving: 280 calories, 3.7 g. fat (11% of calories), 12.4 g. dietary fiber, 0 mg. cholesterol, 78 mg. sodium.

1	tablespoon margarine	1	sweet red pepper, thinly sliced
½	cup chopped onions	¾	cup water, divided
½	cup chopped celery	½	cup raisins
2	garlic cloves, minced	2	tablespoons unsweetened shredded coconut
1	teaspoon ground cumin	1	tablespoon honey
1	teaspoon ground cinnamon	2	teaspoons lemon juice
1	teaspoon turmeric	2	cups hot cooked couscous
½	teaspoon dry mustard		
⅛	teaspoon ground cloves		
1	medium head cauliflower, separated into small florets		

1. In a large no-stick frying pan over medium-high heat, melt the margarine. Add the onions, celery and garlic; cook, stirring frequently, for 2 minutes. Stir in the cumin, cinnamon, turmeric, mustard and cloves.

2. Add the cauliflower, peppers and ½ cup of the water. Cover and cook, stirring frequently, for 5 to 7 minutes, or until the vegetables are tender.

3. Stir in the raisins, coconut and the remaining ¼ cup water. Cook, stirring frequently, for 6 to 8 minutes, or until the raisins are plump but not mushy. Remove from the heat and stir in the honey and lemon juice.

4. Serve over the couscous.

sweet-and-sour tofu

Sweet and sour is a combination most often associated with Chinese cooking. In this dish, I keep the tofu firm and crisp by stir-frying it first and briefly reheating it toward the end of the cooking time.

Preparation time: 15 minutes
Cooking time: 20 minutes

Makes 4 servings.
Per serving: 360 calories, 12.9 g. fat (29% of calories), 5 g. dietary fiber, 0 mg. cholesterol, 312 mg. sodium.

12 ounces firm tofu, well drained and squeezed dry between paper towels	1 tablespoon rice wine vinegar
1 tablespoon peanut oil	1 tablespoon low-sodium teriyaki sauce
1 large head broccoli, separated into florets	1 tablespoon brown sugar or 1½ teaspoons honey
2 cups sliced yellow peppers	1 tablespoon cornstarch
2 garlic cloves, minced	1 tablespoon water
1 cup low-sodium vegetable stock	1½ cups drained canned pineapple chunks
¼ cup tomato paste	
2 tablespoons chopped fresh flat-leaf parsley	

1. Cut the tofu into 1" cubes.

2. In a large no-stick frying pan or wok over medium-high heat, warm the oil. Add the tofu. Cook, turning frequently, for 4 to 5 minutes, or until golden. Remove from the pan and set aside.

3. Add the broccoli, peppers and garlic to the pan. Stir-fry for 5 to 7 minutes, or until tender. Stir in the stock, tomato paste, parsley, vinegar, teriyaki sauce and sugar or honey.

4. In a cup, dissolve the cornstarch in the water. Add to the pan; stir well and bring to a boil. Reduce the heat to low. Stir in the tofu and pineapple; cook, stirring to coat evenly, for 5 minutes to blend the flavors.

creamy tomatillo soup

Tomatillos are green vegetables that look like small tomatoes covered with paper-thin husks. They're available at specialty stores and at some larger grocery stores. Remove the husks before using.

MAKE AHEAD

Preparation time: 10 minutes
Cooking time: 20 minutes
Makes 4 servings.
Per serving: 208 calories, 3.4 g. fat (14% of calories), 4.5 g. dietary fiber, 0 mg. cholesterol, 194 mg. sodium.

1 tablespoon margarine	3 cups thawed frozen corn, divided
1 cup chopped scallions	½ cup spicy vegetable-cocktail juice
3 tomatillos, quartered	
2 garlic cloves, minced	2 teaspoons brown sugar or 1 teaspoon honey
1½ cups low-sodium vegetable stock	1 teaspoon lemon juice
½ cup thawed frozen lima beans	Pinch of ground red pepper
¼ cup chopped fresh cilantro	

1. In a 3-quart saucepan over medium heat, melt the margarine. Add the scallions, tomatillos and garlic; cook, stirring frequently, for 4 minutes. Stir in the stock, beans, cilantro and 2 cups of the corn. Cook for 1 minute.

2. Working in batches, puree the mixture in a blender until smooth. Return the mixture to the pan. Stir in the vegetable juice, sugar or honey, lemon juice, pepper and the remaining 1 cup corn. Simmer for 10 to 15 minutes to blend the flavors.

refried-bean burritos

For variety, you may serve these burritos open-faced. You may also serve the beans over baked potatoes or rice.

1 can (15 ounces) red kidney beans, rinsed and drained	4 large flour tortillas
	1 cup shredded lettuce
	1 cup chopped tomatoes
½ teaspoon ground cumin	½ cup minced scallions
½ teaspoon chili powder	¼ cup salsa
½ teaspoon dried oregano	

Preparation time: 15 minutes
Cooking time: 5 minutes
Makes 4 servings.
Per serving: 210 calories, 2.8 g. fat (12% of calories), 7 g. dietary fiber, 0 mg. cholesterol, 411 mg. sodium.

1. In a food processor, combine the beans, cumin, chili powder and oregano; process until coarsely pureed. Transfer to a 1-quart saucepan. Place over medium heat and cook, stirring frequently, for 2 to 3 minutes, or until heated through and bubbly.

2. Heat a medium no-stick frying pan over medium heat. Warm 1 tortilla at a time for 30 seconds per side. (Do not heat them longer or they'll crack when rolled.)

3. Divide the bean mixture among the tortillas. Top with the lettuce, tomatoes, scallions and salsa.

4. Fold in the sides of each tortilla and roll up to enclose the filling.

spaghetti squash stir-fry

Sesame seeds and shredded coconut make an interesting topping for this stir-fry. This is one dish where some ahead-of-time prep work is needed to get dinner on the table fast—you'll want to precook the spaghetti squash and the lentils.

Preparation time: 20 minutes
Cooking time: 15 minutes
Makes 4 servings.
Per serving: 215 calories, 7.7 g. fat (30% of calories), 7.6 g. dietary fiber, 0 mg. cholesterol, 192 mg. sodium.

2 tablespoons sesame seeds	2½ cups flaked cooked spaghetti squash
2 tablespoons unsweetened shredded coconut	1½ cups cooked brown lentils
1 tablespoon sesame oil	2 garlic cloves, minced
3 cups shredded red cabbage	1 tablespoon low-sodium soy sauce
2 cups broccoli florets	½ teaspoon chili powder
1 cup chopped (1" pieces) scallions	¼ teaspoon ground cumin

1. In a small frying pan over medium heat, brown the sesame seeds and coconut, stirring constantly.

2. In a large no-stick frying pan or wok over medium heat, warm the oil. Add the cabbage, broccoli and scallions; stir-fry for 5 minutes. Add the squash, lentils, garlic, soy sauce, chili powder and cumin. Stir-fry for 5 to 7 minutes, or until the vegetables are just tender.

3. Sprinkle with the coconut mixture.

tofu burgers

I have found that chilling the tofu mixture for a short time makes forming the patties a little easier. If you just can't spare the time, flour your hands before forming the patties, so they don't stick.

Preparation time: 15 minutes
+ chilling time
Cooking time: 15 minutes
Makes 4 servings.
Per serving: 416 calories, 12.6 g. fat (27% of calories), 5.2 g. dietary fiber, 0 mg. cholesterol, 565 mg. sodium.

3 teaspoons sesame oil, divided
¼ cup chopped scallions
2 garlic cloves, minced
8 ounces firm tofu, well drained and squeezed dry between paper towels
1 cup cooked white rice
¼ cup oat bran
¼ cup whole wheat flour
½ cup egg substitute
2 tablespoons sesame seeds
2 teaspoons low-sodium soy sauce
½ teaspoon ground cumin
4 English muffins, split and toasted

1. In a small no-stick frying pan over medium-high heat, warm 1 teaspoon of the oil. Add the scallions and garlic; cook, stirring frequently, for 2 to 3 minutes, or until tender. Set aside.

2. In a large bowl, mash the tofu until smooth. Add the scallions, rice, oat bran, flour, egg, sesame seeds, soy sauce and cumin. Cover and refrigerate for 15 minutes.

3. Shape the mixture into 4 patties. In a large no-stick frying pan over medium heat, warm the remaining 2 teaspoons oil. Add the patties. Cook for 5 to 7 minutes on each side, or until golden. Serve on the English muffins.

middle eastern pilaf

I love the combination of cinnamon and cloves with fruit—flavors typical of Middle Eastern cuisines. For variety, you may use apricots or raisins instead of prunes.

Preparation time: 10 minutes
Cooking time: 30 minutes
Makes 4 servings.
Per serving: 521 calories, 9.3 g. fat (16% of calories), 6.1 g. dietary fiber, 0 mg. cholesterol, 179 mg. sodium.

5	teaspoons margarine, divided	¾	cup green split peas, rinsed and drained
½	cup chopped onions	2	cups low-sodium vegetable stock
½	cup shredded carrots		
½	teaspoon ground cinnamon	¼	cup orange juice
		1	bunch spinach
¼	teaspoon ground cardamom	2	garlic cloves, minced
		½	cup chopped prunes
⅛	teaspoon ground cloves	¼	cup chopped peanuts
1¼	cups basmati or other long-grain aromatic white rice	2	teaspoons lemon juice

1. In a 2-quart saucepan over medium heat, melt 3 teaspoons of the margarine. Add the onions, carrots, cinnamon, cardamom and cloves; cook, stirring frequently, for 2 minutes. Stir in the rice and split peas.

2. Add the stock and orange juice; bring to a boil. Reduce the heat to low. Cover and simmer for 20 to 25 minutes, or until the split peas are tender and the liquid has been absorbed.

3. Meanwhile, wash the spinach in cold water to remove any grit. Shake off the leaves, but don't dry them.

4. About 5 minutes before the rice is scheduled to be finished cooking, melt the remaining 2 teaspoons margarine in a large frying pan over medium heat. Add the garlic; cook, stirring constantly, for 2 minutes. Add the spinach; cook for 1 to 2 minutes, or until wilted. Spoon onto a serving platter.

5. Remove the rice from the heat and stir in the prunes, peanuts and lemon juice. Fluff the mixture with a fork and spoon over the spinach.

fusilli with creamy walnut sauce

12	ounces long fusilli	1½	teaspoons lemon juice
12	sun-dried tomatoes	2	tablespoons chopped
1	cup boiling water		fresh flat-leaf parsley
1	cup nonfat ricotta cheese	2	garlic cloves, minced
¾	cup skim milk	¼	teaspoon freshly ground
⅓	cup walnuts, lightly toasted		black pepper
1	tablespoon coarse Dijon mustard		

Make sure to toast the walnuts—it really brings out their flavor. If you don't have any sun-dried tomatoes, you may substitute chopped tomatoes.

Preparation time: 10 minutes
Cooking time: 10 minutes
Makes 4 servings.
Per serving: 567 calories, 18.7 g. fat (29% of calories), 2.7 g. dietary fiber, 20 mg. cholesterol, 119 mg. sodium.

1. In a large pot of boiling water, cook the fusilli for 8 to 10 minutes, or until just tender. Scoop out ¼ cup of the cooking liquid and set it aside. Drain the pasta and place in a large serving bowl.

2. Meanwhile, in a small bowl, combine the tomatoes and water. Let stand for 2 minutes. Drain and chop. Set aside.

3. In a food processor, combine the ricotta, milk, walnuts, mustard and lemon juice. Process until the nuts are well chopped. Spoon over the pasta. Add the parsley, garlic, pepper, tomatoes and the reserved cooking liquid. Toss well.

vegetarian vegetable kabobs

You may also grill these kabobs rather than broil them.

Preparation time: 15 minutes
Cooking time: 15 minutes
Makes 4 servings.
Per serving: 462 calories, 15.5 g. fat (29% of calories), 6.6 g. dietary fiber, 0 mg. cholesterol, 314 mg. sodium.

1 tablespoon olive oil	3 tablespoons nonfat mayonnaise
1 pound firm tofu, well drained and squeezed dry between paper towels	2 tablespoons nonfat yogurt
2 cups small mushrooms	2 tablespoons fat-free Italian dressing
1 pint cherry tomatoes	1 tablespoon Dijon mustard
2 green peppers, cut into 1" pieces	1 teaspoon prepared horseradish

1. In a large no-stick frying pan over medium heat, warm the oil. Add the block of tofu; cook, turning the piece often, for 5 to 7 minutes, or until browned on all sides. Set aside until cool enough to handle. Cut into 8 cubes.

2. Place the tofu in a large bowl. Add the mushrooms, tomatoes and peppers.

3. In a small bowl, stir together the mayonnaise, yogurt, dressing, mustard and horseradish. Pour over the tofu mixture; toss to mix well.

4. Preheat the broiler.

5. Divide the tofu and vegetables evenly among 8 metal skewers; brush with any remaining marinade. Place on a broiler rack. Broil about 5" from the heat for about 6 minutes. Turn the kabobs and broil for another 6 minutes, or until the vegetables are tender but the tomatoes have not collapsed.

chilaquiles

Chilaquiles is a Mexican entrée that's somewhat like lasagna. You'll need only three tortillas for this. To store the remainder of the package, tightly seal them in a plastic bag and place in the refrigerator or freezer.

Preparation time: 10 minutes
Cooking time: 10 minutes
Baking time: 20 minutes

Makes 4 servings.
Per serving: 322 calories, 10.4 g. fat (28% of calories), 8.1 g. dietary fiber, 14 mg. cholesterol, 443 mg. sodium.

1 tablespoon canola oil	2 tablespoons chopped canned green chili peppers (wear plastic gloves when handling)
1 cup chopped onions	
2 garlic cloves, minced	
2 cups shredded carrots	½ teaspoon chili powder
1 can (16 ounces) red kidney beans, rinsed and drained	3 large flour tortillas
	1 cup shredded low-fat Cheddar cheese
1 large tomato, chopped	
½ cup tomato sauce	2 tablespoons minced scallions

1. Preheat the oven to 400°. Coat an 8" soufflé dish or a 2-quart casserole with no-stick spray; set aside.

2. In a large no-stick frying pan over medium-high heat, warm the oil. Add the onions and garlic; cook, stirring frequently, for 2 to 3 minutes, or until tender. Add the carrots; cook for 2 minutes.

3. Stir in the beans, tomatoes, tomato sauce, peppers and chili powder; bring to a boil. Cook for 5 minutes, or until slightly thick. Scoop out ¼ cup and set aside.

4. Place 1 tortilla in the bottom of the prepared dish. Top with half of the vegetable mixture and ⅓ cup of the Cheddar.

5. Add another tortilla, the remaining vegetables and ⅓ cup of the remaining Cheddar. Top with the final tortilla and the reserved vegetables. Sprinkle with the scallions and the remaining ⅓ cup Cheddar.

6. Bake for 15 to 20 minutes, or until heated through. Let stand for 5 minutes before cutting into wedges.

balsamic lentils and potatoes

Balsamic vinegar really adds zip to the lentils and potatoes. I like to serve this homey dish in the autumn, when the weather suddenly turns cold.

Preparation time: 10 minutes
Cooking time: 25 minutes
Makes 4 servings.
Per serving: 320 calories, 4.2 g. fat (11% of calories), 8.7 g. dietary fiber, 0 mg. cholesterol, 32 mg. sodium.

4 cups water	1 tablespoon olive oil
1¼ cups red lentils, rinsed and drained	1 cup chopped scallions
	1 cup shredded carrots
2 medium baking potatoes, cubed	1 cup shredded zucchini
	2 garlic cloves, minced
1 teaspoon dried tarragon	2 tablespoons balsamic vinegar
¼ teaspoon freshly ground black pepper	

1. In a 3-quart saucepan, combine the water, lentils, potatoes, tarragon and pepper; bring to a boil. Cover and simmer for 15 to 20 minutes, or until the potatoes are just tender. Drain off any excess water.

2. Meanwhile, in a large no-stick frying pan over medium heat, warm the oil. Add the scallions, carrots, zucchini and garlic. Cook, stirring frequently, for 8 to 10 minutes, or until the carrots are tender. Reduce the heat to very low.

3. Add the lentil mixture to the frying pan. Sprinkle with the vinegar and stir to mix well. Increase the heat slightly and cook for 2 minutes longer to blend the flavors.

artichoke and herb pizza

Pizza is one of my favorite foods. Using premade pizza dough lets you have the take-out classic in your own kitchen in less time than it would take to have a pizza delivered. And you get to control both the toppings and the fat content. I particularly enjoy this artichoke version.

Preparation time: 15 minutes
Baking time: 20 minutes
Makes 4 servings.
Per serving: 305 calories, 12.5 g. fat (28% of calories), 2.4 g. dietary fiber, 2 mg. cholesterol, 683 mg. sodium.

2 tablespoons cornmeal	½ cup chopped roasted sweet red peppers
1 tube (10 ounces) refrigerated pizza dough	4 ounces feta cheese, crumbled
1 tablespoon olive oil	2 tablespoons grated Parmesan cheese
1 teaspoon dried oregano	¼ teaspoon freshly ground black pepper
½ teaspoon dried rosemary, crushed	
1 box (9 ounces) frozen artichoke hearts, thawed	
1 cup thawed frozen chopped broccoli	

1. Preheat the oven to 425°.

2. Sprinkle the bottom of a 12" pizza pan with the cornmeal. Unroll the dough and press it evenly into the pan. Brush with the oil and sprinkle with the oregano and rosemary. Bake the dough for 6 to 8 minutes, or until the dough just begins to brown. Remove from the oven.

3. Sprinkle the dough evenly with the artichokes, broccoli, red peppers, feta, Parmesan and black pepper.

4. Bake for 10 to 12 minutes, or until the crust is golden and the vegetables are heated through. Let stand for 5 minutes before cutting.

vegetable toast

Chinese shrimp toast is one of my all-time favorites. Unfortunately, it's usually high in fat because it's deep-fried. This version gives somewhat the same taste but without all the fat. I often serve it as a super-quick dinner.

Preparation time: 10 minutes
Cooking time: 15 minutes
Makes 4 servings.
Per serving: 228 calories, 7.6 g. fat (30% of calories), 4 g. dietary fiber, 0 mg. cholesterol, 398 mg. sodium.

1 egg white	4 medium mushrooms, quartered
2 tablespoons minced scallions	1 large carrot, cut into 1" pieces
2 garlic cloves, minced	¼ cup chopped fresh cilantro
2 teaspoons cornstarch	8 slices rye bread, cut in half to form triangles
1 teaspoon hoisin sauce	
½ teaspoon honey	1½ tablespoons peanut oil, divided
¼ teaspoon powdered ginger	
Pinch of freshly ground black pepper	
1 can (5 ounces) sliced water chestnuts, drained	

1. In a small bowl, mix the egg white, scallions, garlic, cornstarch, hoisin sauce, honey, ginger and pepper.

2. In a food processor, combine the water chestnuts, mushrooms, carrots and cilantro. Process with on/off turns to chop finely. Add the egg white mixture; process until the mixture forms a paste.

3. Spread 1 side of each bread piece with about 1 tablespoon of the paste.

4. In a large no-stick frying pan over medium heat, warm 1 tablespoon of the oil. Add as many bread pieces, vegetable side down, to the pan as will fit in a single layer. Sauté for 2 to 3 minutes, or until golden. Carefully spread the top of each bread piece with another 1 tablespoon each of the paste. Flip the pieces and sauté for 2 to 3 minutes longer.

5. Repeat to use all the remaining bread and paste; add the remaining ½ tablespoon oil to the pan as needed.

ratatouille

You can serve this classic dish many ways—hot or cold, spread on crusty Italian bread, tossed with pasta or spooned over rice.

MAKE
AHEAD

Preparation time: 10 minutes
Cooking time: 30 minutes
Makes 4 servings.
Per serving: 118 calories, 4.1 g. fat (28% of calories), 5.6 g. dietary fiber, 0 mg. cholesterol, 110 mg. sodium.

1 tablespoon olive oil	2 tablespoons tomato paste
1 cup chopped red onions	2 tablespoons capers, rinsed and drained
4 garlic cloves, minced	
1 medium eggplant, cubed	2 tablespoons chopped fresh basil or 1 teaspoon dried
2 large zucchini, cut into ½" pieces	
	½ teaspoon dried rosemary, crushed
1 green pepper, cut into ½" pieces	
	½ teaspoon dried oregano
2 large tomatoes, chopped	

1. In a large no-stick frying pan over medium heat, warm the oil. Add the onions and garlic; cook, stirring frequently, for 2 minutes. Add the eggplant, zucchini and peppers; cook, stirring frequently, for 5 minutes.

2. Stir in the tomatoes, tomato paste, capers, basil, rosemary and oregano. Reduce the heat to low. Simmer for 15 to 20 minutes, stirring occasionally, until the vegetables are tender and the liquid thickens slightly.

tempeh-stuffed pitas

Sandwiches are a great time-saver for midweek meals. This version uses tempeh, a fermented soybean food that's pressed into flat cakes.

Preparation time: 10 minutes
Cooking time: 10 minutes

Makes 4 servings.
Per serving: 322 calories, 9.1 g. fat (25% of calories), 2.6 g. dietary fiber, <1 mg. cholesterol, 451 mg. sodium.

¼ cup nonfat yogurt
2 tablespoons chili sauce
1 teaspoon prepared horse-radish
½ teaspoon sesame oil
2 teaspoons peanut oil
1 tablespoon minced fresh ginger
10 ounces tempeh, cut into 8 thin slices

1½ cups snow peas
2 teaspoons low-sodium soy sauce
4 large pita breads, halved and split open
1 cup shredded red leaf lettuce
1 cup chopped tomatoes

1. In a small bowl, combine the yogurt, chili sauce, horse-radish and sesame oil; set aside.

2. In a large no-stick frying pan over medium-high heat, warm the peanut oil. Add the ginger; cook, stirring frequently, for 1 minute. Add the tempeh and snow peas. Sprinkle with the soy sauce. Stir-fry for 4 to 5 minutes, or until the tempeh is golden on both sides and the snow peas are just tender.

3. Divide the tempeh mixture among the pita halves. Top with the lettuce, tomatoes and yogurt mixture.

moo shu vegetables

You may use either fresh or canned bean sprouts for this dish. Be sure to dry them well, so you don't dilute the vegetable mixture. If dried mushrooms are hard to find, use some additional fresh mushrooms. I usually serve these vegetables over brown rice.

Preparation time: 15 minutes
Cooking time: 15 minutes
Makes 4 servings.
Per serving: 110 calories, 2.7 g. fat (20% of calories), 3.1 g. dietary fiber, 0 mg. cholesterol, 248 mg. sodium.

1 cup boiling water	1 tablespoon low-sodium soy sauce
½ ounce dried mushrooms	
1 cup egg substitute	1 tablespoon chopped fresh ginger
2 teaspoons sesame oil, divided	
¼ cup low-sodium vegetable stock	2 garlic cloves, minced
	1 cup julienned snow peas
2 large carrots, thinly sliced	1 cup sliced mushrooms
1 sweet red pepper, thinly sliced	1 cup bean sprouts
	½ cup shredded Boston lettuce
2 tablespoons rice wine vinegar	

1. In a small bowl, combine the water and dried mushrooms. Let stand for 5 minutes; drain and set aside.

2. Meanwhile, in a medium bowl, whisk together the egg and 1 teaspoon of the oil.

3. Coat a large no-stick frying pan or wok with no-stick spray. Warm over medium-high heat. Add the egg mixture. Cook for 2 to 3 minutes, or until the egg is set. Remove from the pan and set aside until cool enough to handle. Shred finely and set aside.

4. In the same pan over medium-high heat, warm the stock. Add the carrots, peppers, vinegar, soy sauce, ginger and garlic. Stir-fry for 2 minutes.

5. Add the snow peas, sliced mushrooms, sprouts, lettuce, softened dried mushrooms and the remaining 1 teaspoon oil. Stir-fry for 3 to 4 minutes longer, or until the vegetables are just tender.

pepper and eggplant stacks

These stacks are perfect for a light dinner. If you don't like goat cheese, substitute another cheese—pepper-flavored Monterey Jack is particularly good.

Preparation time: 10 minutes
Cooking time: 10 minutes
Makes 4 servings.
Per serving: 142 calories, 7 g. fat (22% of calories), 1.3 g. dietary fiber, 14 mg. cholesterol, 125 mg. sodium.

1 cup finely chopped mushrooms	2 garlic cloves, minced
1 cup chopped roasted sweet red peppers	1 tablespoon balsamic vinegar
4 ounces goat cheese, crumbled	1 tablespoon chopped fresh flat-leaf parsley
2 tablespoons chopped sun-dried tomatoes	1 medium eggplant
1 tablespoon chopped capers	1 tablespoon olive oil
	¼ teaspoon freshly ground black pepper

1. In a small bowl, mix the mushrooms, red peppers, goat cheese, tomatoes, capers, garlic, vinegar and parsley.

2. Preheat the broiler. Coat the broiler rack with no-stick spray.

3. Cut the eggplant into 4 lengthwise slices, about ½" to ¾" thick. Brush both sides of each slice with the oil. Place on the broiler rack. Sprinkle with the black pepper. Broil about 5" from the heat for 3 minutes per side.

4. Remove the pan from the oven. Divide the mushroom mixture among the eggplant slices and spread it evenly to coat each piece. Broil for 2 to 3 minutes, or until the cheese has melted and the eggplant is tender.

hearty sweet potato stew

I like to serve this dish with a simple tossed salad. For variety, you may replace the sweets with white potatoes.

Preparation time: 15 minutes
Cooking time: 30 minutes
Makes 4 servings.
Per serving: 254 calories, 8.9 g. fat (30% of calories), 3.4 g. dietary fiber, <1 mg. cholesterol, 133 mg. sodium.

¼ cup low-sodium vegetable stock	1 cup chopped tomatoes
1 cup chopped onions	¾ cup thawed frozen chopped broccoli
2 garlic cloves, minced	¼ cup water
1 teaspoon curry powder	¼ cup chunky peanut butter
½ teaspoon ground cumin	½ cup nonfat yogurt
3 medium sweet potatoes, peeled and diced	1 tablespoon rice wine vinegar
1½ cups shredded green cabbage	Pinch of ground red pepper

1. In a large no-stick frying pan over medium heat, warm the stock. Add the onions and garlic; cook, stirring frequently, for 2 to 3 minutes, or until tender. Stir in the curry powder and cumin; cook for 1 minute.

2. Stir in the sweet potatoes, cabbage, tomatoes, broccoli and water. Cover and simmer for 15 to 20 minutes, or until the potatoes are tender.

3. Remove the pan from the heat. Add the peanut butter, yogurt, vinegar and pepper. Stir until the peanut butter is smooth and well incorporated.

4. Reduce the heat to low. Return the pan to the heat and cook for 1 minute, or until the stew is heated through; do not let the mixture come to a boil.

cilantro peanut rice pilaf

This unusual pilaf is so easy to prepare.

Preparation time: 10 minutes
Cooking time: 20 minutes

Makes 4 servings.
Per serving: 381 calories, 10.2 g. fat (23% of calories), 8.7 g. dietary fiber, 0 mg. cholesterol, 429 mg. sodium.

2½ cups water	½ teaspoon onion powder
1 cup long-grain white rice	¼ cup low-sodium vegetable stock
2 carrots, thinly sliced	¼ cup smooth peanut butter
1 cup thawed frozen chopped broccoli	2 tablespoons chopped fresh cilantro
1 cup diced sweet red peppers	1 can (16 ounces) chick-peas, rinsed and drained
2 teaspoons minced fresh ginger	

1. In a 3-quart saucepan over high heat, bring the water to a boil. Stir in the rice, carrots, broccoli, peppers, ginger and onion powder. Reduce the heat to low. Cover and simmer for 20 minutes, or until the rice is tender and all the water has been absorbed.

2. Meanwhile, in a 1-quart saucepan, combine the stock, peanut butter and cilantro. Cook over medium heat, stirring constantly, for 1 to 2 minutes, or until the peanut butter is smooth. Set aside.

3. When the rice is ready, stir in the chick-peas and peanut butter mixture. Cook for 2 minutes, or until the chick-peas are heated through. (If the rice gets too thick, thin it with a little stock or water.)

orzo-stuffed peppers

Although you can certainly serve these peppers hot, they make a refreshing cold entrée on hot summer evenings. You may also use the orzo mixture all by itself as a delicious cold salad on a buffet.

MAKE AHEAD

Preparation time: 15 minutes
Baking time: 25 minutes
Makes 4 servings.
Per serving: 183 calories, 6.2 g. fat (29% of calories), 3.6 g. dietary fiber, 22 mg. cholesterol, 318 mg. sodium.

2 cups cooked orzo	2 tablespoons chopped fresh mint
1¼ cups chopped tomatoes	
1 box (10 ounces) frozen chopped spinach, thawed and squeezed dry	1 tablespoon nonfat sour cream
½ cup chopped scallions	4 sweet red peppers
3 ounces feta cheese, crumbled	

1. In a medium bowl, mix the orzo, tomatoes, spinach, scallions, feta, mint and sour cream; set aside.

2. Preheat the oven to 350°. Coat a 9" × 9" baking dish with no-stick spray; set aside.

3. Slice the tops off the peppers. Remove and discard the membranes and seeds. Stand the peppers upright; if necessary, cut a small slice off the bottom so that they're stable. Divide the orzo mixture among the peppers. Place upright in the prepared baking dish.

4. Bake for 20 to 25 minutes, or until heated through.

updated macaroni and cheese

I updated this classic family favorite to fit today's healthy lifestyle by using skim milk and low-fat cheeses. For variety, you may replace the macaroni with no-yolk medium egg noodles.

Preparation time: 10 minutes
Cooking time: 10 minutes
Makes 4 servings.
Per serving: 474 calories, 8.6 g. fat (16% of calories), 0.9 g. dietary fiber, 17 mg. cholesterol, 266 mg. sodium.

10 ounces macaroni	1¼ cups shredded low-fat Cheddar cheese
1 tablespoon margarine	
½ cup chopped scallions	2 tablespoons grated Parmesan cheese
2 garlic cloves, minced	
¼ cup unbleached flour	1 cup chopped tomatoes
2 teaspoons dry mustard	2 tablespoons seasoned dry bread crumbs
1 teaspoon dried basil	
2¼ cups skim milk	

1. In a large pot of boiling water, cook the macaroni for 8 to 10 minutes, or until just tender. Drain.

2. Meanwhile, in a 3-quart saucepan over medium heat, melt the margarine. Add the scallions and garlic; cook, stirring frequently, for 2 minutes. Stir in the flour, mustard and basil; cook, stirring constantly, for 2 minutes. Whisk in the milk. Cook, stirring constantly, for 3 to 4 minutes, or until thick and bubbly.

3. Remove from the heat and stir in the Cheddar and Parmesan. Add the tomatoes and macaroni; mix well.

4. Preheat the broiler.

5. Coat a 2-quart casserole with no-stick spray. Add the macaroni mixture. Sprinkle with the bread crumbs. Broil about 5″ from the heat for 1 to 2 minutes, or until the crumbs are browned.

greek baguette

Baguette is another name for a long loaf of French bread. Some are much too thin to be stuffed, so look for a nice thick one. I particularly like to make this dish with a sourdough loaf. An alternative is to stuff the filling into large pitas.

MAKE
AHEAD

Preparation time: 20 minutes
Makes 4 servings.
Per serving: 257 calories, 4.8 g. fat (17% of calories), 3.7 g. dietary fiber, 7 mg. cholesterol, 328 mg. sodium.

1½ cups shredded romaine lettuce	2 tablespoons red wine vinegar
1 cup cut (1" pieces) green beans, cooked	1 tablespoon olive oil
1 cup chopped zucchini	1 tablespoon water
1 cup chopped tomatoes	½ teaspoon dried oregano
½ cup chopped cucumbers	¼ teaspoon freshly ground black pepper
¼ cup chopped red onions	1 large baguette, halved lengthwise
2 ounces goat cheese or feta cheese, crumbled	½ cup fresh basil leaves
2 tablespoons chopped fresh mint	

1. In a medium bowl, combine the lettuce, beans, zucchini, tomatoes, cucumbers, onions, goat cheese or feta and mint.

2. In a small bowl, whisk together the vinegar, oil, water, oregano and pepper. Pour over the lettuce mixture; toss to mix well.

3. Line the bottom of the baguette with the basil. Spread with the lettuce mixture. Replace the top of the loaf. Cut into 4 equal pieces.

vegetable fajitas with papaya salsa (p. 254)

orzo-stuffed peppers (p. 278)

vegetarian vegetable kabobs (p. 267)

cellophane noodle chow mein (p. 258) 287

chilaquiles (p. 268)

290 roasted garlic soup (p. 327) and appetizer parmesan toasts (p. 318)

red lentil pâté (p. 307), cheesy dip (p. 306), mushroom triangles (p. 326) **291**

snap pea stir-fry (p. 338)

curried tofu with fruit and quinoa (p. 345)

tofu stir-fry (p. 340) 295

roasted brussels sprouts and squash (p. 353)

pasta with endive and artichokes

Frozen artichoke hearts are a godsend. They let you make an otherwise labor-intensive vegetable part of any midweek dinner. Here I combine them with pasta, lots of garlic and other seasonings for a dish that's light but full of flavor.

Preparation time: 10 minutes
Cooking time: 15 minutes
Makes 4 servings.
Per serving: 357 calories, 12.3 g. fat (29% of calories), 5.5 g. dietary fiber, 15 mg. cholesterol, 198 mg. sodium.

8 ounces spaghetti	¼ teaspoon dried sage
2 tablespoons olive oil, divided	⅓ cup shredded Fontina cheese
4 garlic cloves, minced	2 tablespoons Parmesan cheese
¼ teaspoon red-pepper flakes	
2 cups thawed frozen artichoke hearts	2 tablespoons chopped fresh flat-leaf parsley
2 heads Belgian endive, coarsely chopped	1 tablespoon lemon juice
¼ cup low-sodium vegetable stock	¼ teaspoon freshly ground black pepper

1. In a large pot of boiling water, cook the spaghetti for 9 to 11 minutes, or until tender. Drain and keep warm.

2. Meanwhile, in a large no-stick frying pan over medium heat, warm 1 tablespoon of the oil. Add the garlic and pepper flakes; cook, stirring constantly, for 1 minute. Add the artichokes, endive, stock and sage. Cook, stirring frequently, for 4 to 5 minutes, or until the endive is tender.

3. Stir in the Fontina, Parmesan, parsley, lemon juice, black pepper and the remaining 1 tablespoon oil. Add the spaghetti and toss over heat for about 1 minute to melt the cheese.

artichoke and potato stew

The combination of mustard seeds and tarragon vinegar gives this dish a unique flavor. Using vinegar is a great way to increase flavor in many recipes without adding fat and calories. For variety, you may use any other vinegar, such as dill, basil, thyme or red or white wine vinegar.

Preparation time: 15 minutes
Cooking time: 30 minutes
Makes 4 servings.
Per serving: 131 calories, 3.5 g. fat (21% of calories), 5 g. dietary fiber, 0 mg. cholesterol, 203 mg. sodium.

1 tablespoon margarine	2 cups thawed frozen artichoke hearts
½ cup chopped scallions	
4 garlic cloves, minced	½ cup low-sodium vegetable stock
1 pound small potatoes, quartered	
	2 tablespoons tarragon vinegar
1 cup cut (1" pieces) green beans	
	2 teaspoons low-sodium soy sauce
1 cup sliced mushrooms	
1 teaspoon dried thyme	2 tablespoons chopped fresh flat-leaf parsley
½ teaspoon mustard seeds	
¼ teaspoon freshly ground black pepper	1 bunch spinach or kale

1. In a large no-stick frying pan over medium heat, melt the margarine. Add the scallions and garlic; cook, stirring frequently, for 2 minutes. Add the potatoes, beans, mushrooms, thyme, mustard seeds and pepper. Cook, stirring frequently, for 15 minutes.

2. Stir in the artichokes, stock, vinegar and soy sauce; bring to a boil. Reduce the heat to low. Cover and simmer for 5 minutes. Stir in the parsley; simmer, uncovered, for 5 minutes, or until the vegetables are tender and the liquid has been absorbed.

3. Meanwhile, wash the spinach or kale in cold water to remove any grit. Shake off the leaves, but don't dry them. Place in a 3-quart saucepan. Cover and cook over medium heat for 5 minutes, or until wilted. Drain and transfer to a large platter. Spoon the vegetable mixture on top.

crispy stir-fry

If you're like me, you always make too much spaghetti. Here's how I use the leftovers. You can use this same basic idea with any stir-fry—the crispy noodles are an interesting alternative to rice.

Preparation time: 15 minutes
Cooking time: 25 minutes

Makes 4 servings.
Per serving: 221 calories, 6.9 g. fat (27% of calories), 3.2 g. dietary fiber, 0 mg. cholesterol, 389 mg. sodium.

1 tablespoon sesame oil	1 cup low-sodium vegetable stock
2 cups cold cooked spaghetti	⅓ cup orange juice
2 teaspoons peanut oil	2 tablespoons oyster sauce
1 cup chopped scallions	2 tablespoons rice wine vinegar
2 garlic cloves, minced	1 teaspoon low-sodium teriyaki sauce
1 sweet red pepper, cut into strips	1 tablespoon cornstarch
4 ounces green beans or snow peas	1 tablespoon water
2 cups quartered mushrooms	½ cup sliced water chestnuts
1½ cups chopped celery	

1. In a large no-stick frying pan over medium-high heat, warm the sesame oil. Reduce the heat to medium. Add the spaghetti. Press down with a spatula to make the noodles conform to the shape of the pan. Cook for 10 to 15 minutes, or until well browned on the bottom.

2. Flip the noodles over, trying to keep them in 1 piece. (If they break, turn them in sections and press them firmly into the pan.) Cook for 10 minutes, or until browned.

3. Meanwhile, in a wok over medium-high heat, warm the peanut oil. Add the scallions and garlic; stir-fry for 1 minute. Add the peppers, beans or snow peas, mushrooms and celery; stir-fry for 2 minutes.

4. In a small bowl, combine the stock, juice, oyster sauce, vinegar, teriyaki sauce, cornstarch and water. Add to the wok. Bring to a boil. Stir in the water chestnuts. Cook until the sauce thickens.

5. To serve, slide the spaghetti onto a platter. Spoon the vegetables on top.

entertaining in style

What about holidays? Or birthdays, barbecues and parties? How do you handle them when you're vegetarian? And how do you create meals for those occasions that even nonvegetarians will relish?

Those were my challenges as I began working on this chapter. What I came up with were six individual menus covering brunch, a barbecue and four holidays. I also added a couple of pizza recipes that can form the centerpiece of a spur-of-the-moment party. Although I've formally grouped the recipes into specific menus, you should feel free to mix them to suit yourself. And by all means, don't hesitate to expand the menus with some of your family's favorite dishes—including desserts.

In my experience, the key to successful entertaining is to do as much work as possible ahead. You never want your guests to see you frazzled by last-minute details. That's why most of these recipes can be prepared entirely or partially in advance.

Remember that entertaining should be a joyous occasion. So relax and have fun at your own party.

menus for festive occasions

an elegant sunday brunch
Hearts of Palm Salad
Herbed Asparagus Frittatas
Sesame Oat Scones
Red Berry Spread
Cheesy Bell Pepper Dip

the flavors of easter
Red Lentil and Scallion Pâté
Stuffed Tomatoes with Angel Hair
Orange Couscous Salad
Dill Vichyssoise

a midsummer cookout
Garlic Grilled Baby Eggplants
Roasted Red–Pepper Corn
Oriental Orzo Salad
Tempeh-Tofu Shish Kabobs

an impromptu party
Pepper and Mushroom Pizzas
Oven-Roasted Vegetables Pizzas

a thanksgiving feast
Appetizer Parmesan Toasts
Acorn Squash Stuffed with
    Quinoa and Fruit
Carrot and Zucchini Puff
Warm Sweet Potato Salad

a hanukkah dinner
Barley Bean Soup
Sweet Potato Pancakes
Golden Cinnamon Applesauce
Fruit and Noodle Kugel

festive christmas fare
Tarragon Mushroom Triangles
Roasted Garlic Soup
Red and Green Lasagna
Citrus Fennel Salad

hearts of palm salad

This is a wonderful brunch salad. If you don't care for Gorgonzola cheese, substitute goat cheese or feta. Look for hearts of palm in the specialty food section of your supermarket.

MAKE AHEAD

Preparation time: 20 minutes
Cooking time: 2 minutes

Makes 8 servings.
Per serving: 216 calories, 10.2 g. fat (30% of calories), 1.7 g. dietary fiber, 8 mg. cholesterol, 157 mg. sodium.

1 pound thin green beans
1 cup chopped roasted sweet red peppers
½ cup diced red onions
2 cans (14 ounces each) hearts of palm, drained
¼ cup olive oil
2 tablespoons red wine vinegar
1 tablespoon balsamic vinegar
½ teaspoon freshly ground black pepper
3 ounces Gorgonzola cheese, crumbled
   Romaine lettuce leaves

1. In a large pot of boiling water, blanch the beans for 2 minutes. Drain and immediately plunge into a bowl of ice water. Drain and cut the beans into ½" pieces. Place in a large bowl.

2. Add the red peppers and onions.

3. Cut each heart of palm in half lengthwise and remove its woody center. Cut crosswise into ½" pieces. Add to the bowl with the other vegetables.

4. In a small bowl, whisk together the oil, red wine vinegar, balsamic vinegar and black pepper. Pour over the salad. Sprinkle on the Gorgonzola. Toss to mix well. Serve on salad plates lined with the lettuce.

herbed asparagus frittatas

This is a terrific brunch dish. To save time, you may prepare the frittatas ahead. They're delicious warm, cold or at room temperature. If you don't have two large frying pans, make one frittata at a time, using half of the ingredients for each. For variety, replace the asparagus with broccoli florets.

MAKE AHEAD

Preparation time: 20 minutes
Cooking time: 5 minutes
Baking time: 25 minutes

Makes 8 servings.
Per serving: 99 calories, 2.9 g. fat (25% of calories), 0.6 g. dietary fiber, 4 mg. cholesterol, 222 mg. sodium.

4	teaspoons margarine	2	tablespoons chopped fresh chives
1½	pounds thin asparagus, cut diagonally into ½" slices	2	tablespoons chopped fresh tarragon
2	cups chopped scallions	½	teaspoon freshly ground black pepper
4	garlic cloves, minced		
3	cups egg substitute	6	tablespoons grated Parmesan cheese, divided
¼	cup chopped fresh flat-leaf parsley		

1. Preheat the oven to 350°.

2. In a large ovenproof frying pan over medium-low heat, melt the margarine. Add the asparagus, scallions and garlic; cook, stirring frequently, for 5 minutes, or until just tender. Transfer half of the mixture to a second large ovenproof frying pan. Spread the vegetables in the bottoms of the pans.

3. In a large bowl, mix the egg, parsley, chives, tarragon, pepper and 4 tablespoons of the Parmesan. Pour half of the mixture into each frying pan. Sprinkle the remaining 2 tablespoons Parmesan over the eggs.

4. Bake for 20 minutes, or until the eggs are mostly set but the top is still slightly wet. Broil about 5" from the heat for 5 minutes, or until the top is golden and dry. Slide onto large plates. Cut into wedges.

sesame oat scones

The combination of oat flour and sesame seeds really gives these scones a nutty flavor. Look for oat flour in health food stores. If you don't have a biscuit cutter, dip the rim of a glass in flour and use it as a cutter.

MAKE AHEAD

Preparation time: 20 minutes
Baking time: 20 minutes

Makes 12 scones.
Per scone: 191 calories, 6.8 g. fat (31% of calories), 0.9 g. dietary fiber, 0 mg. cholesterol, 167 mg. sodium.

1⅓	cups oat flour	7	tablespoons margarine, well chilled
1⅓	cups unbleached flour	½	cup currants
3	tablespoons brown sugar	½	cup + 2 teaspoons skim milk, divided
2	teaspoons sesame seeds		
2	teaspoons cream of tartar		
1	teaspoon baking soda		

1. Preheat the oven to 375°. Coat a large baking sheet with no-stick spray.

2. In a large bowl, mix the oat flour, unbleached flour, sugar, sesame seeds, cream of tartar and baking soda.

3. Using a pastry blender, cut in the margarine until the mixture resembles coarse crumbs. Stir in the currants. Add ½ cup of the milk; stir to combine and moisten all the flour. Knead a few times to thoroughly combine the ingredients.

4. Working on a lightly floured board with well-floured hands, pat the dough to a circle about ½" thick. Using a 2½" fluted biscuit cutter, cut rounds from the dough and place them on the prepared baking sheet. Gather the scraps into a ball, pat them out, and cut more scones until all the dough has been used.

5. Brush the tops of the scones with the remaining 2 teaspoons milk.

6. Bake for 15 to 20 minutes, or until golden. Transfer the scones to a wire rack. Serve warm or at room temperature.

red berry spread

This spread is good with the Sesame Oat Scones (opposite page) as well as with any other breakfast or brunch bread.

MAKE
AHEAD

Preparation time: 5 minutes
Cooking time: 45 minutes

Makes 1 cup.
Per tablespoon: 11 calories, 0.1 g. fat (4% of calories), 0.4 g. dietary fiber, 0 mg. cholesterol, 0 mg. sodium.

1 cup fresh or thawed frozen whole strawberries	2 teaspoons brown sugar
½ cup fresh or thawed frozen raspberries	1 cinnamon stick
1 tablespoon honey	1 tablespoon grated lemon peel

1. In a 1-quart saucepan, combine the strawberries, raspberries, honey, sugar, cinnamon and lemon peel. Bring to a boil over medium heat. Reduce the heat to low. Simmer, stirring frequently, for 30 to 40 minutes, or until the mixture is thick. Remove and discard the cinnamon stick.

2. Cool, then transfer to a bowl or jar. Store, tightly covered, in the refrigerator.

cheesy bell pepper dip

This is an easy make-ahead dip. Let your guests munch on it while you put the final touches on your brunch or other festive meal. Serve the dip with bagel chips and crudités, such as cherry tomatoes and blanched snow peas.

MAKE
AHEAD

Preparation time: 10 minutes
Cooking time: 10 minutes

Makes 1½ cups.
Per tablespoon: 21 calories, 0.3 g. fat (13% of calories), 0.3 g. dietary fiber, 3 mg. cholesterol, 42 mg. sodium.

1 teaspoon olive oil	½ cup fresh basil leaves
1 small red onion, quartered	6 ounces nonfat cream
2 garlic cloves, crushed	cheese
½ cup chopped roasted sweet red peppers	2 teaspoons lemon juice

1. In a small no-stick frying pan over medium heat, warm the oil. Add the onions and garlic. Cook, stirring constantly, for 6 to 8 minutes, or until soft; do not let the garlic brown.

2. Transfer to a food processor. Add the peppers and basil. Process until smooth. Add the cream cheese and lemon juice; process until just blended.

red lentil and scallion pâté

I like to make this pâté in the spring around Easter, but it's good any time of year. Serve the pâté with flatbreads and crispbreads. If you like, you may serve it warm—let it stand for 10 minutes after it comes out of the oven, then unmold it onto a platter.

MAKE
AHEAD

Preparation time: 20 minutes
+ chilling time
Cooking time: 5 minutes
Baking time: 45 minutes
Makes 8 servings.
Per serving: 83 calories, 0.5 g. fat (6% of calories), 3.2 g. dietary fiber, 0 mg. cholesterol, 58 mg. sodium.

¼ cup low-sodium vegetable stock	¾ teaspoon curry powder
1 cup chopped scallions	½ teaspoon paprika
2 garlic cloves, minced	½ teaspoon no-salt herb blend
2 cups cooked red lentils	Pinch of ground nutmeg
¼ cup egg substitute	Pinch of freshly ground black pepper
1 cup fresh rye bread crumbs	
¼ cup chopped fresh cilantro	
2 tablespoons chopped fresh flat-leaf parsley	

1. Preheat the oven to 350°. Line a 9" × 5" loaf pan with foil. Coat with no-stick spray.

2. In a 1-quart saucepan over medium heat, bring the stock to a boil. Add the scallions and garlic; cook, stirring frequently, for 2 to 3 minutes, or until tender.

3. In a large bowl, mash the lentils and mix in the egg. Stir in the stock mixture and combine well.

4. Add the bread crumbs, cilantro, parsley, curry powder, paprika, herb blend, nutmeg and pepper. Mix well.

5. Spoon into the prepared pan. Smooth the top with a spatula. Bake for 30 to 45 minutes, or until golden. Let cool for 20 minutes, then chill for at least 4 hours. To serve, unmold the pâté onto a plate and peel off the foil.

stuffed tomatoes with angel hair

Although this recipe appears lengthy, it really is quite simple to prepare. You may stuff the tomatoes ahead and put them into the oven just before company arrives. For a light dinner dish, you may prepare just the pasta.

Stuffed Tomatoes

- 1 tablespoon olive oil
- 1 red onion, diced
- 1 yellow onion, diced
- 4 garlic cloves, minced
- 1 tablespoon dried basil
- 1 tablespoon dried marjoram
- 1 eggplant, peeled and diced
- ¼ cup balsamic vinegar
- ¼ cup low-sodium vegetable stock
- 1 can (28 ounces) tomatoes in thick puree
- 1 medium yellow squash, cubed
- 1 sweet red pepper, diced
- 8 ounces mushrooms, thinly sliced
- ¼ teaspoon freshly ground black pepper
- 8 large firm tomatoes

Angel Hair

- 1 pound angel hair
- 1 tablespoon olive oil
- 1 bunch scallions, chopped
- ¼ teaspoon red-pepper flakes
- ½ cup toasted pistachios
- 2 tablespoons chopped pitted kalamata olives
- 2 tablespoons chopped fresh basil
- 1 tablespoon lemon juice
- 1 tablespoon grated Parmesan cheese

1. To make the stuffed tomatoes: In a large no-stick frying pan over medium heat, warm the oil. Add the red onions, yellow onions, garlic, basil and marjoram. Cook, stirring frequently, for 6 to 8 minutes, or until the onions are tender.

2. Add the eggplant; cook for 2 minutes. Stir in the vinegar and stock; cook for 8 to 10 minutes, or until the eggplant is tender.

3. Add the canned tomatoes (with their puree), squash, red peppers, mushrooms and black pepper. Cook, stirring frequently and mashing the tomatoes with the back of a spoon, for 10 minutes, or until the vegetables are tender and the mixture is thick. Set aside.

Preparation time: 30 minutes
Cooking time: 30 minutes
Baking time: 40 minutes

Makes 8 servings.
Per serving: 390 calories, 9.9
g. fat (22% of calories), 6.3 g.
dietary fiber, <1 mg. cholesterol, 211 mg. sodium.

4. Preheat the oven to 350°.

5. Cut a ½" slice off the top of each tomato. Carefully scoop out and discard the pulp, leaving a sturdy shell. Set the tomatoes upside down on a flat surface to drain for a few minutes.

6. Use the vegetable mixture to fill the tomatoes. Place upright in a 9" × 13" baking dish. Bake for 30 to 40 minutes, or until the tomatoes are soft but not ready to collapse.

7. To make the angel hair: In a large pot of boiling water, cook the angel hair for 5 minutes, or until tender. Drain.

8. Meanwhile, in a large no-stick frying pan over medium heat, warm the oil. Add the scallions and pepper flakes; cook, stirring frequently, for 2 to 3 minutes, or until tender. Add the pistachios, olives, basil and lemon juice; toss lightly.

9. Add the angel hair to the pan. Sprinkle with the Parmesan. Toss to mix well.

10. Divide the pasta among individual serving plates. Top each with a tomato.

orange couscous salad

If whole wheat couscous is hard to find, use regular couscous. I prefer the whole wheat variety because it has a nuttier taste.

MAKE AHEAD

Preparation time: 20 minutes + chilling time

Makes 8 servings.
Per serving: 244 calories, 4.4 g. fat (16% of calories), 8.1 g. dietary fiber, 0 mg. cholesterol, 161 mg. sodium.

2 cups water	1/2 cup chopped red onions
1 1/2 cups whole wheat couscous	1/2 cup golden raisins
3/4 teaspoon turmeric	1/4 cup lemon juice
1/4 teaspoon freshly ground black pepper	2 tablespoons olive oil
1 can (16 ounces) chick-peas, rinsed and drained	1 tablespoon grated orange peel
1 cup drained canned mandarin oranges	1 tablespoon minced fresh chives
	Red leaf lettuce

1. In a 1-quart saucepan over high heat, bring the water to a boil. Add the couscous, turmeric and pepper. Remove from the heat, cover, and let stand for 5 minutes, or until the couscous is soft. Fluff with a fork. Transfer to a large bowl.

2. Stir in the chick-peas, oranges, onions and raisins.

3. In a small bowl, whisk together the lemon juice, oil, orange peel and chives. Pour over the salad and toss to mix well. Cover and refrigerate for at least 1 hour. Serve on plates lined with the lettuce.

dill vichyssoise

Nothing is easier for holiday entertaining than a dish that can be made completely ahead of time and does not even need to be re-heated. This soup has become a standard on my table for just that rea-son. I particularly like to serve it at Easter.

MAKE
AHEAD

Preparation time: 20 minutes
+ chilling time
Cooking time: 20 minutes
Makes 8 servings.
Per serving: 89 calories, 1.6 g. fat (16% of calories), 2.5 g. dietary fiber, <1 mg. choles-terol, 63 mg. sodium.

1 tablespoon margarine	3–4 drops hot-pepper sauce
1 cup thinly sliced leeks (white part only)	2 cups nonfat cottage cheese
1 cup thinly sliced scallions	2 tablespoons chopped fresh dill
3 cups peeled and sliced potatoes	1 tablespoon lemon juice
3 cups low-sodium vegetable stock	1 cup skim milk, divided

1. In a 3-quart saucepan over medium heat, melt the mar-garine. Add the leeks and scallions; cook, stirring frequently, for 4 to 5 minutes, or until tender.

2. Add the potatoes, stock and hot-pepper sauce; bring to a boil. Reduce the heat to low; cover and simmer for 10 to 15 minutes, or until the potatoes are tender. Remove from the heat and cool for 20 minutes.

3. In a blender, combine the cottage cheese, dill, lemon juice and ½ cup of the milk. Blend until smooth; pour into a large bowl.

4. Working in batches, blend the potato mixture until smooth. Add to the bowl. Whisk in enough of the remaining ½ cup milk to get the desired consistency. Cover and chill well.

garlic grilled baby eggplants

These eggplants are perfect to serve at a midsummer party. And they're so pretty they'll make any table look special.

Preparation time: 10 minutes + marinating time
Grilling time: 15 minutes
Makes 8 servings.
Per serving: 57 calories, 1.9 g. fat (26% of calories), 2.2 g. dietary fiber, 0 mg. cholesterol, 104 mg. sodium.

8 baby eggplants (4–5 ounces each)	2 teaspoons white wine vinegar
1 tablespoon sesame oil	2 teaspoons no-salt lemon-herb blend
4 teaspoons low-sodium soy sauce	½ teaspoon freshly ground black pepper
4 garlic cloves, minced	

1. Place the eggplants on a flat cutting surface. With a sharp knife, make parallel lengthwise cuts ¼" apart that run from the tips to within 1" of the stem ends. Place in a single layer in a large baking dish or roasting pan; fan out the slices slightly, making sure to keep them attached to the stem.

2. In a small bowl, combine the oil, soy sauce, garlic, vinegar, herb blend and pepper. Brush over the eggplants. Let stand for 15 minutes. Flip the pieces and brush with the remaining marinade. Let stand for 15 to 30 minutes.

3. Prepare an outdoor grill. When the coals are hot, place a mesh grill rack over the top. Add the eggplants. Grill for 5 minutes. Flip the pieces; grill for 5 to 10 minutes, or until tender.

roasted red-pepper corn

Grilling corn brings out a nutty flavor you won't get from boiling. If you don't enjoy spicy food, replace the chili peppers and chili powder with finely chopped sun-dried tomatoes and a little grated Parmesan cheese. You can ready the ears of corn ahead of time and grill them just before serving.

Preparation time: 10 minutes + soaking time
Grilling time: 30 minutes
Makes 8 servings.
Per serving: 107 calories, 3.4 g. fat (24% of calories), 6.7 g. dietary fiber, 0 mg. cholesterol, 63 mg. sodium.

8 ears corn (in the husk)	2 tablespoons finely chopped roasted sweet red peppers
6 teaspoons margarine, softened	1 teaspoon chili powder
2 tablespoons finely chopped canned green chili peppers (wear plastic gloves when handling)	½ teaspoon garlic powder

1. Peel back the corn husks, but do not detach them. Remove and discard the silk. Soak the corn in very cold water for 30 minutes. Shake off as much water as possible.

2. Meanwhile, in a small bowl, mix the margarine, chili peppers, red peppers, chili powder and garlic powder.

3. Rub the mixture all over the corn kernels. Pull the husks back over the corn and twist them shut. Tightly wrap each ear in foil.

4. Prepare an outdoor grill. When the coals are very hot, place the corn on a rack and cover. Grill for a total of 30 to 35 minutes, turning the ears every 10 minutes.

oriental orzo salad

The longer you chill this summer pasta salad, the more intense the flavor becomes. Tahini is sesame seed paste; if it's hard to find, substitute peanut butter. I have also used kidney beans instead of chick-peas.

MAKE
AHEAD

Preparation time: 15 minutes + chilling time

Makes 8 servings.
Per serving: 301 calories, 8.3 g. fat (24% of calories), 5.9 g. dietary fiber, 0 mg. cholesterol, 461 mg. sodium.

8 cups cooked orzo	4 garlic cloves, minced
2 sweet red peppers, diced	4 teaspoons honey
2 cups canned chick-peas, rinsed and drained	4 teaspoons sesame oil
¼ cup minced scallions	2 teaspoons rice wine vinegar
2 tablespoons tahini	1 teaspoon dry mustard
2 tablespoons chili sauce	2 tablespoons lemon juice
2 tablespoons low-sodium soy sauce	

1. In a large bowl, mix the orzo, peppers and chick-peas.

2. In a small bowl, mix the scallions, tahini, chili sauce, soy sauce, garlic, honey, oil, vinegar and mustard. Pour over the salad and mix well. Cover and refrigerate for at least 1 hour.

3. Sprinkle with the lemon juice. Toss well.

tempeh-tofu shish kabobs

Kabobs are one of my favorite things to do on the grill. And there are endless possibilities to choose from. I like this combination that includes both tofu and tempeh. Because you marinate the ingredients before threading them onto skewers, you can do most of the work ahead.

Preparation time: 25 minutes + marinating time
Grilling time: 15 minutes
Makes 8 servings.
Per serving: 462 calories, 13.1 g. fat (25% of calories), 5.6 g. dietary fiber, 0 mg. cholesterol, 370 mg. sodium.

½ cup orange juice	1 pound firm tofu, well drained and squeezed dry between paper towels
½ cup low-sodium vegetable stock	
¼ cup low-sodium teriyaki sauce	10 ounces tempeh, cut into 1" pieces
2 tablespoons peanut oil	2 green peppers, cut into 1" pieces
2 tablespoons honey	
4 garlic cloves, minced	24 cherry tomatoes
4 teaspoons grated fresh ginger	1 large red onion, cut into 8 wedges
Pinch of ground red pepper	8 cups hot cooked brown rice

1. In a large bowl, whisk together the juice, stock, teriyaki sauce, oil, honey, garlic, ginger and red pepper.

2. Cut the tofu into 1" cubes. Add to the bowl. Add the tempeh, green peppers, tomatoes and onions. Toss to mix well. Cover and refrigerate for at least 1 hour, tossing occasionally.

3. Divide the ingredients among 24 metal or soaked bamboo skewers. Reserve the marinade.

4. Prepare an outdoor grill. When the coals are hot, place the kabobs on the rack. Grill for 15 minutes, turning and brushing with the reserved marinade every 5 minutes. Serve the kabobs with the rice.

quick pizza

Sometimes unexpected company comes calling. For those occasions, you might want to whip up some homemade pizzas for snacks. The following dough is quite quick. And the two pizza recipes are also easy to make. Naturally, you can substitute any other vegetables, herbs or cheese that you might have on hand for those specified in the recipes.

pizza dough

2½	cups unbleached flour	¼	teaspoon salt
1	cup whole wheat flour	1⅓	cups hot tap water
1	package quick-rising yeast		

1. In the bowl of a food processor, combine the unbleached flour, whole wheat flour, yeast and salt. Process briefly with on/off turns to mix. With the machine running, slowly pour in the water. Process until the mixture forms a ball of dough. Place the dough on a lightly floured surface and knead for about 1 minute to form a smooth ball.

2. Coat a large glass bowl with no-stick spray. Add the dough and turn to coat all sides. Cover with vented plastic wrap. Microwave on low (10% power) for 5 minutes, or until the dough has risen slightly. Punch down and divide into 4 pieces. Form each piece into an 8" circle.

Preparation time: 15 minutes.

Makes 4 pizza shells (8" each).

Per shell: 316 calories, 1.1 g. fat (3% of calories), 5.9 g. dietary fiber, 0 mg. cholesterol, 139 mg. sodium.

pepper and mushroom pizzas

1	tablespoon olive oil	1	recipe Pizza Dough (above), formed into 4 shells
1	large sweet red pepper, thinly sliced	½	cup tomato sauce
1	large yellow pepper, thinly sliced	1	cup shredded nonfat or low-fat mozzarella cheese
12	tiny pattypan squash, halved	4	large plum tomatoes, thinly sliced
4	large chanterelle mushrooms, cut into 6 wedges each		Fresh oregano leaves
1	tablespoon cornmeal		

1. Preheat the oven to 500°. In a large no-stick frying pan over medium-high heat, warm the oil for 1 minute. Add the red peppers, yellow peppers, squash and mushrooms. Sauté for 5 minutes, or until crisp-tender.

2. Coat a large baking sheet with no-stick spray. Sprinkle with the cornmeal. Place the pizza shells on the sheet. Divide the tomato sauce among them. Sprinkle with the mozzarella. Top with the tomatoes and sautéed vegetables. Bake for 12 to 15 minutes, or until the cheese is bubbly and the shells are nicely browned underneath. Sprinkle with the oregano. Cut each pizza into 4 wedges.

Preparation time: 20 minutes. Cooking time: 5 minutes. Baking time: 15 minutes.

Makes 16 wedges.

Per wedge: 106 calories, 1.6 g. fat (14% of calories), 1.9 g. dietary fiber, 1 mg. cholesterol, 146 mg. sodium.

oven-roasted vegetables pizzas

4 baby eggplants, cut lengthwise into ½" slices	½ teaspoon freshly ground black pepper
2 red onions, cut into 8 wedges each	1 tablespoon cornmeal
6 large shiitake mushrooms, cut into ½" slices	1 recipe Pizza Dough (opposite page), formed into 4 shells
1 large yellow pepper, thinly sliced	½ cup tomato sauce
1 tablespoon olive oil	1 cup shredded nonfat or low-fat mozzarella cheese
1 tablespoon balsamic vinegar	
½ teaspoon dried thyme	Fresh thyme leaves

1. Preheat the oven to 400°. In a large baking dish, combine the eggplant, onions, mushrooms and yellow peppers. In a cup, mix the oil, vinegar, dried thyme and black pepper. Drizzle over the vegetables and toss to mix well. Bake for 20 minutes, or until the vegetables are tender.

2. Increase the oven temperature to 500°. Coat a large baking sheet with no-stick spray. Sprinkle with the cornmeal. Place the pizza shells on the sheet. Divide the tomato sauce among them. Sprinkle with the mozzarella. Top with the roasted vegetables. Bake for 12 to 15 minutes, or until the cheese is bubbly and the shells are nicely browned. Sprinkle with the fresh thyme.

Preparation time: 20 minutes. Baking time: 35 minutes.

Makes 16 wedges.

Per wedge: 115 calories, 1.5 g. fat (12% of calories), 2.4 g. dietary fiber, 1 mg. cholesterol, 145 mg. sodium.

appetizer parmesan toasts

2	small loaves French bread	2	tablespoons grated
4	teaspoons olive oil		Parmesan cheese
¼	cup chopped sun-dried	1	teaspoon garlic powder
	tomatoes		

These toasts are a light way to start a Thanksgiving feast or another traditionally heavy meal. And you can do most of the preparation ahead, so you just broil them at the last minute.

Preparation time: 5 minutes
Broiling time: 5 minutes
Makes 8 servings.
Per serving: 192 calories, 2.7 g. fat (13% of calories), 1.6 g. dietary fiber, 1 mg. cholesterol, 318 mg. sodium.

1. Preheat the broiler.

2. Cut each loaf into 8 thick (½") slices. Brush the tops with the oil. Sprinkle with the tomatoes, Parmesan and garlic powder. Place on a baking sheet. Broil about 5" from the heat for 2 to 3 minutes, or until the bread is golden and the topping is heated through.

acorn squash stuffed with quinoa and fruit

This is a good main dish for Thanksgiving or other winter dinners. You may prepare the stuffing mixture ahead and fill the squash as directed just before the meal. For variety, you may bake the stuffing in a casserole as a side dish.

Preparation time: 15 minutes
Cooking time: 30 minutes
Baking time: 45 minutes
Makes 8 servings.
Per serving: 406 calories, 8.5 g. fat (18% of calories), 8.5 g. dietary fiber, 0 mg. cholesterol, 83 mg. sodium.

4 medium acorn squash	2 tablespoons chopped walnuts
4 cups low-sodium vegetable stock	2 tablespoons honey
2 cups quinoa, rinsed and drained	1 teaspoon ground cinnamon
2 tablespoons margarine	½ teaspoon ground mace
2 cups chopped apples	¼ teaspoon ground allspice
1 cup chopped pears	¼ teaspoon ground cardamom
½ cup chopped dried apricots	

1. Preheat the oven to 350°. Coat a large baking dish or roasting pan with no-stick spray.

2. Cut the squash in half lengthwise; scoop out and discard the seeds. Place the halves, cut side down, in the prepared dish. Bake for 30 minutes.

3. Meanwhile, in a 2-quart saucepan over medium-high heat, bring the stock to a boil. Add the quinoa; stir and reduce the heat to low. Cover and simmer for 20 to 25 minutes, or until the liquid has been absorbed. Remove from the heat and let stand for 5 minutes. Fluff with a fork.

4. In a large no-stick frying pan, melt the margarine. Add the apples, pears, apricots and walnuts; cook, stirring frequently, for 5 minutes. Stir in the honey, cinnamon, mace, allspice and cardamom; cook for 2 minutes.

5. Transfer to a large bowl. Add the quinoa and mix well.

6. Turn the squash cut side up. Divide the quinoa mixture among them. (If there is any extra filling, place it in a small casserole dish.) Bake for 15 minutes, or until the squash are tender.

carrot and zucchini puff

This dish is appropriate for any holiday table. The flavors really remind me of Thanksgivings when I was growing up. You may assemble the dish early in the day and bake it later.

Preparation time: 25 minutes
Baking time: 1 hour

Makes 8 servings.
Per serving: 103 calories, 0.3 g. fat (2% of calories), 3.7 g. dietary fiber, 0 mg. cholesterol, 107 mg. sodium.

5 cups shredded carrots	2 tablespoons grated orange peel
2 cups shredded zucchini	
2 cups shredded yellow squash	4 teaspoons grated fresh ginger
2 cups chopped scallions	¼ teaspoon grated nutmeg
2 cups egg substitute	Pinch of freshly ground black pepper
¼ cup packed brown sugar or 2 tablespoons honey	

1. Preheat the oven to 350°. Coat a 4-quart baking dish with no-stick spray.

2. In a large bowl, mix the carrots, zucchini, squash, scallions, egg, sugar or honey, orange peel, ginger, nutmeg and pepper. Spoon into the prepared baking dish.

3. Bake for 1 hour, or until puffed and golden and a knife inserted in the center comes out clean.

warm sweet potato salad

To me, Thanksgiving would not be complete without sweet potatoes. Here they make an entrance in a new way—as a salad instead of a side dish. Try them this way and pleasantly change your traditional meal.

Preparation time: 20 minutes
Cooking time: 15 minutes
Makes 8 servings.
Per serving: 212 calories, 6.3 g. fat (25% of calories), 3.2 g. dietary fiber, 19 mg. cholesterol, 246 mg. sodium.

½ cup low-sodium vegetable stock, divided	4 cups torn spinach leaves
4 medium sweet potatoes, peeled and diced	1 pound Fontina cheese, cubed
1 teaspoon ground coriander	4 garlic cloves, minced
1 teaspoon ground mace	¼ cup red wine vinegar
2 tablespoons lemon juice	¼ cup balsamic vinegar
2 small heads curly endive, leaves coarsely chopped	¼ cup grated Parmesan cheese

1. In a large no-stick frying pan over medium heat, warm ¼ cup of the stock. Add the sweet potatoes, coriander and mace; cook, stirring frequently, for 8 to 10 minutes, or until tender. Sprinkle with the lemon juice. Transfer to a large bowl.

2. Add the endive, spinach and Fontina. Toss lightly.

3. In the same frying pan, heat the remaining ¼ cup stock. Add the garlic; cook, stirring frequently, for 1 to 2 minutes. Add the red wine vinegar and balsamic vinegar; simmer for 1 minute.

4. Pour over the salad and toss to mix well and gently wilt the greens. Sprinkle with the Parmesan.

barley bean soup

The addition of beans to this soup really makes it different from traditional barley soup. For variety, replace the cannellini beans with chick-peas or kidney beans. As is the case with most soups, this one can be prepared ahead.

MAKE AHEAD

Preparation time: 15 minutes
Cooking time: 1 hour 10 minutes

Makes 8 servings.
Per serving: 210 calories, 3.9 g. fat (17% of calories), 6.6 g. dietary fiber, 0 mg. cholesterol, 375 mg. sodium.

1 tablespoon canola oil	3 garlic cloves, minced
3 celery ribs, diced	1 tablespoon low-sodium soy sauce
3 carrots, diced	
1½ cups chopped onions	¼ teaspoon hot-pepper sauce
9 cups low-sodium vegetable stock	1 can (19 ounces) cannellini beans, rinsed and drained
¾ cup medium pearled barley	

1. In a 4-quart saucepan over medium heat, warm the oil. Add the celery, carrots and onions. Cook, stirring frequently, for 6 to 7 minutes, or until tender.

2. Add the stock, barley, garlic, soy sauce and hot-pepper sauce; bring to a boil. Reduce the heat to low; cover and simmer for 50 minutes to 1 hour, or until the barley is just tender.

3. Stir in the beans; simmer for 5 to 10 minutes, or until heated through.

sweet potato pancakes

This is a good dish to make during Hanukkah or for any winter occasion. I like to serve these pancakes with nonfat sour cream and Golden Cinnamon Applesauce (page 324). You may prepare the pancakes ahead and reheat them in a microwave or in an oven set at low heat.

Preparation time: 25 minutes
Cooking time: 30 minutes
Makes 8 servings.
Per serving: 199 calories, 5.5 g. fat (25% of calories), 4.4 g. dietary fiber, 0 mg. cholesterol, 69 mg. sodium.

6	cups peeled and finely shredded sweet potatoes	1½	cups egg substitute
2	cups finely shredded zucchini	1⅔	cups unbleached flour
1	cup finely shredded onions	¼	cup chopped fresh flat-leaf parsley
¼	cup lemon juice	6	teaspoons canola oil, divided
1	teaspoon no-salt herb blend		

1. In a large bowl, mix the sweet potatoes, zucchini, onions, lemon juice, herb blend, egg, flour and parsley.

2. In a large no-stick frying pan or griddle over medium-high heat, warm 2 teaspoons of the oil. Drop a tablespoon of the batter into the pan and spread it with a spatula to form a thin pancake. Add more batter to fill the pan without crowding the pancakes. Cook for about 2 minutes per side, or until golden and crispy. Remove from the pan and keep warm.

3. Repeat, adding the remaining 4 teaspoons oil as needed, until all the batter has been used.

golden cinnamon applesauce

Sometimes I make extra batches of the applesauce to give away as holiday gifts. This is good served over Sweet Potato Pancakes (page 323) as well as spread on toast, muffins or rice cakes. And naturally, it's delicious all by itself.

MAKE AHEAD

Preparation time: 10 minutes + chilling time
Cooking time: 30 minutes

Makes 8 servings.
Per serving: 108 calories, 0.5 g. fat (4% of calories), 2.8 g. dietary fiber, 0 mg. cholesterol, 0 mg. sodium.

9 Golden Delicious apples, chopped	2 tablespoons water
3 tablespoons lemon juice	½ teaspoon ground cinnamon
3 tablespoons brown sugar or 1½ tablespoons honey	

1. In a 4-quart saucepan, combine the apples, lemon juice, sugar or honey, water and cinnamon. Cover and place over medium-low heat. Cook, stirring frequently, for 20 to 30 minutes, or until the apples are very tender.

2. Transfer to a large bowl, coarsely mash, cover, and chill.

fruit and noodle kugel

This pudding is reminiscent of one my husband's grandmother makes for Hanukkah. I added extra fruit to sweeten the pudding instead of using a lot of sugar. Since this kugel is equally good served warm or cold, you could make it ahead.

MAKE AHEAD

Preparation time: 15 minutes
Cooking time: 12 minutes
Baking time: 45 minutes

Makes 8 servings.
Per serving: 258 calories, 2.7 g. fat (9% of calories), 1.3 g. dietary fiber, 3 mg. cholesterol, 177 mg. sodium.

12	ounces no-yolk broad egg noodles
1	apple, diced
1	pear, diced
¼	cup golden raisins
¼	cup chopped prunes
2	tablespoons margarine, softened
1	cup egg substitute
1	cup nonfat cottage cheese
1	tablespoon honey
½	teaspoon ground cinnamon

1. Preheat the oven to 350°. Coat a 9" × 13" baking dish with no-stick spray.

2. In a large pot of boiling water, cook the noodles for 10 to 12 minutes, or until tender. Drain and place in a large bowl.

3. Add the apples, pears, raisins, prunes and margarine. Mix well. Stir in the egg, cottage cheese, honey and cinnamon.

4. Spoon into the prepared baking dish. Bake for 35 to 45 minutes, or until the top is golden.

tarragon mushroom triangles

These triangles are perfect for a special occasion. They take a little practice to make if you're not familiar with phyllo dough, but once you have the knack, they're really easy. Look for phyllo dough in the freezer section of your supermarket. Follow the package directions for defrosting it. You can form the triangles ahead and store them in the refrigerator for about a day before baking. Or you can freeze them and bake them later. If you'd like, you may add some finely chopped almonds to the filling.

Preparation time: 30 minutes
Cooking time: 15 minutes
Baking time: 15 minutes

Makes 24 triangles.
Per triangle: 56 calories, 2 g. fat (29% of calories), 0.3 g. dietary fiber, 2 mg. cholesterol, 34 mg. sodium.

2 teaspoons olive oil	¼ cup chopped roasted sweet red peppers
4 tablespoons low-sodium vegetable stock, divided	2 ounces feta cheese, crumbled
½ cup chopped red onions	Pinch of grated nutmeg
2 teaspoons dried tarragon	16 sheets phyllo dough (thawed, if frozen)
⅛ teaspoon ground red pepper	2 teaspoons margarine, melted
8 ounces mushrooms, coarsely chopped	
½ cup thawed frozen chopped spinach, squeezed dry	

1. In a large no-stick frying pan over medium heat, warm the oil and 2 tablespoons of the stock. Add the onions, tarragon and ground pepper; cook, stirring frequently, for 4 minutes. Add the mushrooms; cook for 6 to 8 minutes, or until all the liquid given off by the mushrooms has evaporated.

2. Transfer to a large bowl. Add the spinach and red peppers; mix well. Stir in the feta and nutmeg.

3. Preheat the oven to 350°.

4. Unroll the phyllo and cover it with a piece of plastic to keep it from drying out. Peel off 2 sheets and lay the double layer in front of you on your work surface.

5. In a cup, mix the margarine with the remaining 2 tablespoons stock. Lightly brush the top layer of the phyllo with some of the mixture. Cut the phyllo into thirds lengthwise. Place a tablespoon of filling in the bottom corner of each strip. Fold over once to make a triangle; continue rolling as if folding a flag. Place on a baking sheet.

6. Repeat to use all the remaining phyllo and filling as well as most of the remaining margarine mixture.

7. Brush the tops of the triangles with the remaining margarine mixture. Bake for 12 to 15 minutes, or until golden.

roasted garlic soup

If you're not a strict vegetarian, you might want to use beef stock as the base of this soup. It gives the soup extra flavor. Don't be concerned about the amount of garlic used. Roasting turns it sweet and mild. I like to serve this soup around the Christmas holidays.

MAKE
AHEAD

Preparation time: 10 minutes
Cooking time: 1 hour 10 minutes
Baking time: 50 minutes
Makes 8 servings.
Per serving: 113 calories, 3.4 g. fat (25% of calories), 1.6 g. dietary fiber, 0 mg. cholesterol, 149 mg. sodium.

2	garlic bulbs	2	medium leeks (white part only), sliced
3	teaspoons olive oil, divided		
1½	cups boiling water	2	teaspoons balsamic vinegar
2	yellow onions, cut into ½" wedges	2	teaspoons low-sodium soy sauce
1	red onion, cut into ½" wedges	1–2	teaspoons steak sauce
1	tablespoon dried thyme	¼	teaspoon freshly ground black pepper
8	cups low-sodium vegetable stock, divided		

1. Preheat the oven to 400°.

2. Slice about ¼" off the top of each garlic bulb to expose the cloves. Brush the tops with 1 teaspoon of the oil. Place, cut side down, in an 8" × 8" baking dish. Add about ¼" of cold water to the dish. Bake for 40 to 50 minutes, or until the garlic is soft and fragrant. Remove from the dish and set aside.

3. Pour the boiling water into the dish; scrape the bottom with a wooden spoon to loosen any brown bits. Pour into a bowl and reserve.

4. Gently squeeze the garlic cloves from their skins. Mash and set aside.

5. Meanwhile, in a 4-quart saucepan over medium-low heat, warm the remaining 2 teaspoons oil. Add the yellow onions and red onions; cook for 4 minutes. Add the thyme and ¼ cup of the stock. Cover and cook over low heat for 40 to 45 minutes, or until very tender.

6. Add the leeks; cook for 2 minutes. Stir in ½ cup of the remaining stock; cook for 10 minutes, or until the leeks are tender. Add the garlic, vinegar, soy sauce, steak sauce and pepper; stir well.

7. Add the remaining 7¼ cups stock and the reserved garlic liquid. Simmer for 5 to 10 minutes to blend the flavors.

red and green lasagna

This festive lasagna freezes well, so you can assemble it ahead and bake it when needed. The red and green colors are especially appropriate for a Yuletide celebration.

MAKE
AHEAD

Red-Pepper Sauce
2 teaspoons olive oil
2 sweet red peppers, coarsely chopped
2 pounds tomatoes, quartered
½ cup flat-leaf parsley leaves
4 garlic cloves, minced
2 teaspoons balsamic vinegar
¼ teaspoon freshly ground black pepper

Lasagna
9 lasagna noodles
1 teaspoon olive oil
1 green bell pepper, thinly sliced into rings

1 sweet red pepper, thinly sliced into rings
2 cups nonfat ricotta cheese
¼ cup egg substitute
2 tablespoons grated Parmesan cheese
2 teaspoons dried basil
Pinch of grated nutmeg
1 cup canned cannellini beans, rinsed and drained
½ cup shredded nonfat mozzarella cheese

1. To make the red-pepper sauce: In a large no-stick frying pan over medium heat, warm the oil. Add the red peppers; cook for 5 minutes. Add the tomatoes, parsley and garlic; cover and simmer, stirring frequently, for 20 to 25 minutes.

2. Transfer to a blender. Add the vinegar and black pepper; process until smooth.

3. Measure out 1 cup of the sauce and set it aside to serve with the lasagna.

4. To make the lasagna: In a large pot of boiling water, cook the noodles for 10 to 12 minutes, or until tender. Drain and toss with the oil.

5. Meanwhile, coat a large no-stick frying pan with no-stick spray. Warm over medium-high heat. Add the green peppers and red peppers. Cook, stirring frequently, for 2 to 3 minutes, or until just tender; set aside.

Preparation time: 30 minutes
Cooking time: 25 minutes
Baking time: 40 minutes

Makes 8 servings.
Per serving: 218 calories, 3.3 g. fat (13% of calories), 3.8 g. dietary fiber, 2 mg. cholesterol, 252 mg. sodium.

6. In a medium bowl, mix the ricotta, egg, Parmesan, basil and nutmeg.

7. Preheat the oven to 350°.

8. To assemble the lasagna, spread one-quarter of the red-pepper sauce in the bottom of a 9" × 13" baking dish.

9. Lay 3 noodles side by side in the dish. Spread with half of the ricotta mixture, half of the sautéed peppers, half of the beans and one-third of the remaining red-pepper sauce.

10. Repeat to make another layer.

11. Top with the remaining 3 noodles, the remaining red-pepper sauce and the mozzarella.

12. Cover and bake for 30 minutes. Uncover and bake for 10 minutes, or until bubbly. Let stand for 5 minutes before cutting.

13. Reheat the reserved red-pepper sauce and serve it with the lasagna.

citrus fennel salad

The combination of citrus and fennel is ideal for a holiday meal, especially in the winter. I use walnut oil here to take advantage of its robust flavor, but if you can't find any at your store, substitute peanut or sesame oil.

Preparation time: 20 minutes + standing time
Makes 8 servings.
Per serving: 194 calories, 5 g. fat (21% of calories), 2.8 g. dietary fiber, 0 mg. cholesterol, 48 mg. sodium.

1 cup chopped dates	2 heads Boston lettuce, coarsely torn
1 cup golden raisins	1 large head fennel, trimmed and thinly sliced
1/3 cup orange juice	
2 tablespoons lemon juice	1 red onion, thinly sliced crosswise and separated into rings
1 tablespoon minced shallots	
1 garlic clove, minced	
2 tablespoons walnut oil	2 tablespoons coarsely chopped toasted walnuts
2 tablespoons nonfat yogurt	
1/2 teaspoon balsamic vinegar	
1/4 teaspoon freshly ground black pepper	

1. In a medium bowl, combine the dates, raisins, orange juice and lemon juice; set aside for 1 hour. Drain and reserve the liquid.

2. In a small bowl, combine the shallots and garlic. Whisk in the oil, yogurt, vinegar and pepper. Add the reserved liquid; whisk until combined.

3. In a large bowl, combine the lettuce, fennel, onions, walnuts and fruit mixture. Add the dressing and toss well.

cooking for two
(or just you)

Sometimes you need scaled-down recipes. Maybe you live alone or with just one other person. Maybe the rest of the family is out doing something else, and you don't really feel like preparing a lot of food. No matter why you're on your own, these are the recipes you should turn to.

Until just recently, dinner at my house was for my husband and me. And often Dan was out of town, so then I was left to my own devices. I knew I didn't want to deal with a lot of leftovers. And I certainly didn't want to eat a double portion just to use up the food. Nor did I want to get take-out food. That's when I started experimenting with small recipes.

Pasta dishes, stir-fries, mini pizzas, baked potatoes, sandwiches, vegetable patties, crêpes and burritos are particularly adaptable to this treatment. But so are soups, stews, casseroles and even chili. The point is, you can dine in style, even if you're dining solo or as part of a pair.

creamy baked noodles and mushrooms

This easy casserole needs only a tossed salad to turn it into a complete meal. I particularly like bitter greens with a low-fat vinaigrette.

Preparation time: 15 minutes
Cooking time: 10 minutes
Baking time: 40 minutes

Makes 2 servings.
Per serving: 531 calories, 8.9 g. fat (15% of calories), 8.9 g. dietary fiber, 20 mg. cholesterol, 586 mg. sodium.

6 ounces no-yolk broad egg noodles	3 ounces low-fat Monterey Jack cheese, shredded
1 cup broccoli florets	2 teaspoons margarine
1 cup cauliflower florets	1 cup chopped scallions
1 cup nonfat cottage cheese	1 sweet red pepper, diced
1 teaspoon dried oregano	4 ounces mushrooms, thinly sliced
½ teaspoon dry mustard	

1. Preheat the oven to 350°. Coat a 2-quart casserole with no-stick spray; set aside.

2. In a large pot of boiling water, cook the noodles for 8 to 10 minutes, or until just tender. Drain and return the noodles to the pan. Off heat, add the broccoli, cauliflower, cottage cheese, oregano and mustard. Reserve 2 tablespoons of the Monterey Jack; add the remainder to the pan. Toss well.

3. Meanwhile, in a large no-stick frying pan over medium-high heat, melt the margarine. Add the scallions and peppers; cook, stirring frequently, for 3 to 4 minutes, or until the vegetables are just tender. Add the mushrooms; cook for 2 minutes.

4. Add the mushroom mixture to the noodle mixture. Toss to mix well.

5. Spoon into the prepared casserole. Sprinkle with the reserved Monterey Jack.

6. Bake for 30 to 40 minutes, or until the vegetables are tender.

potato and egg crêpes

If you're ambitious, you may make your own crêpes. (See Lentil-Stuffed Crêpes on page 118 for a recipe.) But you can often find ready-made crêpes in the produce or dairy section of supermarkets. If they're unavailable, substitute flour tortillas or even taco shells. In any case, warm them before filling.

Preparation time: 15 minutes
Cooking time: 15 minutes
Makes 2 servings.
Per serving: 427 calories, 8.4 g. fat (17% of calories), 5.6 g. dietary fiber, <1 mg. cholesterol, 552 mg. sodium.

2 teaspoons margarine	1 teaspoon ground cumin
1 cup chopped onions	1 cup egg substitute
2 small baking potatoes, peeled and cubed	2 tablespoons skim milk
1 cup chopped sweet red peppers	2 teaspoons Dijon mustard
	4 crêpes, warmed
	½ cup salsa, warmed

1. In a large no-stick frying pan over low heat, melt the margarine. Add the onions; cook, stirring frequently, for 2 minutes. Add the potatoes, peppers and cumin; cook, stirring frequently, for 10 to 15 minutes, or until the potatoes are tender and lightly browned.

2. In a small bowl, whisk together the egg, milk and mustard. Add to the pan. Cook, stirring constantly, for 3 to 4 minutes, or until the eggs are set.

3. Divide the eggs evenly among the crêpes. Fold to enclose the filling. Serve topped with the salsa.

zucchini-couscous bake

Couscous is a wonderful grain to use when you're pressed for time because it cooks very quickly.

Preparation time: 20 minutes
Cooking time: 10 minutes
Baking time: 30 minutes
Makes 2 servings.
Per serving: 424 calories, 11.1 g. fat (23% of calories), 12.8 g. dietary fiber, 12 mg. cholesterol, 621 mg. sodium.

2 teaspoons olive oil	½ cup canned black beans, rinsed and drained
½ cup chopped onions	½ cup couscous
2 garlic cloves, minced	6 kalamata olives, pitted and chopped
1½ cups thinly sliced zucchini	1 tablespoon grated Parmesan cheese
1 cup chopped green peppers	¼ cup shredded low-fat Cheddar cheese
½ cup chopped celery	
½ teaspoon dried basil	
1 cup canned low-sodium stewed tomatoes	

1. Preheat the oven to 350°. Coat a 1½-quart casserole with no-stick spray; set aside.

2. In a medium no-stick frying pan over medium heat, warm the oil. Add the onions and garlic; cook, stirring frequently, for 2 minutes. Add the zucchini, peppers, celery and basil; cook, stirring frequently, for 4 to 5 minutes, or until tender.

3. Stir in the tomatoes, beans, couscous, olives and Parmesan.

4. Spoon into the prepared casserole. Sprinkle with the Cheddar. Cover and bake for 15 minutes. Uncover and bake for 15 minutes.

creamy rice and lentils with peanuts

The combination of buttermilk and sour cream really gives this dish a tangy taste.

Preparation time: 15 minutes
Cooking time: 20 minutes

Makes 2 servings.
Per serving: 696 calories, 13.7 g. fat (18% of calories), 7.1 g. dietary fiber, 2 mg. cholesterol, 324 mg. sodium.

1¾ cups water
½ cup brown lentils, rinsed and drained
½ cup chopped scallions
1 tablespoon chopped canned green chili peppers (wear plastic gloves when handling)
2 garlic cloves, minced
½ teaspoon dried thyme
2½ cups low-sodium vegetable stock
1 cup long-grain white rice

½ cup buttermilk
2 tablespoons nonfat sour cream
2 tablespoons chopped fresh chives
1 tablespoon chopped fresh flat-leaf parsley
2½ teaspoons walnut or peanut oil
Pinch of ground red pepper
2 tablespoons coarsely chopped unsalted peanuts

1. In a 3-quart saucepan, combine the water, lentils, scallions, chili peppers, garlic and thyme; bring to a boil over medium-high heat. Reduce the heat to low and simmer for 15 to 20 minutes, or until the lentils are tender. Drain and return the mixture to the pan. Set aside.

2. Meanwhile, in a 2-quart saucepan, bring the stock to a boil over medium-high heat. Stir in the rice. Reduce the heat to low; cover and simmer for 20 minutes, or until the rice is tender and the liquid has been absorbed. Fluff with a fork and add to the pan with the lentils.

3. In a small bowl, whisk together the buttermilk, sour cream, chives, parsley, oil and red pepper. Pour over the lentils and rice. Toss to mix well. Sprinkle with the peanuts.

manicotti shells with chili-corn sauce

If you're in a hurry, you may microwave the filled manicotti instead of baking them. Cover the pan with wax paper and microwave on high for about 10 minutes, or until the manicotti are heated through.

Preparation time: 20 minutes
Cooking time: 15 minutes
Baking time: 25 minutes

Makes 2 servings.
Per serving: 302 calories, 2.9 g. fat (8% of calories), 2.9 g. dietary fiber, 15 mg. cholesterol, 707 mg. sodium.

4 manicotti shells	¼ cup thawed frozen chopped spinach, squeezed dry
1 can (14½ ounces) low-sodium stewed tomatoes	
½ cup drained canned corn	¼ cup shredded nonfat mozzarella cheese
2 tablespoons chopped canned green chili peppers (wear plastic gloves when handling)	1 tablespoon grated Parmesan cheese
¼ teaspoon ground coriander	1 large egg white, lightly beaten
½ cup low-fat cottage cheese	

1. Preheat the oven to 350°.

2. In a large pot of boiling water, cook the manicotti for 10 to 12 minutes, or until just tender. Drain and place in a bowl of cold water.

3. Meanwhile, in a 1-quart saucepan, combine the tomatoes, corn, peppers and coriander; bring to a boil over medium heat. Reduce the heat to low and simmer for 6 to 8 minutes, or until the liquid is reduced and the sauce thickens slightly.

4. In a small bowl, mix the cottage cheese, spinach, mozzarella, Parmesan and egg white.

5. Drain the manicotti and pat dry. Carefully spoon the cheese mixture into the shells.

6. Place half of the corn sauce in the bottom of an 8" × 8" baking dish. Top with the manicotti and the remaining sauce. Cover with foil and bake for 20 to 25 minutes, or until hot and bubbly.

red pepper pasta

8	ounces ziti	1	tablespoon grated
½	cup sun-dried tomatoes		Parmesan cheese
½	cup boiling water	½	teaspoon dried basil
1	tablespoon olive oil	1	cup shredded spinach
4	garlic cloves, minced		
¼	teaspoon red-pepper flakes		

Red-pepper flakes really give this dish a nice kick. If you prefer your food on the milder side, reduce the amount. I call for ziti here, but you may replace it with other types of pasta—especially flavored ones.

Preparation time: 15 minutes
Cooking time: 15 minutes
Makes 2 servings.
Per serving: 522 calories, 9.5 g. fat (15% of calories), 11.8 g. dietary fiber, 2 mg. cholesterol, 110 mg. sodium.

1. In a large pot of boiling water, cook the ziti for 10 to 12 minutes, or until tender. Drain and place in a large bowl; keep warm.

2. In a small bowl, combine the tomatoes and water. Let stand for 5 minutes. Drain, reserving the soaking liquid. Chop the tomatoes.

3. Meanwhile, in a medium no-stick frying pan over medium heat, warm the oil. Add the garlic and pepper flakes; cook, stirring constantly, for 2 minutes. Add the Parmesan and basil. Stir in the tomatoes and the reserved tomato soaking liquid. Simmer for 5 to 7 minutes, or until the liquid is reduced by half.

4. Pour over the pasta. Add the spinach and toss well.

snap pea stir-fry

Sugar snap peas are a special springtime treat. If they're unavailable, substitute snow peas.

Preparation time: 30 minutes
Cooking time: 10 minutes

Makes 2 servings.
Per serving: 462 calories, 7 g. fat (13% of calories), 21.2 g. dietary fiber, 0 mg. cholesterol, 383 mg. sodium.

1¼ cups water, divided	1 teaspoon peanut oil
1 tablespoon minced fresh ginger	1 small head broccoli, separated into florets
½ cup couscous	8 ounces snap peas
2 teaspoons cornstarch	1 sweet red pepper, cut into 1" pieces
2 garlic cloves, minced	
1 tablespoon low-sodium soy sauce	1 yellow pepper, cut into 1" pieces
1 teaspoon sesame oil	1 medium zucchini, cut into 1" pieces
1 teaspoon rice wine vinegar	
½ teaspoon dry mustard	1 cup drained canned corn
¼ teaspoon red-pepper flakes	

1. In a 1-quart saucepan over high heat, bring ¾ cup of the water and the ginger to a boil. Add the couscous. Cover and remove from the heat. Set aside for 5 minutes, or until the couscous is soft.

2. In a small bowl, dissolve the cornstarch in the remaining ½ cup water. Add the garlic, soy sauce, sesame oil, vinegar, mustard and pepper flakes; set aside.

3. In a large no-stick frying pan or wok over medium-high heat, warm the peanut oil. Add the broccoli, snap peas, red peppers, yellow peppers and zucchini; stir-fry for 4 minutes. Add the cornstarch mixture and corn; stir-fry for 2 to 3 minutes, or until the liquid thickens slightly.

4. Fluff the couscous with a fork. Place on a serving platter. Top with the vegetables.

spinach and cheese quesadillas

I have found that the easiest way to cut quesadillas is with kitchen scissors. But be sure to let the quesadillas stand for at least 5 minutes before cutting or the tortillas will slide apart.

Preparation time: 20 minutes
Baking time: 15 minutes
Makes 2 servings.
Per serving: 332 calories, 9.6 g. fat (21% of calories), 5.6 g. dietary fiber, 7 mg. cholesterol, 312 mg. sodium.

½ cup canned chick-peas, rinsed and drained
2 garlic cloves, minced
1 tablespoon water
4 large flour or corn tortillas
1 teaspoon canola oil
½ cup thawed frozen chopped spinach, squeezed dry
¼ cup chopped roasted sweet red peppers
¼ cup shredded low-fat Cheddar cheese
¼ teaspoon chili powder

1. Preheat the oven to 350°. Coat a baking sheet with no-stick spray.

2. In a small food processor, process the chick-peas, garlic and water until smooth. (Or place in a bowl and mash well.)

3. Brush 1 side of each tortilla with a little of the oil. Place 2 tortillas, oiled side down, on the prepared baking sheet. Spread both evenly with the bean puree to within ½" of their edges. Sprinkle with the spinach, peppers, Cheddar and chili powder.

4. Top with the remaining 2 tortillas, oiled sides up.

5. Bake for 10 to 12 minutes, or until golden. Let cool for at least 5 minutes. Cut each quesadilla into 4 triangles.

tofu stir-fry

There are no hard-and-fast rules for stir-frying, so use whatever vegetables you have on hand.

Preparation time: 20 minutes
Cooking time: 10 minutes
Makes 2 servings.
Per serving: 458 calories, 14.7 g. fat (29% of calories), 5.5 g. dietary fiber, 0 mg. cholesterol, 37 mg. sodium.

2 teaspoons sesame oil	½ cup sliced water chestnuts
2 garlic cloves, minced	1 teaspoon grated fresh ginger
1 cup sliced green peppers	
1 cup cut (1" pieces) green beans	½ teaspoon ground cinnamon
1 cup cubed tofu	Pinch of grated nutmeg
½ cup chopped (½" pieces) scallions	Pinch of ground red pepper
	2 cups hot cooked no-yolk egg noodles
½ cup sliced bamboo shoots	

1. In a large no-stick frying pan or wok over medium-high heat, warm the oil. Add the garlic; stir-fry for 1 minute.

2. Stir in the green peppers, beans, tofu, scallions, bamboo shoots, water chestnuts, ginger, cinnamon, nutmeg and red pepper. Stir-fry for 4 to 5 minutes, or until the vegetables are crisp-tender.

3. Serve over the noodles.

cheesy spinach gratin

This dish tastes very similar to the filling for the Greek specialty spanakopita. Serve this either as a filling side dish or as a main course.

2 cups nonfat ricotta cheese	3 tablespoons unbleached flour
2 cups thawed frozen chopped spinach, squeezed dry	½ teaspoon dried oregano
¾ cup egg substitute	2 tablespoons shredded provolone cheese
½ cup chopped onions	½ teaspoon paprika
¼ cup shredded low-fat Jarlsberg cheese	

Preparation time: 15 minutes
Baking time: 35 minutes

Makes 2 servings.
Per serving: 434 calories, 4.6
g. fat (10% of calories), 5.4 g.
dietary fiber, 12 mg. cholesterol, 663 mg. sodium.

1. Preheat the oven to 350°. Coat 2 small oval gratin dishes with no-stick spray; set aside.

2. In a medium bowl, mix the ricotta, spinach, egg, onions, Jarlsberg, flour and oregano. Divide the mixture between the prepared dishes. Sprinkle with the provolone and paprika.

3. Bake for 30 to 35 minutes, or until set and golden. Let stand for 5 minutes before serving.

mexican stuffed potatoes

Here's a good way to use leftover baked potatoes. If you don't have any already cooked, either bake them as usual for about 1 hour or microwave them for about 10 minutes. You can easily prepare the salsa ahead. The longer it stands, the stronger the flavors become.

1 cup canned black beans, rinsed and drained	2 tablespoons minced scallions
½ cup drained canned Mexican-style corn	½ teaspoon ground cumin
¼ cup chopped fresh cilantro	2 large baked potatoes, warmed
¼ cup chopped tomatoes	¼ cup shredded low-fat Cheddar cheese
2 tablespoons minced red onions	

1. In a medium bowl, mix the beans, corn, cilantro, tomatoes, onions, scallions and cumin. Cover and refrigerate for at least 1 hour.

2. Split the potatoes in half lengthwise. Top with the salsa. Sprinkle with the Cheddar. Bake for 5 minutes or microwave for 1 minute to melt the cheese.

Preparation time: 15 minutes
Baking time: 35 minutes

Makes 2 servings.
Per serving: 434 calories, 4.6
g. fat (10% of calories), 5.4 g.
dietary fiber, 12 mg. cholesterol, 663 mg. sodium.

vegetable patties

I like to serve these patties in pitas with some shredded chicory, chopped tomatoes and low-cal Russian dressing. Sometimes I also put a slice of tomato on each patty before baking.

Preparation time: 20 minutes
Cooking time: 25 minutes
Baking time: 30 minutes

Makes 2 servings.
Per serving: 364 calories, 12.5 g. fat (31% of calories), 6.7 g. dietary fiber, 0 mg. cholesterol, 525 mg. sodium.

¾ cup water	2 tablespoons pecan halves
¼ cup millet	2 teaspoons low-sodium soy sauce
2 teaspoons canola oil	
½ celery rib, diced	½ cup shredded zucchini
¼ cup diced red onions	½ cup seasoned dry bread crumbs
2 slices bread, coarsely torn	
¼ cup fresh basil leaves	

1. In a 1-quart saucepan over medium-high heat, bring the water to a boil. Stir in the millet. Reduce the heat to low; cover and simmer for 20 to 25 minutes, or until the water has been absorbed. Transfer to a large bowl.

2. Meanwhile, in a medium no-stick frying pan over medium heat, warm the oil. Add the celery and onions; cook, stirring frequently, for 4 to 5 minutes, or until tender. Add to the bowl.

3. In a food processor, combine the bread, basil, pecans and soy sauce; process with on/off turns until coarsely chopped. Add to the bowl with the millet. Add the zucchini and mix well with your hands.

4. Preheat the oven to 400°. Coat a baking sheet with no-stick spray.

5. Form the millet mixture into 4 patties. Coat the patties with the bread crumbs. Place on the prepared sheet. Bake for 15 minutes. Flip the patties and bake for another 10 to 15 minutes, or until golden.

bell pepper burritos with guacamole

Tortillas are a staple at my house. I know that I can always use them to whip up quick meals. All I need is something to fill them with, and the possibilities are endless. Here's a filling I made when I had some avocado on hand.

Preparation time: 20 minutes + marinating time
Cooking time: 5 minutes
Makes 2 servings.
Per serving: 310 calories, 10.3 g. fat (29% of calories), 5.2 g. dietary fiber, 0 mg. cholesterol, 21 mg. sodium.

1 green pepper, cut into strips	¼ ripe avocado, lightly mashed
1 sweet red pepper, cut into strips	2 tablespoons grated red onions
¼ cup lemon juice	1 teaspoon grated lime peel
2 tablespoons chopped fresh cilantro	1 teaspoon lime juice
½ teaspoon ground cumin	1 teaspoon olive oil
½ teaspoon chili powder	4 flour tortillas, warmed
¼ teaspoon freshly ground black pepper	1½ cups shredded romaine lettuce
½ cup chopped tomatoes	½ cup shredded jícama

1. In a medium bowl, mix the green peppers, red peppers, lemon juice, cilantro, cumin, chili powder and black pepper. Let stand for 30 minutes.

2. In another medium bowl, mix the tomatoes, avocado, onions, lime peel and lime juice. Cover and refrigerate until needed.

3. In a large no-stick frying pan over medium heat, warm the oil. Add the pepper mixture. Cook, stirring frequently, for 4 to 5 minutes, or until the peppers are tender and the liquid has evaporated.

4. Divide the mixture among the tortillas. Sprinkle with the lettuce and jícama. Roll to enclose the filling. Serve with the avocado mixture.

squash stuffed with wild rice

A nice plump winter squash makes a perfect meal for two. Just split it in half and stuff with your choice of filling. This recipe calls for butternut squash, but you may use acorn, buttercup or any other variety. If using small squash, such as sweet dumpling or delicata, allow one per person.

Preparation time: 20 minutes
Cooking time: 15 minutes
Baking time: 1 hour
Makes 2 servings.
Per serving: 435 calories, 6 g. fat (11% of calories), 11.1 g. dietary fiber, 2 mg. cholesterol, 239 mg. sodium.

1 large butternut squash	1 cup cooked wild rice
½ teaspoon no-salt herb blend	¼ cup low-sodium vegetable stock
2 teaspoons margarine	¼ cup nonfat sour cream
½ cup fresh bread crumbs	1 tablespoon grated Parmesan cheese
½ teaspoon dried thyme	
1 cup sliced mushrooms	
½ cup chopped celery	
½ cup chopped sweet red peppers	

1. Preheat the oven to 375°.

2. Cut the squash in half lengthwise; remove and discard the seeds. Place the squash, cut side down, in a baking dish. Bake for 45 minutes, or until just tender. Flip the pieces and sprinkle with the herb blend.

3. Meanwhile, in a large no-stick frying pan over medium heat, melt the margarine. Add the bread crumbs and thyme; cook, stirring frequently, for 4 to 5 minutes, or until golden. Transfer to a small bowl and set aside.

4. In the same pan, cook the mushrooms, celery and peppers for 4 to 5 minutes, or until tender. Stir in the wild rice and stock; cook for 2 minutes. Remove from the heat and stir in the sour cream and Parmesan.

5. Spoon the filling into the squash cavities, mounding it as necessary to use all of it. Sprinkle with the bread crumbs. Bake for 10 to 15 minutes, or until heated through.

curried tofu with fruit and quinoa

This dish combines many foods typical of Indian cuisine: curry, fruit, grains and yogurt. Many Indian dishes are vegetarian or nearly so, with grains being the focus of the meal. Although quinoa isn't a typical Indian grain, I like the way it complements the other ingredients.

Preparation time: 20 minutes
Cooking time: 15 minutes

Makes 2 servings.
Per serving: 497 calories, 17.2 g. fat (29% of calories), 9 g. dietary fiber, <1 mg. cholesterol, 51 mg. sodium.

1 cup water	2 tablespoons chopped almonds
½ cup quinoa, rinsed and drained	¾ teaspoon curry powder
2 teaspoons margarine	¼ teaspoon ground cumin
½ cup diced onions	¼ teaspoon turmeric
6 ounces firm tofu, well drained and squeezed dry between paper towels	¼ teaspoon freshly ground black pepper
1 McIntosh apple, thinly sliced	2 tablespoons nonfat yogurt
¼ cup coarsely chopped dried apricot halves	

1. In a 1-quart saucepan over high heat, bring the water to a boil. Add the quinoa; cover, reduce the heat to medium-low, and simmer for 20 to 25 minutes, or until tender and transparent. Drain off any water. Let stand for 5 minutes; fluff with a fork.

2. Meanwhile, in a large no-stick frying pan over medium heat, melt the margarine. Add the onions; cook, stirring frequently, for 3 to 4 minutes, or until tender.

3. Cube the tofu and add to the pan, along with the apples, apricots, almonds, curry powder, cumin, turmeric and pepper. Stir gently. Cook, stirring occasionally, for 6 to 8 minutes, or until the apples are tender.

4. Add the quinoa. Mix well. Serve topped with the yogurt.

boboli potato pizza

You can easily multiply this recipe for a crowd. If Boboli bread is unavailable, substitute refrigerated pizza dough. Roll it into an 8" circle and prebake according to the package directions.

•

Preparation time: 20 minutes
Cooking time: 20 minutes
Baking time: 20 minutes

Makes 2 servings.
Per serving: 504 calories, 15.8 g. fat (27% of calories), 5.3 g. dietary fiber, 15 mg. cholesterol, 838 mg. sodium.

8 ounces small red potatoes	½ cup chopped tomatoes
1 small package (8 ounces) Boboli bread	½ cup chopped arugula
2 teaspoons olive oil	¼ cup chopped red onions
¼ cup tomato sauce	¼ cup crumbled blue cheese
2 garlic cloves, minced	¼ teaspoon freshly ground black pepper
⅛ teaspoon red-pepper flakes	

1. Scrub the potatoes and cook in water to cover for 15 to 20 minutes, or until tender. Drain and let cool slightly. Cut into ¼" slices.

2. Preheat the oven to 400°.

3. Place the Boboli bread on a large baking sheet. Brush with the oil and top with the tomato sauce. Sprinkle with the garlic and pepper flakes.

4. Top with the potatoes. Sprinkle with the tomatoes, arugula, onions, blue cheese and black pepper.

5. Bake for 15 to 20 minutes, or until the bread is golden and the cheese has melted.

cauliflower ragoût

A ragoût is a thick stew. I like to serve this version over wide noodles or rice. If you don't have balsamic vinegar, substitute red wine vinegar.

Preparation time: 15 minutes
Cooking time: 15 minutes
Makes 2 servings.
Per serving: 402 calories, 9.9 g. fat (21% of calories), 15.2 g. dietary fiber, 2 mg. cholesterol, 153 mg. sodium.

2 teaspoons olive oil	1 can (19 ounces) cannellini beans, rinsed and drained
2 cups cauliflower florets	
½ cup chopped celery	1 tablespoon grated Parmesan cheese
½ cup sliced zucchini	
¼ teaspoon red-pepper flakes	1 teaspoon balsamic vinegar
1 cup tomato sauce	½ teaspoon dried basil
¼ cup coarsely chopped sun-dried tomatoes	1 tablespoon chopped fresh flat-leaf parsley

1. In a large no-stick frying pan over medium heat, warm the oil. Add the cauliflower, celery, zucchini and pepper flakes; cook, stirring frequently, for 6 to 8 minutes, or until tender.

2. Stir in the tomato sauce and tomatoes; bring to a boil. Reduce the heat to low. Stir in the beans, Parmesan, vinegar and basil. Simmer for 5 to 7 minutes longer, or until the sauce thickens slightly. Sprinkle with the parsley.

artichoke lasagna rolls

Lasagna rolls are a perfect way to use up leftover lasagna noodles. I always seem to have a few left in the box—not enough for a whole pan of lasagna. You may assemble the rolls ahead and refrigerate them until you're ready to bake them. Any leftover rolls reheat nicely—just microwave them for 1 to 2 minutes each.

MAKE AHEAD

Preparation time: 25 minutes
Cooking time: 15 minutes
Baking time: 30 minutes

Makes 2 servings.
Per serving: 545 calories, 12.7 g. fat (18% of calories), 8.4 g. dietary fiber, 10 mg. cholesterol, 547 mg. sodium.

4   lasagna noodles
2   cups spaghetti sauce
½   cup chopped fresh basil
¼   cup chopped sun-dried tomatoes
½   teaspoon dried oregano
4   teaspoons olive oil
1   cup sliced mushrooms
½   cup chopped onions
1   cup nonfat ricotta cheese
1   cup coarsely chopped thawed frozen artichoke hearts
¼   cup chopped roasted sweet red peppers
2   tablespoons grated Parmesan cheese
½   cup shredded nonfat mozzarella cheese

1. In a large pot of boiling water, cook the noodles for 10 to 12 minutes, or until tender. Drain and rinse with cold water.

2. Meanwhile, in a 1-quart saucepan over medium heat, simmer the spaghetti sauce, basil, tomatoes and oregano for 5 minutes. Set aside.

3. In a large no-stick frying pan over medium heat, warm the oil. Add the mushrooms and onions; cook, stirring frequently, for 4 to 5 minutes, or until tender. Transfer to a large bowl. Add the ricotta, artichokes, peppers and Parmesan; mix well.

4. Preheat the oven to 350°. Spread ½ cup of the tomato sauce in the bottom of an 8" × 8" baking dish.

5. Lay the noodles flat on a work surface. With a small spatula, spread about 1 tablespoon of the tomato sauce along the length of each noodle. Spread each with equal amounts of the ricotta mixture. Roll up the noodles to enclose the filling.

6. Place, seam side down, in the baking dish. Top evenly with the remaining tomato sauce and the mozzarella. Bake for 25 to 30 minutes, or until bubbly.

open-faced bean sandwiches

Sandwiches are always quick and easy. You can easily halve this recipe to serve one or double it for a family. I call for Italian bread, but you could use hard rolls, English muffins or another type of bread. And you may vary the beans according to what's on hand. No matter what your choices, this is a very filling meal.

Preparation time: 15 minutes
Cooking time: 8 minutes
Broiling time: 5 minutes

Makes 2 servings.
Per serving: 527 calories, 10.6 g. fat (18% of calories), 12.9 g. dietary fiber, 14 mg. cholesterol, 868 mg. sodium.

1	can (19 ounces) red kidney beans, rinsed and drained
2	tablespoons low-sodium ketchup
2	teaspoons brown sugar or 1 teaspoon honey
1	teaspoon steak sauce
1	teaspoon white wine vinegar
¼	teaspoon chili powder
4	thick (1") slices Italian bread
2	teaspoons olive oil
1	garlic clove, halved
½	cup thawed frozen chopped spinach, squeezed dry
4	low-fat Cheddar cheese slices
4	tomato slices

1. In a 2-quart saucepan, mix the beans, ketchup, sugar or honey, steak sauce, vinegar and chili powder. Simmer over medium heat for 6 to 8 minutes, or until the liquid is reduced slightly.

2. Preheat the broiler. Place the bread on a baking sheet. Broil about 5" from the heat for 1 minute per side, or until lightly browned. Brush the top of each slice with the oil and rub with the garlic.

3. Divide the spinach among the slices. Spoon on the bean mixture. Top with the Cheddar and tomatoes. Broil for 2 to 3 minutes, or until the cheese is bubbly.

brown rice with nutty eggplant sauce

This eggplant sauce is one of my basic recipes. I serve it over baked potatoes, pasta, rice and other grains. It's even good as a pizza topping; cook it until it's quite thick.

Preparation time: 20 minutes
Cooking time: 45 minutes
Makes 2 servings.
Per serving: 346 calories, 11.9 g. fat (29% of calories), 8.4 g. dietary fiber, 0 mg. cholesterol, 116 mg. sodium.

1¼ cups water	½ cup chopped onions
½ cup brown rice	½ teaspoon dried oregano
2 teaspoons olive oil	Pinch of ground red pepper
1½ cups peeled and cubed eggplant	2 plum tomatoes, chopped
½ cup chopped scallions	¼ cup low-sodium vegetable stock
2 garlic cloves, minced	1 tablespoon capers, rinsed, drained and chopped
1 green pepper, cut into strips	2 tablespoons toasted pine nuts
2 cups sliced mushrooms	

1. In a 2-quart saucepan over high heat, bring the water to a boil. Stir in the rice. Reduce the heat to low; cover and simmer for 45 minutes, or until the rice is tender and the water has been absorbed.

2. Meanwhile, in a large no-stick frying pan over medium heat, warm the oil. Add the eggplant, scallions and garlic; cook, stirring frequently, for 5 to 7 minutes, or until the eggplant is just tender.

3. Add the green peppers, mushrooms, onions, oregano and red pepper; cook, stirring frequently, for 4 minutes. Add the tomatoes, stock and capers; simmer for 2 minutes. Keep warm.

4. Fluff the rice with a fork and spoon onto a serving platter. Top with the eggplant mixture and sprinkle with the pine nuts.

creamy lentil soup

Sometimes you really *don't* want to make a big pot of soup. I like to make this soup for myself on nights when my husband is out of town. The leftovers make a wonderful lunch the next day.

MAKE
AHEAD

Preparation time: 10 minutes
Cooking time: 1 hour
Makes 2 servings.
Per serving: 266 calories, 4.6 g. fat (15% of calories), 7.8 g. dietary fiber, 0 mg. cholesterol, 407 mg. sodium.

1 teaspoon canola oil	2 cups low-sodium vegetable stock
½ cup chopped scallions	
2 teaspoons grated fresh ginger	1 can (14½ ounces) tomatoes with juice
1 garlic clove, minced	1 tablespoon chopped fresh thyme or 1 teaspoon dried
½ teaspoon curry powder	
¼ teaspoon cumin seeds	1 teaspoon white wine vinegar
½ cup red lentils	

1. In a 2-quart saucepan over medium heat, warm the oil. Add the scallions, ginger and garlic; cook, stirring frequently, for 2 to 3 minutes, or until tender. Stir in the curry powder and cumin seeds; cook for 1 minute.

2. Stir in the lentils, stock and tomatoes (with their liquid); bring to a boil. Reduce the heat to low; cover and simmer for 40 to 45 minutes, or until the lentils are tender.

3. Transfer half of the soup to a blender and process until smooth. Return to the saucepan. Stir in the thyme and vinegar; simmer for 10 minutes.

bulgur with spinach and oranges

You may also serve this dish as a cold salad. For variety, use pineapple chunks instead of oranges.

Preparation time: 20 minutes
Cooking time: 5 minutes
Makes 2 servings.
Per serving: 234 calories, 7.8 g. fat (27% of calories), 6.8 g. dietary fiber, 1 mg. cholesterol, 153 mg. sodium.

¼ cup water	1 tablespoon red wine vinegar
¼ cup bulgur	
4 cups coarsely chopped spinach	1 tablespoon minced scallions
¼ cup low-sodium vegetable stock	2 teaspoons olive oil
1 cup drained canned mandarin oranges	½ teaspoon ground cumin
	¼ teaspoon freshly ground black pepper
½ cup nonfat yogurt	1 tablespoon sesame seeds

1. In a 2-quart saucepan over high heat, bring the water to a boil. Stir in the bulgur. Remove from the heat, cover, and let stand for 10 minutes. Fluff with a fork.

2. Add the spinach, stock and oranges. Simmer over low heat for 2 to 3 minutes, or until the spinach is wilted. Remove from the heat.

3. In a small bowl, mix the yogurt, vinegar, scallions, oil, cumin and pepper. Pour over the bulgur. Mix well. Sprinkle with the sesame seeds.

roasted brussels sprouts and squash

To me, a bowl of roasted winter vegetables makes a very filling and satisfying main dish. Round out this meal with steamed rice and maybe some cheese or yogurt for extra protein.

Preparation time: 25 minutes
Baking time: 50 minutes
Makes 2 servings.
Per serving: 275 calories, 3 g. fat (9% of calories), 11.6 g. dietary fiber, 0 mg. cholesterol, 286 mg. sodium.

½	cup apple juice	2	cups peeled and cubed butternut squash
¼	cup raisins		
2	teaspoons lemon juice	1½	cups cut (1" pieces) green beans
1	teaspoon Dijon mustard		
½	teaspoon caraway seeds	1	cup sliced carrots
3	cups halved brussels sprouts	1	tablespoon poppy seeds

1. Preheat the oven to 350°.

2. In a small bowl, mix the apple juice, raisins, lemon juice, mustard and caraway seeds.

3. In a 9" × 13" baking dish, mix the brussels sprouts, squash, beans and carrots. Pour on the juice mixture and toss well.

4. Cover with foil and roast for 25 to 30 minutes, or until the vegetables are just tender. Stir. Roast, uncovered, for 15 to 20 minutes, or until the liquid is reduced and the vegetables are tender. Sprinkle with the poppy seeds.

chili for a small family

This is a scaled-down version of chili, so you don't have to make a big potful for only one or two people.

MAKE AHEAD

Preparation time: 15 minutes
Cooking time: 50 minutes

Makes 2 servings.
Per serving: 470 calories, 16.7 g. fat (29% of calories), 11.2 g. dietary fiber, 0 mg. cholesterol, 395 mg. sodium.

2	teaspoons canola oil
1	cup chopped scallions
½	cup chopped sweet red peppers
½	cup chopped green peppers
2	garlic cloves, minced
8	ounces firm tofu, well drained and squeezed dry between paper towels
1	tablespoon unbleached flour
1	tablespoon chili powder
1	teaspoon cocoa powder
⅛	teaspoon ground red pepper
1	can (14½ ounces) low-sodium stewed tomatoes with juice
2	tablespoons red wine vinegar
1¼	cups canned black beans, rinsed and drained
1	tablespoon chopped fresh cilantro

1. In a 2-quart saucepan over medium heat, warm the oil. Add the scallions, red peppers, green peppers and garlic; cook, stirring frequently, for 4 to 5 minutes, or until tender.

2. Crumble the tofu and add to the pan. Cook, stirring often, for 5 to 7 minutes, or until golden.

3. Add the flour, chili powder, cocoa powder and ground pepper. Cook, stirring constantly, for 2 minutes. Add the tomatoes (with their liquid) and vinegar; bring to a boil. Reduce the heat to low and simmer for 20 to 30 minutes, or until slightly thick.

4. Stir in the beans and cilantro. Simmer for 5 minutes.

a month's worth of vegetarian meals

Most people have no trouble planning meals around meat. It's easy. You take a hefty portion of beef, chicken, fish, lamb or whatever and add some starch, a vegetable or two, maybe some salad or soup, probably some bread. Then you top it off with a nice dessert. There's no question what the "main course" is.

Things aren't so clear-cut when you remove the meat from a meal. Most of us can throw together a fairly traditional vegetarian dinner such as cheese pizza, a hearty vegetable soup, pasta with tomato sauce or bean enchiladas. But when we try to be a little more creative, our resources fail us. We're not really sure what foods go together or what dishes will give us enough protein to carry us through the day.

That's why I created these menus—to show you how to pair filling meatless entrées with easy accompaniments. I've used many of the recipes featured in this book. But I've intentionally limited the number of actual recipes called for at any given meal. I know you're busy and you don't want to be overwhelmed with having to cook too many new dishes at a time. As you become more comfortable with this way of eating, I hope you'll substitute more book recipes for the simple salads, steamed vegetables and other straightforward side dishes listed in the menus.

week one

	breakfast	**lunch**
day 1	Grapefruit sections • Raisin-Barley Pudding (page 235)	Curried Fruit and Rice Salad (page 205) • Butter-flavored rice cakes • Carrot sticks • Iced tea
day 2	Pineapple-Banana Breakfast Shake (page 234) • Toasted raisin bread • Nonfat cream cheese	Couscous and Tomato Salad (page 220) • Red kidney beans with low-fat Italian dressing • Chilled lightly steamed broccoli florets • Green grapes
day 3	Orange juice • Apple Pancakes (page 247) • Maple syrup	Cheese and pepper pizza • Bitter Greens with Tangy Dressing (page 206) • Zucchini sticks and cherry tomatoes • Melon balls • Berry-flavored seltzer
day 4	Strawberries • Couscous Breakfast Cereal (page 232)	Meghan's Noodle Soup (page 176) • Melba toast • Low-fat Monterey Jack cheese • Nonfat chocolate pudding
day 5	Peach nectar • Red Pepper Frittata (page 243) • Toasted rye bread	Pita stuffed with nonfat cream cheese, shredded carrots and chives • Couscous with Lentils, Tomatoes and Basil (page 98) • Celery sticks • Nonfat pineapple yogurt • Apple juice
day 6	Guava juice • Vidalia Onion Omelets (page 242) • Toasted bagel • Nonfat cream cheese	Baked potato • Hearty Red Lentil Sauce (page 77) • Mixed green salad with low-fat Dijon dressing • Julienned raw jícama • Mixed dried fruit
day 7	Peanut Butter French Toast (page 232) • Low-fat milk	Boboli Potato Pizza (page 346) • Roasted red peppers and blanched green beans with balsamic vinegar • Nonfat yogurt with raisins, cinnamon and honey

dinner	snack
Minestrone with Cheese Dumplings (page 168) • Steamed snow peas • Boston lettuce salad with low-fat blue cheese dressing • Almond cookies	Rice cakes • All-fruit preserves
Penne with Fresh Vegetable Sauce (page 52) • Grilled eggplant slices • Romaine salad with chick-peas and low-fat Thousand Island dressing • Baked apple with caramel sauce	Hot chocolate made with low-fat milk
Vegetable Patties (page 342) • Pita bread • Shredded lettuce and chopped tomatoes with low-fat Catalina dressing • Brown rice with roasted red peppers • Cinnamon graham crackers	Raisins and lightly smoked almonds
Vermicelli with Chunky Vegetable Sauce (page 80) • Escarole and red onion salad with balsamic vinegar • Italian bread rubbed with garlic and drizzled with olive oil • Steamed asparagus • Sliced kiwifruit and oranges drizzled with honey	Popcorn with sour cream–flavored sprinkles
Sweet-and-Sour Tofu (page 261) • Cellophane noodles • Steamed snow peas • Bibb lettuce with low-fat Oriental soy dressing • Pear poached in cranberry juice	Saltine crackers • Low-fat Swiss cheese
Vegetarian Vegetable Kabobs (page 267) • Baked sweet potato • Couscous with grated orange peel • Banana Fruit Shake (page 234)	Ice milk with chopped walnuts and pineapple topping
Tangy Cuban Beans (page 155) • Brown rice • Steamed green beans with sesame seeds • Tossed green salad with low-fat Russian dressing • Cheese Blintzes with Raspberry Sauce (page 236)	Dried apple rings

week two

	breakfast	**lunch**
day 1	Tangerine sections • Breakfast Fried Rice (page 248) • Low-fat milk	Creamy Lentil Soup (page 351) • Sliced tomatoes and red onions with tarragon vinegar • French bread • Marinated mushrooms • Low-fat coffee cake
day 2	White grapefruit half • Potato and Tofu Scramble (page 244) • Toasted whole wheat bread	Tomato, low-fat mozzarella and basil sandwich on whole wheat bread • Watercress Salad with Scallion Dressing (page 216) • Pear
day 3	Cornmeal Pancakes (page 231) • Blueberry pancake syrup • Sliced bananas	Open-Faced Bean Sandwiches (page 349) • Mixed green salad with low-fat Parmesan dressing • Yellow pepper strips • Peach
day 4	Apple-Bran Muffins (page 239) • Kiwifruit and strawberries • Low-fat Colby cheese	Oriental Orzo Salad (page 314) • Sliced water chestnuts and baby corn • Flatbread • Tomatoes sprinkled with soy sauce and rice wine vinegar • Cherries
day 5	Orange juice • Brown Rice Breakfast Parfaits (page 237) • Low-fat milk	Cream of tomato soup • Cheesy Bell Pepper Dip (page 306) • Broccoli and cauliflower florets and red radishes • Bagel chips • Oat bran cookies
day 6	Apricot nectar • Scrambled Eggs with Limas and Spinach (page 140) • Toasted English muffins	Bell Pepper Burritos with Guacamole (page 343) • Steamed rice • Marinated vegetable salad • Crisp homemade tortilla chips • Nonfat banana pudding
day 7	Citrus fruit salad • Toasted bagel • Low-fat cream cheese • Red Berry Spread (page 305)	Minestrone • Sesame Oat Scones (page 304) • Fig bars

dinner	snack
Red Pepper Pasta (page 337) • Sliced smoked mozzarella cheese • Arugula and radicchio salad with low-fat creamy Italian dressing • Steamed broccoli • Mixed berries with low-fat whipped topping	Low-fat tortilla chips • Salsa
Squash Stuffed with Wild Rice (page 344) • Salad of chick-peas, roasted red peppers and low-fat vinaigrette • Cooked turnips sprinkled with Parmesan cheese • Nonfat chocolate frozen yogurt with blueberries	Gingersnaps
Artichoke Lasagna Rolls (page 348) • Stir-fried red pepper and onion strips • Italian bread brushed with olive oil and sprinkled with oregano • Nonfat vanilla yogurt sprinkled with Breakfast Granola (page 230)	Caramel-flavored rice cakes
Cannellini and Tarragon Ravioli (page 139) • Steamed spinach • Creamy Cucumber Mint Salad (page 216) • Angel food cake with raspberry sauce	Lime gelatin with sliced bananas and low-fat whipped topping
Lentil-Stuffed Crêpes (page 118) • Wild and brown rice with scallions • Steamed carrots • Raspberries topped with nonfat lemon yogurt	Frozen fruit bar
Brown Rice Egg Rolls (page 106) • Hoisin and Black Bean Stir-Fry (page 137) • Lo mein noodles • Tossed green salad with honey-orange dressing • Litchi nuts • Fortune cookies	Pretzels
Red and Green Lasagna (page 328) • Marinated artichoke hearts • Kale salad with creamy yogurt dressing • Italian dinner rolls • Fruit and low-fat cheese platter	Popcorn with peanuts and dried fruit

week three

	breakfast	**lunch**
day 1	Orange-pineapple juice • Herbed Asparagus Frittatas (page 303) • Toasted whole wheat bread	White Herb Chili (page 117) • Shredded zucchini and cabbage salad with low-fat ranch dressing • Melba toast • Banana
day 2	Mango chunks • Scrambled Eggs and Greens (page 245) • Toasted rye bread	Thai Tofu Salad (page 213) • Marinated vegetables • Toasted pita triangles • Nonfat vanilla pudding
day 3	Cantaloupe wedge • Breakfast Granola (page 230) • Nonfat cherry yogurt	Herbed Grilled Vegetables with Spaghetti (page 51) • Sliced low-fat provolone and tomato salad with low-fat Caesar dressing • Bread sticks • Apricot halves
day 4	Cranberry juice • Oat and Fruit Pudding (page 249) • Low-fat milk	Skillet Oats and Tempeh (page 102) • Broccoli and red onion salad with low-fat French dressing • Nonfat butterscotch pudding
day 5	Nutty Peach Cereal (page 233) • Bran muffin • Apple butter	Spinach and Cheese Quesadillas (page 339) • Chunky salsa • Arugula and tomato salad with low-fat Dijon vinaigrette • Red and green grapes
day 6	Pink grapefruit half • Red and Yellow Pepper Omelets (page 241) • Toasted pumpernickel bread	Millet-Stuffed Grape Leaves (page 105) • Romaine salad with feta cheese and low-fat vinaigrette • Flatbread • Nectarine
day 7	Tropical fruit juice • Toasted Bagels with Roasted Red Pepper Spread (page 228) • Sliced banana drizzled with honey	Chilled Avocado-Asparagus Soup with Jícama Salsa (page 182) • Black beans and parsley • Tossed green salad with low-fat onion and chive dressing • Cherries

dinner	snack
Pepper and Eggplant Stacks (page 275) • Spaghetti sauce • Steamed cauliflower and green beans • Wild rice with onions • Low-fat frozen chocolate mousse	Low-fat crackers with olives and nonfat cream cheese
Caponata-Stuffed Shells (page 48) • Endive salad with low-fat coleslaw dressing • Herbed focaccia • Persimmon	Banana split made with nonfat chocolate frozen yogurt and low-fat whipped topping
Mini Kasha Balls with Onion Gravy (page 103) • No-yolk broad egg noodles • Steamed broccoflower with thyme • Red leaf lettuce with low-fat blue cheese dressing • Strawberry ice milk	Popcorn with Cheddar-flavored sprinkles
Saffron Corn Chowder (page 179) • Asparagus and Feta with Cavatelli (page 81) • Sautéed thick onion slices • Low-fat pound cake with apricot sauce	Low-fat strawberry ice milk shake
Curried Brown Rice and Peas (page 92) • Steamed cauliflower • Pita bread • Chutney • Papaya slices drizzled with honey and sprinkled with poppy seeds	Low-fat tapioca pudding
Radiatore with Three-Onion Sauce (page 84) • Steamed snap peas • Blue Cheese and Mushroom Salad (page 210) • Garlic-flavored bread sticks • Raspberry fruit and yogurt bar	Trail mix
Lentil Burgers with Sautéed Mushrooms and Onions (page 145) • Baked potato • Mango Spinach Salad (page 217) • Low-fat granola bar	Warm fruit compote with low-fat custard sauce

week four

	breakfast	lunch
day 1	Cranberry-apple juice • Strawberry Whole-Grain Waffles (page 229) • Maple syrup	Arugula Gazpacho (page 184) • Three-bean salad • Chilled asparagus spears • Fresh figs • Iced tea
day 2	Peanut Butter Raisin Bread (page 240) • Nonfat cream cheese • Low-fat milk	Dried-Tomato and Barley Soup (page 166) • Dilled cucumber salad with nonfat sour cream dressing • Low-fat herb crackers • Watermelon chunks • Vegetable-cocktail juice
day 3	Red grape juice • Fried Polenta with Cranberry-Maple Topping (page 227)	Tricolor Rotelle and Cucumber Salad (page 204) • Whole wheat pita triangles • Low-fat Muenster cheese • Graham crackers • Lime-flavored seltzer
day 4	Carrot juice • Cornmeal and Oat Bran Muffins (page 238) • Black raspberry preserves • Blueberries with mint	Miso Bean Soup (page 183) • Saltine crackers • Low-fat Cheddar cheese • Tossed salad with green beans and low-fat buttermilk dressing • Nonfat vanilla yogurt with chocolate chips
day 5	Sliced peaches • Scrambled eggs • Rosemary Hash Browns (page 248)	Split Pea Soup with Toasted Caraway Croutons (page 162) • Coleslaw • Apple
day 6	Honeydew chunks and raspberries • Mushroom-Tomato Brunch Bake (page 226)	Gremolata Rice Soup (page 163) • String cheese • Low-fat whole-grain crackers • Carrot and raisin salad • Kiwifruit
day 7	Poached dried figs • South of the Border Scrambled Eggs (page 246) • Toasted oat bread	Corn and Barley Salad (page 206) • Sliced tomatoes with crumbled feta cheese and red wine vinegar • Red pepper strips • Peach yogurt with blueberries

dinner	snack
Grilled vegetables with balsamic vinegar • German Potato Salad with Cornichons (page 222) • Lentils with salsa and nonfat sour cream • Low-fat brownies	Sunflower seeds
Five-Bean Chili Salad (page 218) • Low-fat tortilla chips • Guacamole • Steamed spinach and mushrooms sprinkled with red wine vinegar • Citrus sections with walnuts and toasted coconut	Nonfat pistachio pudding
Pumpkin Soup (page 161) • Chicory salad with goat cheese and low-fat olive oil vinaigrette • Brussel sprouts with lemon and caraway seeds • Dinner rolls • Applesauce with cinnamon	Buttermilk • Low-fat oat crackers
Artichoke Lasagna (page 74) • Mozzarella and Bread Salad (page 207) • Corn on the cob • Anisette toast cookies	Dates stuffed with peanut butter
Ravioli with Sautéed Peppers (page 75) • Fennel salad with low-fat tomato vinaigrette • Peas • Broiled banana with brown sugar • Vanilla ice milk	Sesame seed pretzels
Spaghetti with Spinach Cream Sauce (page 46) • Garlic bread • Steamed Italian beans • Belgian endive salad with low-fat ranch dressing • Strawberries with balsamic vinegar and orange peel	Dried papaya • Low-fat brick cheese
Creamy Mushroom Soup (page 172) • Red lentils with onions and thyme • Baked acorn squash • Boboli bread • Low-fat strawberry cheesecake	Cheddar-flavored rice cakes

index

Note:
Underscored page references indicate boxed text. **Boldface** references indicate photographs.

d

e